BATTLE OVER THE REICH

BATTLE OVER THE REICH

THE STRATEGIC AIR OFFENSIVE OVER GERMANY

VOLUME ONE

1939 - 1943

Dr. Alfred Price

CLASSIC

An imprint of
Ian Allan Publishing

First published 2005

ISBN 1 903223 47 4

Produced by Chevron Publishing Limited

Project Editor: Chevron Publishing Limited

© Text Dr. Alfred Price 2005

© Colour Illustrations: Colour profiles by Tim Brown and Tom Tullis. Unit badges by Eddie J. Creek 2005

With thanks to Mark Postlethwaite at ww2images.com

Published by Classic Publications an imprint of Ian Allan Publishing Ltd, Hersham, Surrey KT12 4RG

Printed in England by Ian Allan Printing Ltd, Hersham, Surrey KT12 4RG

Visit the Classic Publications website at www.ianallanpublishing.com

CONTENTS

PROLOGUE AND
ACKNOWLEDGEMENTS

In writing this book, my purpose has been to present the reader with a broad picture of the air battles fought over Germany during the Second World War, as seen through the eyes of the British, American and German combatants. I have made no attempt to describe every single action, for to do so would have required a book many times the length of this one. Instead, I have chosen as examples those actions which in my view illustrated the general pattern – although, of course, every action contained unique features of its own.

'Battle Over the Reich' would not have been possible without the co-operation of many members of the 'original cast' most of whom, sadly, are no longer with us. Men like General Adolf Galland, General Roderick Cescotti, Colonel Hans-Ulrich Flade, Hans Seyringer, Willi Herget, Hans Kogler, and Hanfried Schliephake of the *Luftwaffe*, Air Marshal Sir Robert Saundby, Group Captain Hamish Mahaddie, Group Captain Bob Braham and Flight Lieutenant Bob Brydon of the RAF, and August Briding, Bernard Dopko, General Tom Marchbanks, William Murphy, Harold Stearns, Lowell Watts, Colonel Hubert Zemke and Colonel Ross Miller of the USAAF.

My good friends Arno Arbendroth, Götz Bergander, Roger Freeman, Werner Girbig, Günther Heise, Norbert Krueger, Danny Morris, Hans Obert, Hans Redemann, Franz Selinger, Hans Ring, and, Richard Smith helped to amass the necessary material and photographs.

Finally I should like to thank my dear wife Jane, for support that went far beyond that laid down in the small print of our marriage contract.

ALFRED PRICE
Uppingham Rutland

Searchlights over Berlin

Their silver scalpels probe the wound of night
seeking our doom, a death to death.
And now no highflung phrase, no braggart gesture of
the hand or jaw can still the double fear.
Who fly ten thousand feet above in the shrill dark
are linked with those who cower under earth to
hear, vague as sea upon an island wind, the murmur
which is, for some eternity, for some an ending.
And he is rising mad who searches here for meaning.

By Pilot Officer T. R. Hodgson,
killed in action in 1940

1

LEARNING THE HARD WAY

August 1939-December 1941

"As Reichsminister for air, I have convinced myself

personally of the measures taken to protect the Ruhr against

air attack. In future I will look after every battery, for we

will not expose the Ruhr to a single bomb dropped by

enemy aircraft."

Hermann Göring, speaking on 9 August 1939

Hermann Göring's declaration concerning the safety of the Ruhr industrial area, much quoted in later years, showed the degree of confidence the *Luftwaffe* had in its air defence system before the outbreak of Second World War. In August 1939 however that confidence was by no means misplaced.

The war planned to commence against Poland in a few weeks would, the German leaders judged, be fought only in and against that country. Less than a year earlier the British and French leaders had conceded Adolf Hitler's demands to annex parts of Czechoslovakia. Few in Germany thought they would now go to war over Poland. If Poland fought alone, her air force possessed only 36 medium bombers with which to attack targets in Germany. That danger could safely be ignored, Göring decided.

If the improbable happened, and Britain and France went to war to assist Poland, the risk to the Ruhr would be increased. The French airfields nearest to the German industrial area were only about 150 miles away, yet although the French Air Force possessed some 370 operational bombers, virtually all were obsolete. In a confidential letter to his Air Minister, two weeks after Göring's statement, the French Chief of Air Staff had written:

"The power of our bomber force has remained unchanged since September 1938, and is as restricted now as it was then. The poor performance of our bombers will make it necessary to be cautious in our operations during the first months of the war. The modern types built in France or expected from overseas have not yet been delivered to the units ..."

From that quarter also, Göring saw little to fear. The only dangerous adversary the Germans might face, if Great Britain entered the war, was the Royal Air Force. At this time RAF Bomber Command operated some 300 modern bombers, Hampdens and Wellingtons, plus about 100 of the older Whitleys. All these aircraft had the range to penetrate deeply into German airspace. In addition there were about 300 medium-range Blenheims, able to reach peripheral areas. Here was a threat Göring could not shrug off; yet the air defence system he had erected was formidable indeed.

On the eve of war the *Luftwaffe* fighter force comprised more than 1,000 Bf 109 interceptor fighters, and nearly 200 twin-engined Bf 110 bomber destroyers. Without doubt, these could inflict crippling losses on bomber formations attempting to penetrate German airspace by day. Since they lacked the necessary electronic systems they were, however, almost powerless to prevent night attacks.

In the summer of 1939 the Flak arm of the *Luftwaffe* (*Flak* was an abbreviation for *Fliegerabwehrkanonen*, anti-aircraft guns) operated 197 heavy anti-aircraft batteries with about one thousand five hundred 88 mm guns. The *Luftwaffe* had devoted considerable effort into developing this form of defence. Against radio-controlled targets flying

◄◄ Hampden Mark Is of No. 144 Squadron pictured over their base at Hemswell, Lincolnshire. This type had a maximum speed of 265 mph and cruised at 217 mph at 15,000 feet. Maximum take-off weight was 21,000 pounds. Its defensive armament comprised one fixed and one moveable .303 inch Vickers gun firing forwards, and twin hand-held Vickers in the dorsal and ventral gun positions. The Hampden flew its last operational sortie with RAF Bomber Command in September 1942. (Sleight, via Garbett/Goulding)

ARMSTRONG WHITWORTH WHITLEY B.Mk.V

Serving with 102 Squadron from RAF Driffield, Yorkshire during 1939-40. Overall standard finish of Dark Earth and Dark Green over Night (black) undersurfaces. Note overpainting of the A1 type roundel to obscure the visibility of the yellow surround.

► Of the three bomber types that bore the brunt of the RAF bomber offensive during the first three years of war, the Whitley had the lowest performance. This example, a Mark V, belonged to No. 102 Squadron based at Finningley in Yorkshire before the war. At the outbreak of war the type was relegated to the role of night raider, and it flew many of the early leaflet dropping missions over Germany. The main production version of the Whitley, the Mark V, had a maximum speed of 230 mph and it cruised at 210 mph at 15,000 feet. Maximum take-off weight was 33,500 pounds. Defensive armament was four Browning .303 inch machine guns in the rear turret, and one in the nose turret. The Whitley passed out of front line service in Bomber Command early in 1942.

straight and level at altitudes below 10,000 feet, in clear skies, the heavy guns had demonstrated their effectiveness. To counter low flying raiders there were 48 light Flak batteries equipped with 37 mm or 20 mm light automatic weapons.

Raiders could lessen the danger from Flak by flying at very high altitude, by flying a weaving course in the target area, or by attacking on moonless nights; but if they did any of these things their bombing would be inaccurate. And if the enemy's bombs could not inflict serious damage to targets in Germany, would the enemy consider it worth risking his aircraft in this way?

All of this was deterrent enough for a would-be attacker attempting to hit targets in Germany, but an even more powerful counter was the ability of the *Luftwaffe* to exact retribution. Its bomber force comprised more than 1,000 modern twin-engined bombers. Any nation foolhardy enough to attempt attacks on the most heavily defended targets in the world, faced the certainty of powerful retaliatory attacks on its homeland.

So, when Göring made his famous assertion on the invulnerability of the Ruhr, it was with what seemed to be a soundly based confidence. What he did not foresee was that Germany would find itself at war with a nation so unperceptive that it was not cowed by the *Luftwaffe* bomber force. This enemy was, moreover, so naïve as to believe that its air attacks were having a serious effect on

"The Whitley was not the sort of vehicle in which one should go to pursue the King's enemies ..."

the German war economy, and so stubborn that it continued with these attacks even after their ineffectiveness had become clear. Yet that was precisely what happened.

The Second World War opened on 1 September 1939, when German troops invaded Poland. Two days later, following a rejection of an ultimatum for the German forces to withdraw, France and Great Britain declared war. The air threat from the east soon evaporated, as Göring had expected: the small Polish bomber force smashed itself in brave attacks on the advancing German columns, and there were no retaliatory attacks on the homeland. Within a month, Poland had surrendered.

In the west, RAF Bomber Command began operations on 4 September, the day following the outbreak of war, yet, as Göring had foreseen, there was no British or French willingness to attack targets in Germany and trigger a massive retaliation by the *Luftwaffe*. The C-in-C Bomber Command, Air Chief Marshal Sir Edgar Ludlow-Hewitt, had orders to restrict his attacks to enemy warships off the coast, where there was little risk of incurring civilian casualties.

The targets for the first RAF attack were the heavy

◄ Heinkel He 111 bombers under construction at the Heinkel factory at Rostock late 1339/1940.

cruiser *Admiral Scheer* and the cruiser *Emden*, both lying at anchor in Wilhelmshaven Roads. Low cloud forced the raiders to attack from low altitude, and the ten Blenheims roared over the warships at little more than mast-top height. At least three bombs hit the *Admiral Scheer* but, released from too low an altitude for the

◄ A Whitley of No. 78 Squadron is prepared for a night operation over Germany in early 1941.

"The Wellington is very inflammable, and burns readily."

▲ The fabric-covered Wellington, with its unusual geodetic construction, was the type best able to resist the effects of Flak damage. Often the blast and fragments from an exploding shell blew away the fabric covering but left the essential structure of the aircraft intact. (IWM)

► The primary damage mechanism of the heavy anti-aircraft shell was the high velocity splinters from the shell's casing. The effects of this damage can be seen on the tail of this Stirling. Against an aircraft of normal stressed-skin construction, the 88 mm shell would inflict lethal damage if it exploded within about 30 feet. (IWM).

weapons to arm themselves before impact, they failed to detonate and caused only superficial damage. The *Emden* suffered damage and some casualties when a Blenheim was shot down and crashed into her. A similar force of Wellingtons set out to attack targets at the mouth of the Kiel canal, but had no greater success. Return fire from the warships and anti-aircraft batteries caused the destruction of five Blenheims and two Wellingtons. It was a poor omen for the future of British daylight bombing, yet it could be argued that the unusually poor weather conditions had forced the bombers to attack at low level, where the light Flak was lethal. Attacks from higher altitude would put the raiders beyond the reach of that particular threat.

There followed a series of small-scale raids on warship targets, all of them inconclusive. Then, on 18 December 1939, came the first stand-up fight between an RAF bomber formation and *Luftwaffe* fighters. That afternoon 24 Wellingtons of Nos. 9, 37 and 149 Squadrons took off for an armed reconnaissance over the Heligoland Bight. The bombers formed up into a diamond-shaped formation comprising four flights, each consisting of two 'V's of three aircraft. Two Wellingtons returned early with mechanical trouble; the remainder continued eastwards at 14,000 feet. In the Heligoland Bight the bomber crews found the sky clear of cloud, but the sea was clear of warships. Having failed to find a legitimate target for their bombs, the bombers turned for home.

On the pre-war holiday island of Wangerooge, one of the new *Freya* early warning radars had observed the approaching Wellingtons at a range of 70 miles, and tracked their movements. The operator reported the formation to the nearby fighter station at Jever and defending fighters, 16 Bf 110s and 34 Bf 109s, took off to engage.

In 1939 the Wellington was the most effective bomber type in the RAF. For its defence it carried three power-operated gun turrets each mounting a pair of rifle-calibre .303 inch machine guns: one in the nose, one in the tail and a retractable turret under the fuselage. It was an article of faith in Bomber Command that the co-ordinated defensive fire from a score of bombers flying in close formation would defeat fighter attacks from almost any quarter. Now that theory was to be put to the test.

It was a clear, winter's day and the German fighter pilots could see the RAF formation from several miles away. They quickly caught up with the raiders and opened their attack. The German tactics varied. Many pilots chose to stand off at long range beyond the effective range of their return fire and engage the

◄ A formation of Wellingtons of No. 9 Squadron in formation just before the war.

bombers with their cannon. Some pilots pressed home attacks to within 50 yards of the bombers before breaking off, while others preferred to attack the bombers from abeam and above, where the individual Wellingtons were virtually defenceless.

A brisk action followed. *Leutnant* Üllenbeck who flew a Bf 110 of I. *Gruppe* of *Zerstörergeschwader* (*ZG*) 76, afterwards reported:

"I was with the second formation on a course of 120 degrees, about 50 km to the north of Ameland. Suddenly, we came upon two Wellingtons flying 300 metres beneath us, on the opposite heading. I attacked the leader from the side and it caught fire. Then I opened fire on the second one, from the left and above. When he didn't budge I moved into position 300 metres behind him, and opened up with everything. The nose of the bomber fell, and it dived towards the sea. It was at this time that I was hit by a bullet, between my neck and left shoulder; the round went clean through me, and hit the radio operator on his left wrist."

Üllenbeck limped back to Jever in his peppered Messerschmitt, and landed successfully; afterwards mechanics counted 23 bullet holes in his fighter.

German pilots noted that the Wellingtons flew considerably slower than the attacking Messerschmitts. Part of the reason was that the bombers had lowered their retractable underneath turrets to increase their defensive fire power. This move reduced the bombers speed by about 15 mph, yet the additional guns had

▲ Hptm. Gunther Reinecke from Stab I./ZG 76 standing in the cockpit of his Bf 110 C, coded M8+DB in early 1940.

little deterrent value. On the other hand, the fighters' greater speed differential allowed them to attack from almost any direction they wished. The commander of I./ZG 76, *Hauptmann* Gunther Reinecke, afterwards commented: *"The Wellington is very inflammable, and burns readily."*

The bombers' return fire destroyed two German fighters and inflicted damage on several others. But of the 22 Wellingtons which took part in the action, only ten regained the shores of Britain and three of those had taken serious damage.

So the RAF learned the hard way – as the *Luftwaffe*

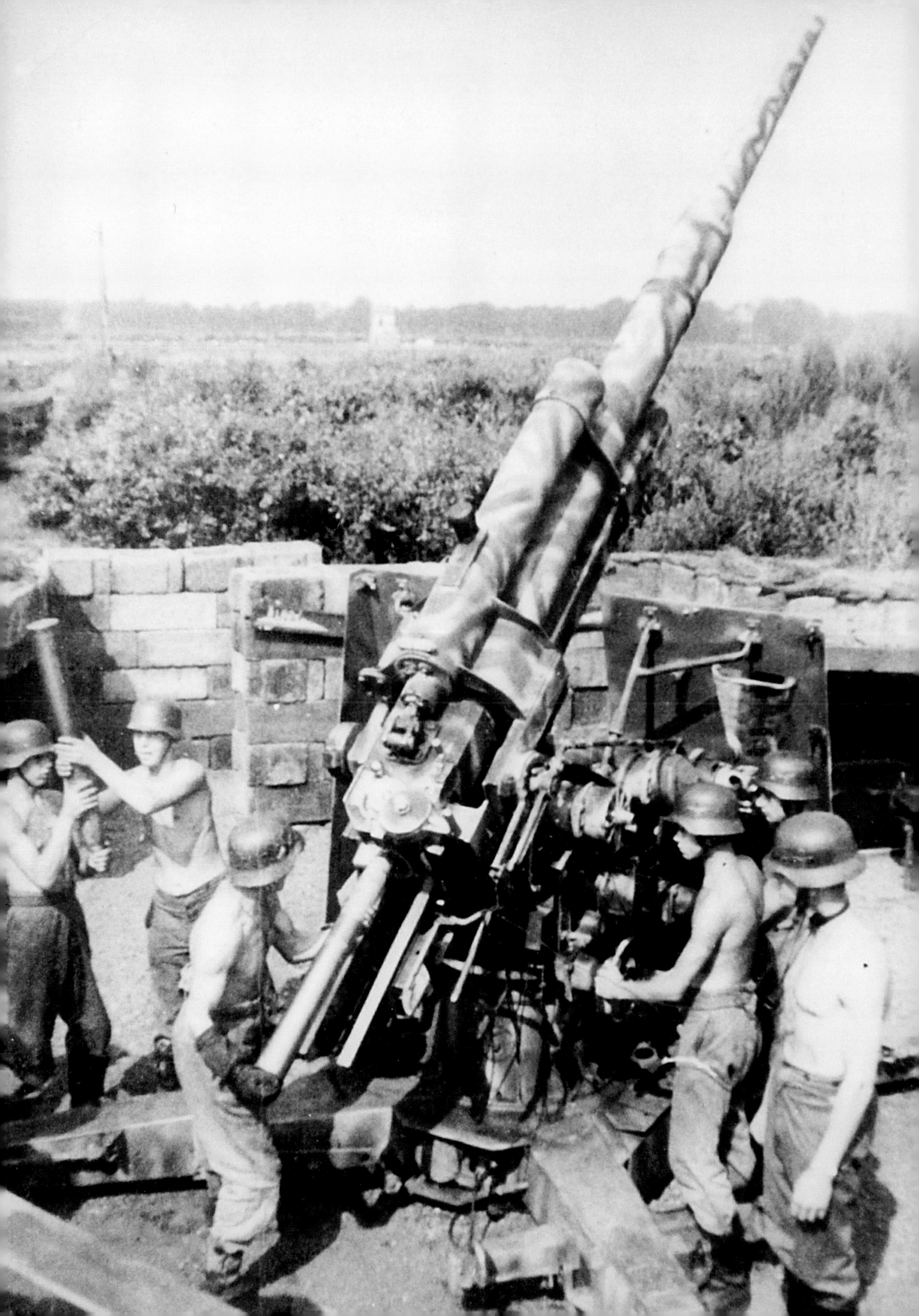

◄ ◄ A close-up of the data transmission windows of an 88 mm gun, conveying information from the nearby predictor. The task of the azimuth and elevation layers (K1 and K2) was to match the pointers on the gun to the pointers on the dials throughout the engagement.

◄ A *Luftwaffe* 88 mm Flak gun and crew at gunnery practice early in the war.

◄ ◄ Initially the *Luftwaffe* relied almost entirely on its heavy Flak batteries to protect targets in the German homeland. The 88 mm Flak 36 was the most-used heavy anti-aircraft weapon at the beginning of the war, and in its early and improved versions it held that position throughout the conflict. Early in the war this gun had a crew of ten: the commander, usually an Unteroffizier; Kanonier 1 (gunner 1) azimuth layer; K 2 elevation layer; K3 loader; K 4 put the shell in the automatic fuse setter; and K5, K6, K7, K 8 and K9 to pass ammunition. Later the positions of K7, K8 and K9 were disestablished.

would learn during the Battle of Britain — that formations of 1939-vintage bombers without fighter escort could not fight their way to targets in daylight in the face of a well-equipped and determined fighter opposition. The lesson was clear: unless bombers could have fighter escorts, or they could achieve surprise by attacking fringe targets and exploiting cloud, they would survive only by attacking under cover of darkness.

Attacking at night produced a new set of problems, however. From the outbreak of war the low-performance Whitley bombers of No. 4 Group had been employed in night operations. Since bombing attacks on enemy populated areas were forbidden, these aircraft flew probing sorties over Germany and Poland dropping millions of propaganda leaflets. These operations revealed the difficulties of finding blacked-out cities deep in enemy territory. Air Vice Marshal Conningham, No. 4 Group's commander, commented, *"I foresee a never-ending struggle to circumvent the law that we cannot see in the dark."* And so it was to prove.

The raids also revealed many of the shortcomings of the outdated Whitley bombers. One pilot who took part in those long-distance night flights during the severe winter of 1939 later commented: *"The Whitley was not the sort of vehicle in which one should go to pursue the King's enemies ..."*

Typical of the problems were those encountered by a Whitley crew of No. 51 Squadron, on the night of 27 October 1939. With difficulty the men reached the Frankfurt-Dusseldorf area and released their pamphlets, but then, in the absence of efficient heating or oxygen systems, the cold and the shortage of oxygen took their toll on the men's faculties. Their report on the mission stated:

"Such was the condition of the navigator and the wireless operator at this stage, that every few minutes they were compelled to lie down and rest on the floor of the fuselage. The cockpit heating system was useless. Everyone was frozen, and had no means of alleviating their distress. The navigator and Commanding Officer were butting their heads on the floor and navigation table in an endeavour to experience some other form of pain as a relief from the awful feeling of frost-bite and the lack of oxygen ..."

The bomber returned to the French airfield at Villeneuve and landed successfully.

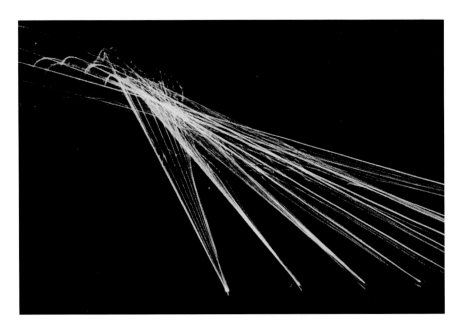

▲ Flying at low level Allied aircraft came within range of the 37 mm and 20 mm anti-aircraft guns. The effect of the tracer shells clearly show the concentration and direction of fire.

▲ ► Barrage balloons were also used by German ground defences to deter low level Allied aircraft attacks.

HANDLEY PAGE HAMPDEN B.Mk I

P5304 JS-L served with No. 16 Operational Training Unit from RAF Upper Heyford in 1941-42. Overall standard finish of Dark Earth and Dark Green over Night (black) undersurfaces.

Of the leaflets dropped during the early part of the war it is difficult to find evidence that they had any useful effect, apart from providing useful training for crews. Everywhere the Wehrmacht had been victorious, German national morale was high and no enemy pamphlet would change that. Speaking of the leaflet operations Air Vice Marshal Arthur Harris, then Deputy Chief of Air Staff, commented that they did little except supply *"... the Continent's requirements of toilet paper"*.

The first deliberate bombing attack on a target on German soil was on the night of 19 March 1940. Still there was no wish to provide the *Luftwaffe* with a pretext for bombing civilian targets in Britain, so the raid was launched against the seaplane base Hörnum on the sparsely populated island of Sylt. Fifty Whitleys and Hampdens set out to attack the base, one failed to return. Forty-one crews claimed to have found and bombed the target, and they reported many direct hits on hangars and living quarters. A subsequent photographic reconnaissance of the seaplane base failed to reveal any serious damage, however. It was the first serious conflict between the bomber crews' claims and the subsequent photographic reconnaissance evidence, and it would not be the last.

In April 1940 Sir Edgar Ludlow-Hewlitt was promoted and appointed to the post of Inspector General of the RAF. In his place came Air Marshal Sir Charles Portal. For the next few weeks the pattern of operations remained unchanged, until mid-May and the devastating *Luftwaffe* attack on Rotterdam. On 15 May, Britain's new Prime Minister, Winston Churchill, lifted the ban on attacks that might place German civilian lives at risk and that very night a force of 99 RAF bombers was sent to bomb oil and railway targets in the Ruhr. The strategic bomber offensive against Germany had begun in earnest.

During the early part of the offensive the vast majority of night attacks were made at high altitude. A rare exception, however, was the low level night precision attack on the Dortmund-Ems canal on 12 August. The specific target was the aqueduct which carried the canal high over the Ems River and the surrounding countryside.

Eleven Hampdens of Nos. 49 and 83 Squadrons, flown by picked crews, took part in the operation. The RAF had attacked the aqueduct previously, and there were powerful light Flak and balloon defences to deter low-flying aircraft. For that reason, five Hampdens were to create a diversion and sever the balloon cables with their wing-mounted cable cutters. The remaining bombers were then to attack the aqueduct with delayed action bombs. At the controls of the last aircraft to attack

was Flight Lieutenant Roderick Learoyd of No. 49 Squadron. In his report he later recounted how he flew at 200 feet past the lane of anti-aircraft guns:

"After a moment three big holes appeared in the starboard wing. They were firing at point-blank range. The navigator continued to direct me on to the target. I could not see it because I was blinded by the glare of the searchlights and had to keep my head below the level of the cockpit top. At last I heard the navigator say 'Bombs gone!'; I immediately did a steep turn to the right and got away, being fired at heavily ..."

Learoyd nursed the crippled bomber to his base at Scampton in Lincolnshire, only to discover that the

▲ The remains of a Bristol Blenheim belonging to No. 80 Squadron shot down during a raid on the airfield at Aalborg, Denmark, on the night of 23/24 April 1940.

▼ Controlling the fire of each four-gun battery was a predictor, usually the Kommandogerät 36 depicted here. The predictor provided the guns' crews with azimuth, elevation and fuse-setting information to detonate the shells close to the moving aircraft.

▲ The 150 cm Flakscheinwerfer 37, the main type of searchlight in use by the *Luftwaffe* Flak arm, projected a beam of nearly a thousand million candlepower. At night the searchlight was an effective method of target defence in its own right, for once a bomber was held in its blinding glare, its crew could not deliver an accurate attack.

▲ Before the introduction of radar, the Flak arm relied on sound locators to establish the initial pick-up of aircraft flying at night and give searchlights a direction in which to search so they could illuminate the target. The system employed two operators, one to align the sound horns in azimuth and the other in elevation. Due to the relatively low velocity of sound waves, however, the position of the aircraft given by the locator lagged behind the machine's real position by as much as a mile. Moreover, bomber crews could render the process extremely difficult by flying with their engines desynchronised to produce a 'waam-waam-waam' note (as *Luftwaffe* bombers did over England).

hydraulic system had been shot through and he could not lower the flaps or undercarriage. Undaunted, he circled the airfield until it was light, then belly-landed. For his exploit Learoyd was awarded the Victoria Cross.

Two Hampdens from the main attack force were shot down, and the remaining machines all suffered damage. Subsequent reconnaissance photographs showed that their bombs had demolished part of the canal embankment, allowing the waters to surge out of the breach. The important canal was not restored to full use for more than a month.

Yet, when labourers had completed the hasty repairs, there was no attempt to mount another low altitude attack. The earlier raid had cost 40 per cent of the main attack force. As Air Vice Marshal Harris later commented: *"Any operation which deserves the VC is, in the nature of things, unfit to be repeated at regular intervals ..."*

During the first four months of its offensive against Germany, RAF Bomber Command flew some 8,000 sorties.

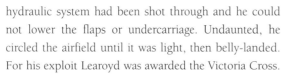

"Any operation which deserves the VC is, in the nature of things, unfit to be repeated at regular intervals ..."

It lost 163 aircraft. In military terms that loss rate, about two per cent of the force engaged, was acceptable, yet we now know that the bombers caused little damage of military value and most of the bombs fell in open country. Compared with those to follow, the raids were little more than gestures of defiance. A few bombs fell on the Ruhr and other German industrial areas, and they struck a raw nerve in Göring; had he not staked his reputation on this very thing being impossible?

At this time the night defence of the German homeland rested almost entirely on the Flak arm of the *Luftwaffe*, which now operated some 450 heavy anti-aircraft gun batteries and over 100 searchlight batteries. These were all positioned to provide point defence for the more important industrial areas.

Typically, each heavy gun battery was equipped with four guns and a predictor, while each searchlight battery operated three lights and had a sound locator. The standard heavy anti-aircraft weapon in the German inventory was the 88 mm Flak 36, which hurled an 18 pound shell to a maximum slant range of 9,000 yards or to a maximum effective engagement altitude of 20,000 feet. A clockwork fuse detonated the shell when it reached its previously set bursting point, splitting the casing into about 1,500 red-hot and jagged splinters which moved outwards at high velocity. Those splinters constituted the shell's main damage mechanism, and they could inflict lethal damage on an aircraft within about 15 yards of the detonation point.

As in any engagement involving a moving target at long range, the accuracy of the guns depended on the effectiveness of the fire-control system – in this case the *Kommandogerät 36* predictor. If, say, the guns engaged an aircraft flying overhead at 12,000 feet, the shells would take about six seconds to reach that altitude. In the meantime, a bomber flying at 180 mph covered 530 yards. Thus, to inflict lethal damage, the gunners needed to aim their weapons at a point precisely 530 yards in front of the target's observed position. An analogue computer in the predictor measured the previous flight path of the aircraft, and from that calculated its future path. It then disgorged that information in the form of azimuth and elevation settings for the guns, and time-of-flight fuze settings for the shells. An electrical data transmission system communicated the results immediately and continuously from the predictor to the guns.

Overall, from the initial tracking of the target to the bursting of the first salvo, the engagement of a target took about 21 seconds: a minimum of ten seconds for the predictor to track the target, five seconds to fuse and load the shell, and six seconds for the shells to reach the target in the above example. Repeat salvoes followed the first at intervals of about five seconds, and a well-drilled crew could maintain this maximum rate of fire for about two minutes.

To assist the searchlights to find their targets, each battery also operated a sound locator, yet this device could provide only an imprecise indication of the target's whereabouts. Due to the relatively low velocity of sound waves, an aircraft's engine noises took about 18 seconds to reach the instrument from 6,000 yards away. Thus, when tracking an aircraft flying at 180 mph, the calculated position lagged behind the machine's real position by almost a mile. Clearly some better system was urgently needed.

For the future, the Flak arm looked forward to receiving a precision radar system to enable gunners to engage bombers at night or in bad visibility. Such a device, code-named *Würzburg* with a maximum range of 25 miles, had entered production at the *Telefunken* company shortly before the outbreak of war. The device seemed to provide the answers to the gunners' main problem, and the optimistic reports that followed its tests had inspired Göring to make his statement that no enemy bomb would fall on the Ruhr. Yet the *Würzburg* was a state-of-the-art radar system, and like most of its ilk had its share of teething troubles. As a result, there were serious delays in introducing the equipment into large-scale service. In the meantime, anti-aircraft guns

FIGHTER UNITS ASSIGNED TO REICH AIR DEFENCE
17 AUGUST 1940

For the most part the initial RAF night raids failed to inflict serious damage to militarily important targets. They were, in truth, little more than gestures of defiance from a nation that was itself close to defeat. While playing down their effect, however, the German leadership saw them as a threat that might develop into something more serious. The nascent nightfighter force received a high priority for key personnel and essential items of equipment. The table below lists the units assigned to the night air defence role on 17 August 1940.

Unit		Total	Serviceable
Jagdgeschwader 52			
III. Gruppe	Bf 109	31	23
Jagdgeschwader 77			
Stab	Bf 109	4	4
I. Gruppe	Bf 109	36	30
Zerstörergeschwader 76			
I. Gruppe	Bf 110	34	20
Nachtjagdgeschwader 1			
Stab	Bf 110	3	2
I. Gruppe	Bf 110	33	24
III. Gruppe	Bf 110	33	20

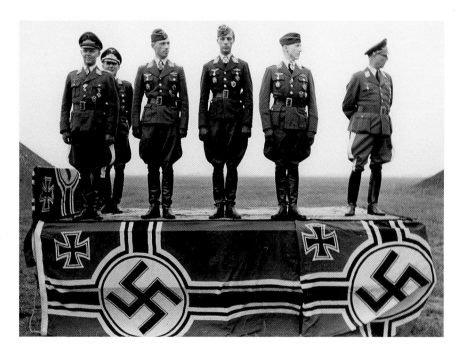

▲ Throughout 1941 the *Luftwaffe* made strenuous efforts to build up an effective nightfighter force. Seen along the front row on the reviewing stand are four of the men who were instrumental in achieving its initial successes. From left to right, in the foreground: Generalmajor Josef Kammhuber, architect of the Himmelbett system; and Helmut Lent, Paul Gildner and Ludwig Becker, three pilots who gained some of the initial successes as nightfighter pilots.

▲ The Wellington was the best of the early war bombers. The Mark IC had a maximum speed of 243 mph and cruised at 180 mph. Maximum take-off weight was 33,000 pounds. Defensive armament comprised two Browning .303 inch guns in the nose turret and two (later four) of these weapons in the rear turret. The Wellington remained in first-line service in Bomber Command until October 1943. The example depicted, in the process of being loaded with incendiary bombs, belonged to No. 301 (Polish) Squadron based at Swinderby. The unit re-equipped with this type in October 1940.

alone did not deter night raiders attacking from altitudes above 12,000 feet.

To counter the leaflet raids, the *Luftwaffe* operated a few single-engined Bf 109s in the nightfighter role. These fighters worked in conjunction with searchlights, which were to illuminate the enemy bombers so they could be engaged. The technique was called *Helle Nachtjagd* (illuminated night fighting). It soon became clear, however, that the single-engined fighters lacked

the endurance necessary for effective night patrols. The first success using these methods was on the night of 9 July 1940, when *Feldwebel* Förster of *Jagdgeschwader JG 2* shot down a Whitley.

With the British attacks becoming an almost nightly event, it was clear to Göring that a more structured nightfighter force was necessary if his wounded pride was not to take a further battering. Accordingly, he ordered *Oberst* Josef Kammhuber to form a nightfighter

► This Ju 88 C-4 from 9./NJG 2, coded R4+MT, made a belly-landing in a corn field in Belgium, just north of the French border during the summer of 1942. Note the variation of the 'Englandblitz' forward of the cockpit.

division. This formation was to operate twin-engined fighters more suitable for this task, with ground radar and searchlights to assist them. By the end of July *Nachtjagdgeschwader 1*, under the command of *Major* Wolfgang Falck, comprised two *Staffeln* of Bf 110s, a few Junkers 88 and Dornier 17 bombers fitted with forward firing guns, and the Bf 109s previously engaged on night fighting. Kammhuber divided his force into two. The Bf 109s and 110s were to operate against the bombers over Germany itself and the occupied territories in the West. The Junkers 88s and Dornier 17s were to take the war to the enemy camp, to catch bombers as they took off or returned to their bases.

During the summer of 1940 the German defensive nightfighter tactics were in their infancy, and there was almost continual change. At first Kammhuber employed the old *Helle Nachtjagd* methods with his twin-engined fighters. He was also allocated a few *Freya* radars, with a maximum range of 100 miles, to provide early warning. On their information the fighters took off and climbed to altitude, then circled their assigned radio beacon close to the searchlight zones and waited for the enemy bombers to come to them.

The drawback of the *Helle Nachtjagd* method soon became clear. Since the searchlights were concentrated at the more important towns and cities, these tactics achieved little outside the actual target area. Moreover, as they orbited over these defended points, the nightfighters were often illuminated and engaged by German anti-aircraft guns.

To overcome this identification problem, Kammhuber redeployed the searchlights assigned to him to a new line in front of the German cities, and therefore well clear of the gun-defended areas. This defensive line

◄ Major Wolfgang Falck was Kommodore of NJG 1 between 26 June 1940 and 30 June 1943.

ran from Schleswig Holstein to Liege and lay astride the approach routes used by RAF bombers. This zone was prohibited to other *Luftwaffe* aircraft at night, allowing the nightfighters to engage any unidentified aircraft detected passing through the area.

The redeployment produced an immediate improvement in the nightfighters' effectiveness, though Kammhuber regarded it merely as a stopgap. Because the searchlights had to illuminate a raider before an interception could take place, *Helle Nachtjagd* was a slave

JUNKERS Ju 88 C-2

This Ju 88 C-2 belonged to 9./NJG 2 which was based in Belgium during the summer of 1942. The top surface was painted in RLM 74 Graugrün and RLM 75 Grauviolet over RLM 65 Lichtblau undersurfaces.

▼ Oblt. Ludwig Becker achieved his first nightfighter victory with 4./NJG 1 on 16 October 1940.

►► The interior of a Wellington bomber shows the Navigator sitting at his table discussing flight information with a cockpit crew member, while another crewman takes a rest on the restbed.

"For a while the Englishman flew on, losing height rapidly. The fire died away but then I saw him spin towards the ground, and burst into flames on crashing."

to the weather: even small amounts of cloud could ruin its working. To overcome this problem, Kammhuber suggested using a *Freya* to provide close control for a nightfighter making an interception. Initially he found an inbuilt resistance to the idea; some experienced pilots argued that *"the fighter pilot's greatest weapon is his courage"*, and such a move would stifle offensive spirit.

Certain of his ground, Kammhuber overruled them.

Luftwaffe signals personnel erected a *Freya* radar with a crude height-finding attachment on the eastern side of the Zuider Zee. Following a series of operational trials, the first successful German radar-assisted night interception took place on the evening of 16 October when *Leutnant* Ludwig Becker of the 4. *Staffel* of *NJG 1*, flying a Dornier 17, followed directions from the ground and intercepted an unidentified aircraft coming in over Holland. He afterwards reported:

> *"I was well positioned at the correct altitude of 3,300 metres ... and directed on to the enemy by means of continual corrections. Suddenly I saw an aircraft in the moonlight, about 100 metres above and to the left; on moving closer I made it out to be a Vickers Wellington. Slowly I closed in from behind, and aimed a burst of 5-6 seconds duration at the fuselage and wing root. The right motor caught fire immediately, and I pulled my machine up. For a while the Englishman flew on, losing height rapidly. The fire died away but then I saw him spin towards the ground, and burst into flames on crashing."*

Becker's interception was a pointer to the future, but no more than that. In truth the *Freya*, though a good early-warning radar, was too imprecise to provide effective close control for nightfighters. Becker's victory had been a lucky kill, made on a clear moonlight night by exceptional men in the air and on the ground.

A few *Würzburg* radars were allocated to the nightfighter force, and during trials a pattern for future nightfighter operations began to evolve. Each fighter control station would employ three separate radars: a *Freya* for general area surveillance and two *Würzburg* sets, one to track the target aircraft and the other to follow the movements of the nightfighter. With such a mix of equipment, ground controllers were able to direct fighter pilots to within visual contact of their prey. The new tactic bore the code-name *Himmelbett*.

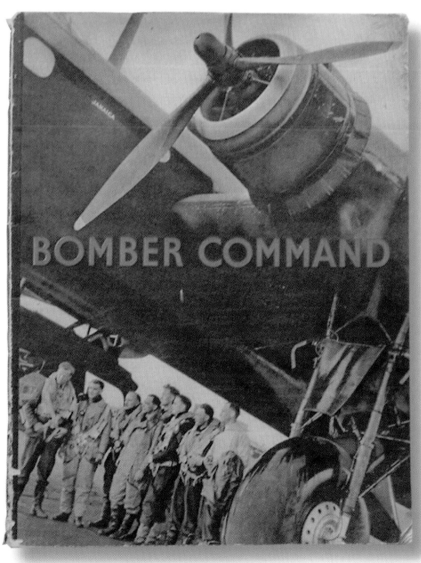

▲ The cover of a British wartime propaganda booklet.

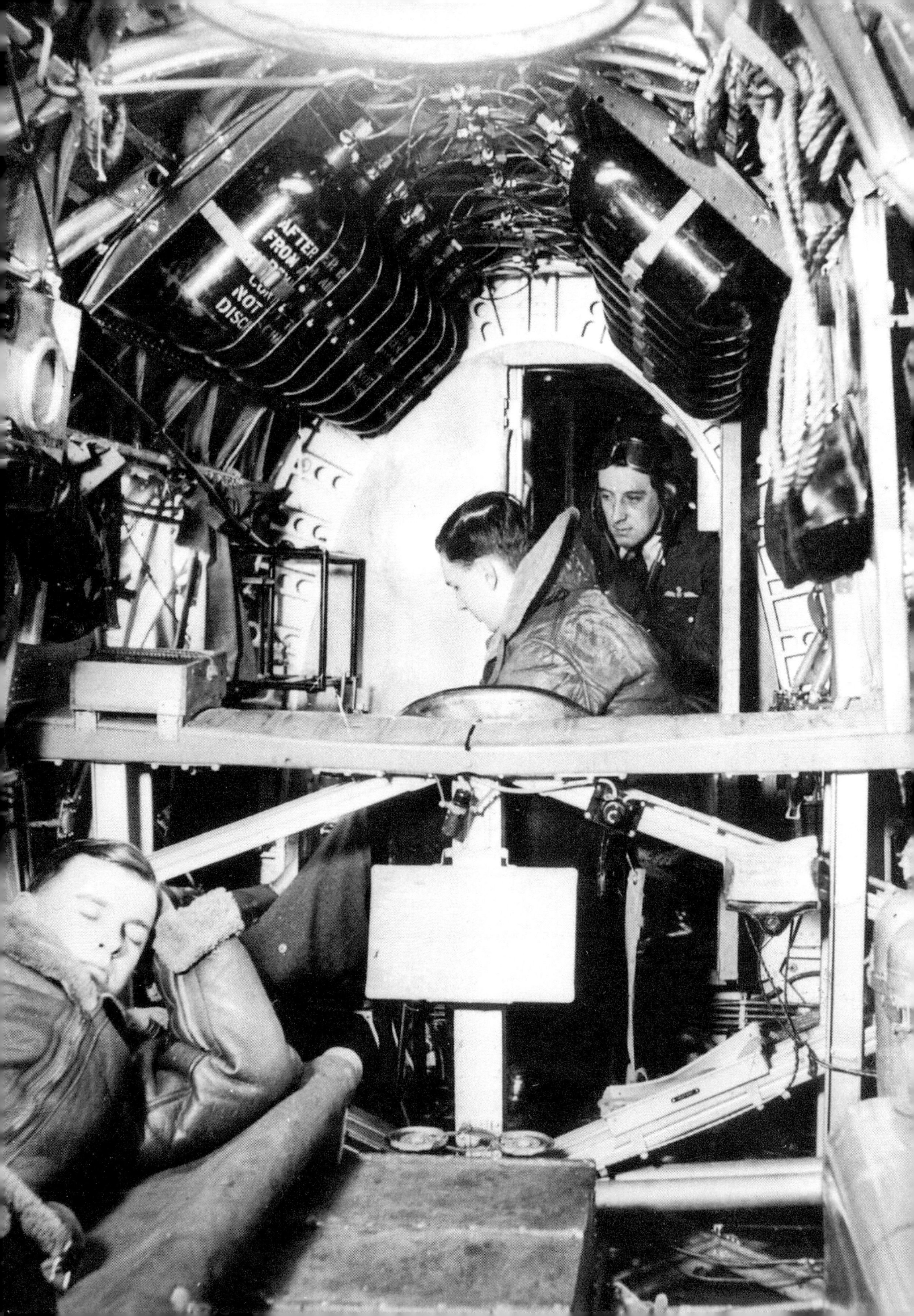
AFTER
FROM
NOT

SPITFIRE PR MK IVD OF NO. 1 PHOTOGRAPHIC RECONNAISSANCE UNIT
This reconnaissance Spitfire was piloted by Belgian P.O. Andre Cantillion of 1 PRU.
He was shot down and killed, crashing on the island of Sylt, on 17 August 1942,
the first victory of Uffz. Heinz Born of 9./JG 1 flying an Fw 190.

▶ Belgian P.O. Andre
Cantillion of 1 PRU, is seen
here on the wing of his
reconnaissance PR Mk IVD
Spitfire.

The *Würzburg* pointed the way to the future, but its limited 25-mile range meant that interceptions had often had to be broken off before the nightfighter pilot made visual contact with the bomber. The clear need was for a precision radar like *Würzburg* but with a maximum range of 50 miles. Accordingly, *Telefunken* modified the *Würzburg* with a much larger reflector dish, to squeeze the available power into a narrower beam. The new radar, the *Giant Würzburg* (*Würzburg Riese*), was ordered into production.

Under Kammhuber's direction, *Himmelbett* nightfighter control stations were erected at 20-mile intervals along his defensive line. The line itself was shaped like an enormous sickle, the 'handle' running through Denmark from north to south and the 'blade' curving through northern Germany, Holland, Belgium and eastern France to the Swiss frontier.

As the ground controlled aspects of the defence took shape, Kammhuber saw that a further item of radar equipment was needed to assist the system to cope with the RAF's attacks. Initially, bombers usually attacked when the moon was full or nearly full, for they needed its light to find their targets. If his new tactics made that practice more dangerous, Kammhuber felt sure the bombers would move their attacks to the darker nights. This meant that the ground radar controllers needed to guide nightfighters much closer to the target, before it came within visual range. The answer was to build a lightweight radar for installation in nightfighters, and engineers at *Telefunken* set to work to meet this requirement.

While the *Luftwaffe* stiffened its defences along Germany's western frontiers, its long-range nightfighters had some success over the RAF bomber bases in England. The First *Gruppe* of *NJG 2*, operating from Gilze-Rijen in Holland, sent aircraft on intruder missions to patrol over RAF bases during raids to catch bombers taking off or approaching to land. Such aircraft had little reserve speed for evasion and were virtual sitting ducks, a fact known only too well to their crews. The effect of these operations on the bomber crews' morale was out of all proportion to the *Luftwaffe* effort involved. Bomber

crews, returning tired at the end of long flights, had to land on dimly lit airfields. Many aircraft were damaged or written-off in heavy landings, for there was no thought of going round again no matter how bad the approach, if intruders were around.

In October 1940 Sir Charles Portal was promoted and appointed to the post of Chief of Air Staff. His successor as C-in-C Bomber Command was Sir Richard Pierse. If the *Luftwaffe* night air defences were improving their ability to locate targets, the same could not yet be said for RAF Bomber Command. For, as was becoming clear, the darkness which protected the bombers from the defences, also hid the targets from the bombers. Air Vice Marshal Conningham's prediction, of a 'never-ending struggle to circumvent the law that we cannot see in the dark,' was being proved correct.

▲ The Commander-in-Chief Bomber Command Air Marshal Sir Charles Portal was promoted to Chief of Air Staff in October 1940.

◄ A Mk 1a Manchester, which was superseded by the Lancaster, is prepared for a mission on 17 April 1942 with two 2000 pound bombs. The type proved troublesome mainly due to the problems suffered by its two Rolls-Royce Vulture engines and was withdrawn from service.

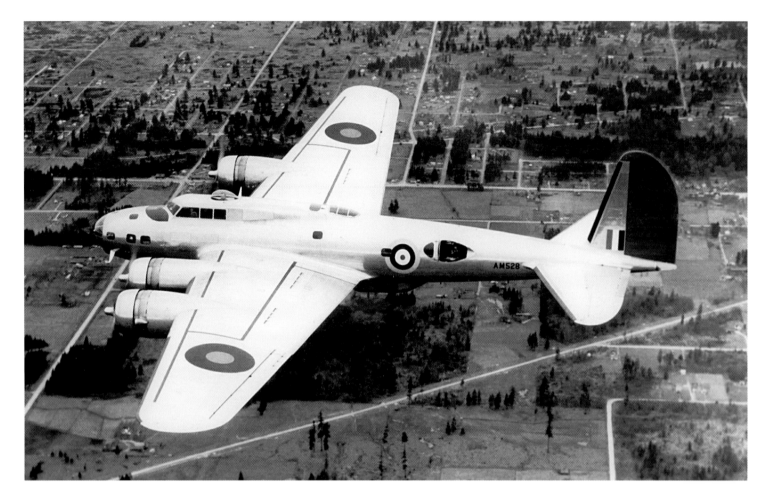

▲ A B-17C in RAF markings being test flown in the USA during 1941, prior to delivery to the UK.

The primary method of navigation used at this time by RAF Bomber Command during the early night attacks was known as 'dead reckoning'. The navigator directed the pilot to fly the aircraft on a calculated heading which, allowing for wind, would bring him to the target at the end of a calculated time of flight. If the pilot was allowed to fly the calculated heading without interference from the enemy, and if the meteorologists predicted correctly the upper-air winds over Germany, it would not have been that difficult for a competent navigator to find his target. But over enemy territory it was almost impossible to predict the wind velocity with any degree of accuracy. From trials flown over Britain, Bomber Command planners knew that, on average,

" ... a never-ending struggle

to circumvent the law that we

cannot see in the dark..."

dead reckoning errors for each 100 miles flown were in the order of 7 miles to either side of the intended track. This was bad enough, but on operational sorties harassment from enemy Flak or fighters could greatly increase the errors. Provided one of the crew could make out ground features, the navigator could update his plot and reduce the area of uncertainty. Yet, flying over blacked-out enemy territory, it was often impossible to obtain a fix off a ground feature after crossing the coast.

If there were clear skies above the aircraft, a navigator could take a fix on three stars to ascertain his position. But this required the aircraft to fly straight and level for several minutes while the navigator took his sextant shots, and there was a further delay while he completed the necessary mathematical calculations. As one airman later recalled, the process was *"... rather like sitting in a freezing cold stair cupboard with the door shut, the Hoover running, and trying to do calculus!"* At the end of it all, the resultant fix was unlikely to have an accuracy better than 12 miles.

Bomber Command crews made frequent use of radio bearings from ground direction-finding stations in England. Up to 200 miles from the ground station these bearings were reasonably accurate and useful, but

◄▲ The Short Stirling was the first of the modern four-engined bomber types to enter service with Bomber Command following the outbreak of war, beginning operations in February 1941. The Mark I, seen here, had a maximum speed of 260 mph and cruised at 215 mph at 15,000 feet. Maximum take-off weight was 70,500 pounds. Defensive armament was four Browning .303 inch machine guns in the rear turret, two of these weapons in the nose turret and two in the dorsal turret.

beyond that distance their value deteriorated rapidly.

Thus, with the primitive methods in use in RAF Bomber Command during the first two years of the war, a navigator was doing well if he arrived at a point within 20 miles of his target at the end of a dead reckoning run of 350 miles. Once in its general area, a crew might spend as long as an hour searching in the darkness for their target.

To provide a further distraction to the raiders, German engineers constructed numerous decoy targets in open countryside. For the most part these consisted of walled enclosures filled with combustible material which, when ignited, produced the effect of a group of burning buildings. These decoys were ignited electrically when enemy bombers arrived in their area. Fake lighting systems conveyed the impression of bad blackout or the opening of a door from a lighted room; simple sparking devices imitated the bright flashes that emanated from street cars on the move. Add to this a few well-placed searchlights and guns, a smoke screen and some explosions to simulate bomb bursts, and it is not difficult to see why many crews bombed the decoys and afterwards reported in good faith that they had hit their briefed targets.

In order to increase the effectiveness of the decoys, there was also a programme to camouflage important potential targets, so that they blended in with the surrounding background.

► The Handley Page Halifax entered service in December 1940. The type flew its first operational mission in March 1941, and was the first of the new RAF four-engined bombers to attack a target in Germany.

As well as the problem of finding their targets, RAF crews had also to learn to cope with the more lethal elements of the enemy air defence system and the *"RAF Manual of Air Tactics"*, 1941 edition, gave crews advice on how to react to the various threats. For example, to upset tracking by sound locators, crews were advised to de-synchronise their engines so that the latter ran at slightly different speeds. The resultant 'waaam-waaam-waaam' note made aural direction finding extremely difficult. (Those who lived through the *Luftwaffe* attacks on Great Britain will remember that the engines of German bombers issued a similar engine note – and for exactly the same reason). Germans who lived through the war said they could distinguish the RAF bombers flying over their homeland, from their varying engine note.

When engaged at high level by heavy anti-aircraft guns, bomber crews were told to make a six degree course change every 20 seconds. A well-drilled gun crew took about ten seconds to loose off a predicted round, and the predictor had to make corrections after

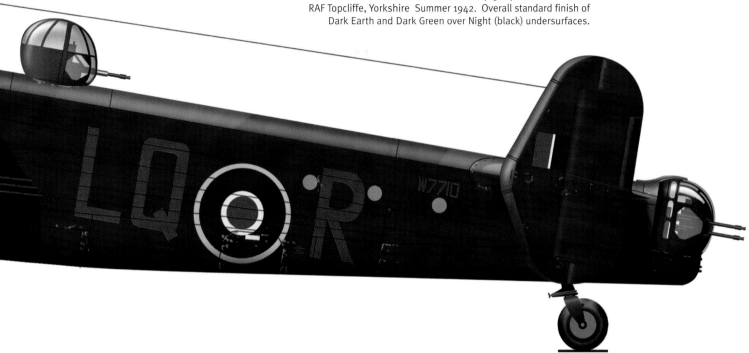

HANDLEY PAGE HALIFAX B II

This Halifax BII served with 405 Squadron RCAF from RAF Topcliffe, Yorkshire Summer 1942. Overall standard finish of Dark Earth and Dark Green over Night (black) undersurfaces.

each change in the target's heading. An 88 mm shell took about 14 seconds to reach 15,000 feet, so there was a good chance that the bomber would be well clear of the shell's lethal sphere when it detonated. If the Flak remained uncomfortably accurate in spite of this, crews were advised to trade height for speed. The manual pointed out that shells bursting above the aircraft were not dangerous, because the speed of the shell heading upwards cancelled out the velocity of the fragments coming down. Similarly, bursts behind the aircraft were less dangerous than those in front of it, since the aircraft's speed decreased the impact velocity of the fragments in the former case and increased it in the latter case.

To shake off an enemy nightfighter, crews were advised to make a diving turn in either direction. That would enable the bomber to pick up speed rapidly, and unless the latter was silhouetted against cloud it would be difficult to see from above at night.

By the middle of 1941, Spitfires modified for the long-range photographic role were ranging far and wide over Germany, going as far as the Baltic port of Stettin. They returned with clear pictures of targets that reportedly had been bombed, yet for the most part, the photographs showed disappointingly little damage. That meant one of two things: either the German damage

camouflage and repair organisations were superbly efficient or, as now seemed increasingly likely, the greater proportion of the bombs fell outside the target areas. Air Vice Marshal Saundby, the Senior Air Staff Officer at Bomber Command headquarters, went so far as to state that when bombers claimed to have dropped 300 tons of bombs on a certain target, all that could be said for certain was that they had *"exported 300 tons of bombs in its direction"*.

The new evidence called into question the effectiveness of the RAF bomber attacks, and the value the nation gained from this massive expenditure of resources. Professor Lindemann, Mr Churchill's scientific adviser, asked Mr D. Butt of the War Cabinet Secretariat to conduct an independent inquiry into the effectiveness of the bombing, using photographs taken at the moment of bomb release and during subsequent reconnaissance missions. Butt's findings were disquieting in the extreme. Only a small proportion of the bombers carried the attack cameras, and these aircraft were usually flown by the most experienced crews. Yet, of the crews that had reported hitting their briefed target, only one in four placed their bombs within five miles of it. During attacks on nights with a full moon, the proportion of crews getting their bombs within five miles of the target increased to two in five. In the Ruhr industrial area, with its almost permanent blanket of industrial haze, the proportion of crews hitting the target was considerably less. While the

MESSERSCHMITT Bf 109 E-3
Flown by Uffz. Hans Schubert, of 3./JG 1 stationed
at De Kooy, Holland in the spring of 1941.

▶ ▼ The first line of defence against daylight bombing
attacks on Germany was the *Luftwaffe* fighter force. Here pilots
of Jagdgeschwader 1 relax while at readiness close to the unit's
Bf 109 Es at De Kooy in Holland, in the summer of 1941. The E-3
variant had a maximum speed of 348 mph at
13,100 feet and its maximum take-off weight was
5,875 pounds. Its armament comprised two Oerlikon
MG/FF 20 mm cannon and two Rheinmetall MG 17, 7.9 mm
machine guns. Whenever the RAF attempted daylight attacks
on targets in Germany during this stage of the war, these
fighters took a heavy toll of the raiders. 'Yellow 4' was flown by
Uffz. Hans Schubert who is sitting at Sitzbereitschaft (cockpit
readiness) waiting for the order to scramble. (Via Obert)

RAF attacks on the Ruhr had dented Göring's pride, they inflicted remarkably few scars on the industrial area.

As a means of reducing German war production, Bomber Command's attacks were ineffectual. The evidence was irrefutable: even under ideal conditions on moonlit nights and in the summer, with Bomber Command's present navigational equipment, standards of crew training and tactical employment, it could not hit its targets with any reasonable degree of accuracy. After reading Butt's report Mr Churchill chided Sir Charles Portal, his Chief of Air Staff, with this: *"It is an awful thought that perhaps three-quarters of our bombs go astray ... If we could make it half and half, we should virtually have doubled our bombing power."*

In June 1941, German troops invaded the Soviet Union and advanced deep into that country. Winston Churchill knew that unless he could take measures to reduce the German pressure, the Soviet government might be forced to sue for peace. His army was far too weak to mount an invasion on the mainland of Europe. The only offensive weapon at his disposal with which he could strike at Germany, was RAF Bomber Command. That gave top priority to making the force into an effective weapon of war.

The first requirement was to provide Bomber Command with the systems necessary to enable its crews to locate and hit their targets. Scientists at the government Telecommunications Research Establishment were moved from tasks with a lower priority, and joined the teams working on radio and radar aids to assist the bombers.

In the autumn of 1941 the first such system, GEE, entered large-scale production, GEE employed three ground transmitters in England operating in concert and radiating a complex train of pulses in a pre-determined order. Using a special receiver, the aircraft navigator measured the minute differences in the time of arrival of the various pulses. Then, by referring those time differences to a special GEE map, he could read off his position. It took an experienced navigator about a minute to fix his position with the system.

In effect, the GEE transmitters laid an invisible radio grid across Europe. Using this grid, an aircraft could fix its position to within six miles at points 400 miles from the most distant transmitter. Closer to the transmitters, the system gave fixes accurate within about half a mile. GEE represented a striking improvement over the position-fixing aids previously in use in Bomber Command, and promised to increase the proportion of

"It is an awful thought that perhaps three-quarters of our bombs go astray ..."

aircraft which found and bombed their targets.

Also during 1941, three new heavy bomber types entered large-scale service with RAF Bomber Command. All of them offered improved performance and load-carrying capability, compared with the Whitleys, Wellingtons and Hampdens they were to replace.

First to enter service was the four-engined Short Stirling, able to carry a bomb load of 14,000 pounds for 740 miles or 5,000 pounds of bombs for nearly 2,000 miles.

Next came the Avro Manchester, which weighed almost as much as the Stirling but was powered by two big Rolls Royce Vulture engines each rated at 1,760 horse power. These powerplants proved unreliable in service, however, and immediately gave the Manchester a bad reputation amongst its crews.

Somewhat better was the other four-engined bomber, the Halifax, although in its early versions it was underpowered and exhibited some nasty handling characteristics when it was heavily loaded and flying slowly.

Thus, of the three heavy bomber types beginning their operational careers only one, the Stirling, could be considered effective in its initial form. The other two

▼ An RAF Sergeant is entertained by members of I./ZG 76, after successfully parachuting to safety from his damaged Wellington bomber on 18 December 1939.

▲ General Josef Kammhuber (centre) was given the task of forming a *Luftwaffe* nightfighter division. He is shown here in 1941 flanked by fighter pilot Lt. Hans 'Assi' Hahn of JG 2 on his right and nightfighter ace Stabsfeldwebel Paul Gildner on his left.

targets by day. The risks incurred during these daylight attacks were known to be great, but they had to be accepted. Even if the attacks caused relatively little damage to the enemy war machine, it was hoped they would constitute an ever-present threat that which hold back fighters that might otherwise go to the Eastern Front.

The scale of these daylight attacks varied greatly. For example on 30 June, just over a week after the invasion of the Soviet Union, six Halifaxes of the newly-equipped No. 35 Squadron bombed Kiel from altitudes of around 20,000 feet; one bomber failed to return. On 4 July, 12 Blenheims of Nos. 105 and 107 Squadrons delivered a low-level attack on the docks at Bremen. Four Blenheims were shot down, and most of the others returned with damage. Afterwards, Wing Commander Hughie Edwards received the Victoria Cross for leading the attack.

would eventually be developed into extremely successful bombers, but that would take time. A further heavy bomber type arrived from the USA during 1941, the Boeing B-17C Flying Fortress. Bomber Command received sufficient aircraft to equip one squadron. This early version of the bomber was only lightly armed, however, and it was much inferior to the developed versions which would follow later.

During 1941 the great majority of Bomber Command attacks on Germany were made at night, but from time to time the Command mounted attacks on

The most ambitious incursion during 1941, with the deepest penetration into enemy airspace by day, was the low altitude attack on the electrical power stations at Knapsack and Quadrath near Cologne on 12 August. Eighteen Blenheims attacked Quadrath, while twice that number attacked Knapsack. Fourteen squadrons of Spitfires and one of Whirlwinds provided penetration and withdrawal cover for the two striking forces, led by two Blenheims which acted as navigation leaders. For the final 100 miles to the target, however, and the first

◀ ▲ A *Luftwaffe* Flak crew run to their 88 mm anti-aircraft gun during an exercise. The red collar patches as worn by the *Luftwaffe* Flakartillerie are clearly shown by the Gefreiter (Private First Class) crew member holding one of the 88 mm Flak shells.

150 miles of the withdrawal, the Blenheims of the two striking forces were on their own. Each Blenheim carried two 500 pound bombs, with fusing delay of 11 seconds to allow the low flying aircraft time to get clear before the weapons detonated.

To draw enemy attention away from the raiders, Bomber Command mounted simultaneous small scale raids on Gosney power station and St. Omer airfield in France, and De Kooy airfield in Holland. The main raid was a bold incursion into enemy territory, and the defending fighter and Flak units reacted vigorously. Ten attacking Blenheims were shot down, as were the two aircraft serving as navigation leaders for the fighters. Several other Blenheims suffered damage. That rate of bomber losses, 12 Blenheims out of 56 dispatched (21 per cent), was far too heavy to contemplate except in rare cases or where an operation was likely to secure important military or political objectives. Four escorting Spitfires were also lost. There were no losses from the aircraft taking part in the diversionary actions.

The two attacks inflicted serious damage at the Cologne power stations, although repairs were effected relatively quickly and both were soon returned to full operation.

Also during this period, the RAF experimented with daylight attacks from very high altitudes, above 30,000 feet, using its newly acquired B-17C Flying Fortresses. No. 90 Squadron, the sole Bomber Command unit to receive this variant, never possessed more than nine of them so there was no question of mounting large-scale attacks on the lines of those which would become common in later years. Instead, the Fortresses attacked either singly or in formations of two or three. Yet even these bombers could not fly high enough or fast enough to avoid the attentions of German fighters. Lacking power-operated gun turrets, their ability to defend themselves was poor. In September 1941, following the loss of three aircraft in action and four more in accidents, the B-17Cs were withdrawn from operations over

▲ In the autumn of 1941 elements of NJG 1 were sent to the Mediterranean theatre of operation. This Bf 110 F belonging to 8./NJG 1 can be identified as one of these aircraft as it has the usual operational theatre markings applied in the form of a white rear fuselage band. On this aircraft the outer underside of the wings have also been painted white.

◄ The Würzburg radar manufactured by the Telefunken Company entered large-scale service in the *Luftwaffe* in 1941, and was a considerable improvement over the sound locators it replaced. The tracking information from the radar was fed into the predictor, enabling gunners to engage high-flying raiders at night or above cloud.

"The most suitable object from an economic point of view, is not worth pursuing if it is not tactically available"

THE NIGHT THE FUEL RAN OUT

On the evening of 7 November 1941, after a frustrating period of poor weather, Bomber Command launched its most powerful attack to date. Some 392 Whitleys, Wellingtons, Hampdens, Manchesters, Halifaxes and Stirlings set out to attack Berlin (the main target) as well as Cologne, Manheim, Essen, Ostend, Boulogne, and to lay mines off the Norwegian coast. Over the North Sea they encountered strong westerly winds, with cloud thicker than forecast and patches of hail.

Of the 169 aircraft sent to the most distant target, Berlin, 21 failed to return. The westerly winds which assisted the raiders on their way out acted against them on their homeward flights. Several crews, recognising the problems which were likely to arise, turned back early and dropped their bombs on targets of opportunity. Of those that continued to the enemy capital, many had problems with severe icing, or ran out of fuel on the way home and crashed into the North Sea.

In all told Bomber Command lost 37 aircraft, more than double its previous highest numerical loss. The attackers failed to achieve any degree of concentration at any of their targets.

▼ The main bomber-destroying weapons carried by German nightfighters during the initial stages of the war was the 20 mm Oerlikon MG/FF cannon. The detachable drum magazine held 45-rounds and when it was empty a crewman had to replace it with a full one – no easy task at night and at altitude.

northern Europe. Although the type was not yet ready for battle in this most testing of theatres, the lessons of its shortcomings during the early high-altitude attacks would be well learnt.

Between May 1940 and the end of July 1941, the *Luftwaffe* nightfighter force was credited with some 250 victories, of which just under half went to the intruder force. During the same period RAF Bomber Command lost 543 aircraft to all causes, so the nightfighters' claim has a ring of truth. By now Josef Kammhuber had been promoted to *Generalmajor*. His force operated some 250 twin-engined fighters, of which about 170 were available for operations at any time. The expansion of the nightfighter arm, both in terms of aircraft and ground radar stations, continued.

In the autumn of 1941, following the invasion of Russia and the general over-extension of the *Luftwaffe*, there was an important change in the pattern of nightfighter operations. The unit conducting the night intruder operations over Britain, some elements of NJG 2, were transferred to the Mediterranean theatre. The intruder missions against the RAF bomber airfields ceased, never to resume as a regular feature. Thus, without firing a shot, the RAF secured the right to develop its bases in England and train its crews virtually without interference from the enemy.

At the end of 1941 the *Luftwaffe* possessed 302 nightfighters, of which about 150 were available for operations at any time. With the strength of the force steadily increasing, and the introduction of new and more effective equipment, it was starting to inflict serious losses on the raiding forces. And this trend was likely to continue, for the nightfighters were about to receive a new airborne radar code-named *Lichtenstein* with a maximum range of some two and a half miles.

In Britain there was a new air of realism in RAF Bomber Command, with the recognition that the night bombers could not hit small industrial targets from high altitude. Attempts to do so had led to many bombs being scattered over open countryside. As Air Chief Marshal Sir Charles Portal was moved to comment: *"The most suitable object from the economic point of view, is not worth pursuing if it is not tactically attainable."*

The result was a gradual shift towards attacking targets which were considered *"tactically attainable"*, i.e. the German cities. Senior Bomber Command officers hoped that this move towards the so-called 'area bombing' would be only temporary. With the introduction of GEE, and with other advanced electronic devices in the planning stage, it was hoped that the force would revert to more precise forms of bombing.

In securing its poor set of bombing results, Bomber Command had incurred serious cumulative losses. Between 7 July and 10 November 1941 the force lost 414 night bombers and 112 day bombers. That was roughly the equivalent of losing Bomber Command's entire strength in aircraft and crews during the four-month period. A few days after the costly operation on the night of 7/8 November (see box on pg 34), the War

Cabinet ordered Air Marshal Sir Richard Pierse to reduce the scale of the bomber offensive during the winter months in order to conserve the force, and allow it to build its strength with the introduction of new aircraft types and, at the same time, provide improved training for the crews.

Sir Richard Pierse's reputation did not survive the scale of Bomber Command's losses, coupled with the relative ineffectiveness of its attacks. To be fair, given the paucity of the equipment during his tenure of office, it is doubtful whether anyone else could have done any better. In January 1942 Pierse was moved sideways to take command of the RAF units in India. For a few weeks Air Vice-Marshal J. Baldwin, the commander of No. 3 Group, acted as temporary C-in-C Bomber Command until a permanent successor could be appointed.

In December 1941, following the Japanese attack on Pearl Harbor, the United States entered the war. America was already in the process of assembling a large strategic bomber force to conduct daylight attacks, and we shall observe its progress in later chapters.

Thus, at the beginning of 1942, both sides in the air war over Germany were in a state of flux. With new equipment on order, however, both sides had reason to feel that the year would see decisive developments in their favour. In that, both sides would be proved wrong.

FIGHTER UNITS ASSIGNED TO REICH AIR DEFENCE

24 JUNE 1941

In recognition of the growing threat to Germany from the RAF, a new headquarters with *Luftflotte* status, **Luftwaffenbefehlshaber Mitte**, had been formed to direct units located in the homeland. The table below gives those units assigned to the role of day and night air defence of metropolitan Germany.

Unit		Total	Serviceable
Jagdgeschwader 1			
Stab	Bf 109	4	4
I. Gruppe	Bf 109	28	24
Nachtjagdgeschwader 1			
Stab	Bf 110	4	2
I. Gruppe	Bf 110	37	28
II. Gruppe	Bf 110 z	32	21
	Do 215	5	2
III. Gruppe	Bf 110	34	28
	Bf 109	11	9
Nachtjagdgeschwader 2			
Stab	Ju 88	4	4
I. Gruppe	Ju 88	32	15
	Do 17	6	4
Nachtjagdgeschwader 3			
Stab	Bf 110	3	3
I. Gruppe	Bf 110	37	32

◄ The effect of the explosive shells fired by the 20 mm Oerlikon MG/FF cannon can be seen on the fuselage of this Avro Manchester of No. 83 Squadron. On average, it required about 20 hits with 20 mm rounds to knock down a heavy bomber. (Lewin, via Garbett/Goulding)

2

THE WEAPONS TAKE SHAPE

January-December 1942

"Tis with our judgements as our watches, none

go just alike, yet each believes his own."

Alexander Pope

The opening of 1942 brought with it an air of optimism in Germany that the war on the Eastern Front might be brought to a victorious conclusion that summer. The front line was at the gates of Moscow and Leningrad, and German troops had taken prisoner more than two and a half million men. When the spring thaw ended and the ground dried out, few doubted that the German army would resume its Blitzkrieg advance and finish the task of destroying the Red Army. In the Atlantic the U-boat arm was inflicting heavy losses on the hard-pressed convoys of merchantmen, and a large expansion of the submarine force was already well in hand. Indeed, the USA had now entered the conflict, but was still building up its military strength. So far its forces had been able to do little except fall back before the powerful Japanese thrusts in the Pacific. With the Soviet Union defeated and the Atlantic blockaded, would the British and Americans have any choice but to negotiate a peace on German terms?

Over Germany itself, the RAF's nocturnal attacks caused little more than a few sleepless nights, although this was soon to change. In February 1942, Air Marshal Arthur Harris assumed command of RAF Bomber Command, at a time when a number of improvements initiated by his predecessor were about to take effect. During March the GEE radar navigational aid became operational, and it was not long before the German people started to feel its effect. On 28 March a force of 234 bombers carried out an attack on Lübeck which razed parts of the city. For the first time, the RAF night bombers had caused serious harm to

such a target. In the following month Rostock suffered similarly , in the course of four successive night attacks. Both targets were outside the 400 mile maximum range of GEE, yet in each case the new navigational aid proved of considerable assistance along the route and the attacks took place on moonlit nights against easily identifiable coastal targets.

However, even when attacks were launched with the assistance of GEE, they could still go seriously wrong. On the night of 4/5 May, for example, 121 RAF bombers took off to attack the Robert Bosch factory at Stuttgart which manufactured dynamos, magnetos and fuel injection pumps for aero and motor engines. But when the raiders arrived in the target, it was blanketed in cloud and bombs were scattered over a wide area. About 15 miles north of the city was a clever decoy site defended by 35 searchlights and 50 heavy anti-aircraft guns. As a result of a spectacular display by this site, more bombs fell wide of the target area. Stuttgart itself therefore suffered little damage that night, and the Robert Bosch factory was untouched. The poor weather also affected the fighter and gun defences, however, and the attacking force lost only one bomber.

During the first 18 months of the night offensive individual bomber crews had been free to choose their own route to and from the target. Many of them attributed their survival to the fact that they did things differently from everyone else. Thus the raiders crossed the German defensive line at widely separated points, one or two at a time, over a

◄◄ A Handley Page Halifax II undergoing maintenance. The Mk II featured a new streamlined nose in an attempt to increase performance.

► In February 1942 Air Marshal Arthur Harris (left) assumed leadership of Bomber Command. Under this vigorous new commander, shown here with his deputy, Air Vice-Marshal Saundby, the force rapidly built up its strength and effectiveness and the night bombers began to make concentrated attacks on targets in Germany. (IWM)

period of several hours. That was the grist for which Josef Kammhuber had designed his *Himmelbett* mill.

With the introduction of the new German airborne and ground fighter-control radars and the expansion of the nightfighter force, the increased potency of the

defences became all too clear to RAF Bomber Command. During the six months to the end of February 1942, night bomber losses had amounted to a bearable 2.7 per cent of the forces involved, but during the following three months the average loss rate climbed to nearly four per cent. The increase was due almost entirely to the nightfighters. Although the higher loss remained bearable, the question arose: might it be reduced if the bombers adopted more effective tactics?

With the improvement in navigation which GEE had made possible, it became feasible to send the entire bomber force along the same route, achieving concentration in space and time. As the working of the *Luftwaffe* night air defence system became known in Britain, the advantages of such concentration became clear. A *Himmelbett* control station and its associated nightfighter could engage only one bomber at a time, and on average the interception took ten minutes. A Flak battery could bring aimed fire to bear on only one bomber at a time, and such an engagement might last about two minutes. Both defensive systems worked best if the bombers came through their respective areas in

ones and twos, with a long interval between each. In that case they could engage almost every target that passed within their range.

If, on the other hand, the bombers passed through the defences in a concentrated mass, the defenders would have a surfeit of targets for a short time, and none for the remainder. An efficient *Himmelbett* station could engage a maximum of about six bombers per hour. So, no matter how many more aircraft flew through its area

"There was a tremendous argument as to whether we should concentrate and accept the resultant risks."

◄ A Stirling of No. 149 Squadron, flown by Sgt J. Jerman, which was shot down during a minelaying operation over the Baltic on 18 May 1942. It is pictured here after it crash-landed near Aabenraa in Denmark. The crew was taken prisoner. (Helme)

SHORT STIRLING Mk. I
Serving with 149 Squadron from RAF Mildenhall, Suffolk, May 1942. Overall standard finish of Dark Earth and Dark Green over Night (black) undersurfaces.

▲ A Bf 110 of II./NJG 1 being re-fuelled at Deelen in readiness for another sortie against Allied bombers during the autumn of 1940. During the latter half of 1940 many of these units operated out of airfields based in Holland which enabled the nightfighters to intercept the bombers before they reached their targets, as well as on their return journeys.

▲ ► Due to the shortage of Bf 110s during 1942, small numbers of Do 217s were modified to serve as nightfighters. Although the type had an excellent endurance, it was sluggish in the climb and insufficiently manoeuvrable. As a result it was unpopular with crews, and after a short period in front line service it was relegated to the training role.

◄ A four-gun heavy battery positioned south-west of Bremen. The annotation represents: A, heavy guns, probably 105 mm; B, light Flak weapons, probably 20 mm; C, searchlights; D, gunfire predictor; E, Würzburg radar for fire control; F, accommodation; G, ammunition storage; H, gun emplacements abandoned, probably used earlier for smaller weapons.

during that time, all except those six unfortunates were safe from fighter attack. Similarly, the Flak defences were limited in the number of targets they could engage.

Concentrating the bomber force in a more compact volume of sky would, of course, increase the risk of collisions between the attacking aircraft. It would also increase the risk of aircraft being hit by bombs dropped from above. Dr Basil Dickins, head of the Operational Research Section at Bomber Command headquarters and a staunch advocate of concentration, told the author:

"There was a tremendous argument as to whether we should concentrate and accept the resultant risks. The interesting point here is that when a crew failed to return from an operation, that was just too bad, but if the crew returned with a hole in the wing caused by an incendiary bomb from above or if there was a jolly near miss, they would tell everyone about their close shave. This highlighted the collision risk. We had to reduce it all to mathematics, and work out the actual chance of a collision. And it became quite obvious to us at ORS that while a collision was a half per cent risk, the chance of being shot down by Flak or fighters was a three or a four per cent risk. So we could allow the collision risk to mount quite a bit, provided that in doing so we would bring down the losses from other causes."

It must be stressed that in this context the term 'concentrate' was relative, to be compared with what had gone before. In fact the bombers would still be spread out quite thinly. Dickins proposed that they should cross any given point on the route at a rate of about ten per minute.

FIGHTER UNITS ASSIGNED TO REICH AIR DEFENCE

27 JULY 1942

By now the RAF had started to mount damaging attacks on the German homeland, forcing the *Luftwaffe* nightfighter force to continue its expansion. It now comprised two full *Geschwader*, and two under-strength *Geschwader*.

Also in England the US Eighth Air Force had started to build its strength, though some months would elapse before it could alter the balance of air power. In recognition of these developments, the home defence day fighter force had been expanded to an overstrength *Geschwader*, with four *Gruppen* of Fw 190s.

Unit		Total	Serviceable
Jagdgeschwader 1			
Stab	Bf 109	4	4
I. Gruppe	Bf 109	28	24
Jagdgeschwader 1			
Stab	Fw 190	4	4
I. Gruppe	Fw 190	37	34
II. Gruppe	Fw 190	38	28
III. Gruppe	Fw 190	40	33
IV. Gruppe	Fw 190	39	28
Nachtjagdgeschwader 1			
Stab	Bf 110	3	2
I. Gruppe	Bf 110	19	14
II. Gruppe	Bf 110	15	15
	Do 217	14	7
III. Gruppe	Bf 110	15	15
	Do 217	3	1
Nachtjagdgeschwader 2			
Stab	Ju 88	3	1
II. Gruppe	Bf 110	23	17
	Do 217	10	1
	Do 215	6	5
III. Gruppe	Ju 88	20	13
	Do 217	15	7
Nachtjagdgeschwader 3			
Stab	Bf 110	2	1
I. Gruppe	Bf 110	20	16
	Do 217	3	1
II. Gruppe	Bf 110	24	21
	Do 217	9	6
III. Gruppe	Bf 110	31	24
	Do 217	1	1
Nachtjagdgeschwader 4			
Stab	Bf 110	1	1
II. Gruppe	Bf 110	15	8
III. Gruppe	Bf 110	19	13
	Do 217	7	5

▲ Backing the German nightfighters were the ground Himmelbett stations which operated a Freya surveillance radar (centre) for area surveillance, and two Giant Würzburg sets to track the movements of the bomber and the attacking nightfighter. (Via Heise)

▲ A close-up of the Giant Würzburg, a development of the small Würzburg used to provide fire control for Flak. The new radar employed a larger reflector, to narrow the transmitted beam and thus increase the effective range of the device.

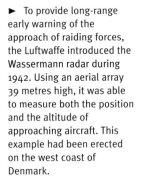

► To provide long-range early warning of the approach of raiding forces, the Luftwaffe introduced the Wassermann radar during 1942. Using an aerial array 39 metres high, it was able to measure both the position and the altitude of approaching aircraft. This example had been erected on the west coast of Denmark.

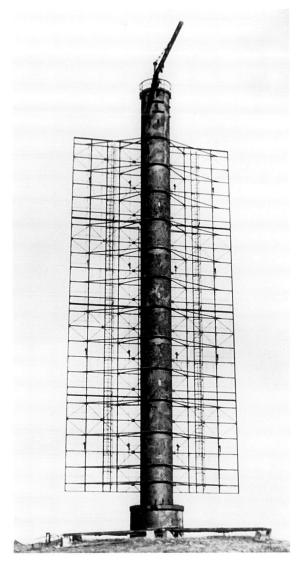

That would mean ten bombers scattered randomly inside a 'box' of sky some three miles long, five or more miles wide, and nearly two miles deep. Thus, even on a clear night, there would be only a slight chance of a crew seeing more than one or two of the other bombers engaged on the operation. The 'bomber stream', as it became known, was in no way comparable to even the loosest formation. Nor would it enable bombers to provide each other with mutual defence against nightfighters though, on occasions, some would attempt it.

The first use of the bomber stream tactic coincided with an important milestone in the RAF bomber offensive: its first 'Thousand Bomber' raid. For political reasons Air Marshal Harris needed to mount such a blow to show that his force really could hit hard at the enemy. Later he wrote: -

"Such a demonstration was, in fact, the only argument I could see which was at all likely to prevent our squadrons being snatched away and our effort diverted to subsidiary targets, or to extract the equipment we so desperately needed, the radar navigational aids and target indicators, from the torpid departments which withheld them for so long."

To assemble the thousand bombers Harris considered necessary, he used his entire operational force as well as nearly 500 bombers from his operational training units. The latter were to be flown by instructors or by crews in the final stages of training. He was, therefore, staking both the present and the future of his

▲ Also during 1942 the Luftwaffe introduced the Mammut early warning radar into service, the example depicted being set up near Den Helder in Holland. The Mammut had a longer range than the Wassermann, but it was unable to measure target altitude.

force on this single attack.

The target for the attack was Cologne, situated in the west of Germany and well within GEE cover. In the van of the attack would be about 100 GEE-equipped aircraft of Nos. 1 and 3 Groups, loaded with incendiary bombs to start fires which would guide in the remainder of the force. The attack was mounted on the night of 30/31 May and 1,047 bombers took off to attack the German city, a force about four times greater than any which Bomber Command had previously committed. The attack was scheduled to take

90 minutes, giving a planned density of about eleven aircraft per minute passing over the target.

Harris' demonstration cost Bomber Command its highest numerical loss to date, 43 aircraft lost. On the other hand the loss expressed as a percentage of the force, 3.9 per cent, was not significantly different from the norm for attacks at this time. The Cologne attack took place on a moonlit night, which greatly increased the danger from nightfighters, and a proportion of the bomber crews lacked previous operational experience. Undoubtedly the losses would have been greater, had the force not used the tactic of concentration. Moreover, the raiders caused widespread damage to a major German city, the first time they had done so.

The bombers' route to and from the target took them through the Himmelbett areas served by the *II. Gruppe* of *Nachtjagdgeschwader 1*, equipped with Bf 110s. As one might expect, this unit enjoyed an abundance of targets

▲ In March 1942 the Avro Lancaster I commenced operations in Bomber Command. This aircraft had a maximum speed of 275 mph and cruised at 220 mph at 20,000 feet. Normal loaded weight was 65,000 pounds. Defensive armament was four Browning .303 inch machine guns in the rear turret, plus two of these weapons in the nose and dorsal turrets.

"...we encountered the first, which we recognised as a Wellington, 500 metres away. At almost exactly the same time the Tommy spotted us..."

and was able to shoot down eight bombers, but for each one destroyed, more than a score passed through the defensive line unscathed.

One of the most noteworthy actions that night, from the German side, was that fought by *Leutnant* Niklas and his radio operator, *Unteroffizier* Wenning, both with *II./NJG 1*. On the approach of the bombers they had taken off from their base at St. Trond in Belgium and orbited the radio beacon at their allocated fighter control station. Then, as Wenning later recalled:

"In our area we did not have long to wait. At 3,000 metres we encountered the first, which we recognised as a Wellington, 500 metres away. At almost exactly the same time the Tommy spotted us. He made a sudden turn to the right, then turned away from us. We went after him, but his fire was so strong that we could not get into a firing position and we overshot the Wellington... Again we moved into a position behind the target and, from short range, we pumped shells into the bomber's left wing. It caught fire and we could see the flames. By this time our victim was down to 2,000 metres. Again we closed in. We

fired another burst into the fuselage and wings, and the flames burnt brighter. Then we moved out for a while, waiting to see whether it would be necessary to go in again. For a short time the Wellington flew on, the blaze growing the whole time. Then it flipped over and went down, trailing sparks like a comet. Close to the ground it exploded, lighting up the surrounding countryside."

Niklas and Wenning climbed back up to operational altitude, and reported to their ground station that they were ready for the next target. Almost immediately they were guided into position behind a second, and sighted it 700 metres in front.

"He was weaving but he did not open fire. Had they seen us? We went straight into the attack. The target grew larger until, suddenly, it seemed enormous. My breath almost stopped: we were going to ram him. From short range we opened fire, hitting him on the wings and on the fuselage. We could see the glow of the flashes on the rear fuselage. I was about to call out "He's on fire!", when suddenly Leutnant Niklas shouted "I've been hit, breaking

▲ Many of the aircraft operated by the German Nachtjagdgeschwader carried the socalled 'Englandblitz' emblem of a diving eagle holding a red lightning strike pointed at London.

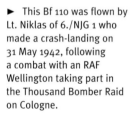

▶ This Bf 110 was flown by Lt. Niklas of 6./NJG 1 who made a crash-landing on 31 May 1942, following a combat with an RAF Wellington taking part in the Thousand Bomber Raid on Cologne.

MESSERSCHMITT Bf 110 E-1

This aircraft was on the strength of 6./NJG 1 based in Holland in 1942. The aircraft is finished in all over black with grey codes. Note the red only sharkmouth marking on the nose.

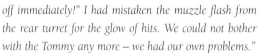

◄ A partial enlargement of the dashed area on the previous photograph revealing a Bf 110 nightfighter parked outside its hangar.

◄ The important bomber and nightfighter airfield at Venlo in Holland, showing the aircraft dispersal area in a nearby wood and the well-camouflaged individual aircraft hangars.

off immediately!" I had mistaken the muzzle flash from the rear turret for the glow of hits. We could not bother with the Tommy any more – we had our own problems."

Niklas' left arm was smashed and unusable, and bleeding profusely. Unable to reach the controls from his position in the rear of the fighter, Wenning improvised a tourniquet and tied it round Niklas' arm. Then he set about the difficult task of directing his pilot back to St Trond, as the latter drifted in and out of consciousness. Wenning continued:

"That was how we flew back to our airfield. Leutnant Niklas was almost over the lights before he caught sight of them. It was too late to land on the runway. So, with a sideslip, he tried to get down on the emergency strip. Trees passed just below us. 'We're too low!' Leutnant Niklas murmured, 'I can't go on any longer', and slumped forward. There was a scraping sound and soil was flung against the cabin. We skidded over the ground for what seemed an eternity. I sat there tensely. So this was what a crash landing was like, I had always imagined that it would be different. The crashing and splintering grew louder, there was a jerk and everything was still. Then Leutnant Niklas shouted:

▲ A Bf 110 F nightfighter of Nachtjagdgeschwader 1. This variant equipped the bulk of the Luftwaffe nightfighter force during the early years of the conflict. It had a maximum speed of 566 km/h at 5,400 metres. Normal take-off weight was 7200 kg. Offensive armament comprised two Oerlikon MG/FF 20 mm cannon and four Rheinmetall MG 17 7.9 mm machine guns on fixed mounting in the nose. In addition there was a single Rheinmetall MG 15 7.9 mm weapon on a hand held mounting firing rearwards.

'Let's get out of here!' He had hit his head but had regained consciousness. He leapt from his seat, trying to run and at the same time to release his parachute harness, but it was no good and he fainted. I laid him out gently on the grass, and opened his blood-soaked flying suit. Soon a doctor and others appeared, and they carried him away. I was surrounded by a lot of people, who began to ask questions; I realised just how lucky I had been."

Having assembled his large force, Air Marshal Harris was anxious to press his advantage. Early in June he mounted two more monster attacks: on the night of 1st/2nd he sent 956 bombers to hit Essen, and on the night of 25th/26th he launched a force of 1,006 bombers

▲ The larger of the two Flak towers at Friedrichshain, showing how the giant 27-metre high structure dominated the skyline.

◄ An RAF reconnaissance photograph of the Flak towers (arrowed) in the Friedrichshain district of Berlin. These massive structures, constructed of ferro-concrete, were built to provide clear fields of fire for AA gun batteries situated in built-up areas. The larger tower, on the right, mounted one heavy gun – either a 105 mm or a 128-mm, at each corner of the upper structure. On smaller platforms at a lower level were lighter 20 mm or 37 mm guns. The smaller tower, on the left, carried the fire control radar, the predictor and the command post as well as some light AA weapons. The towers' lower storeys housed air raid shelters and civil defence headquarters.

► The Kammhuber Line: the German nightfighter defence system at the end of 1942.

▲ Generalmajor Josef Kammhuber, commander of the Nachtjagdwaffe.

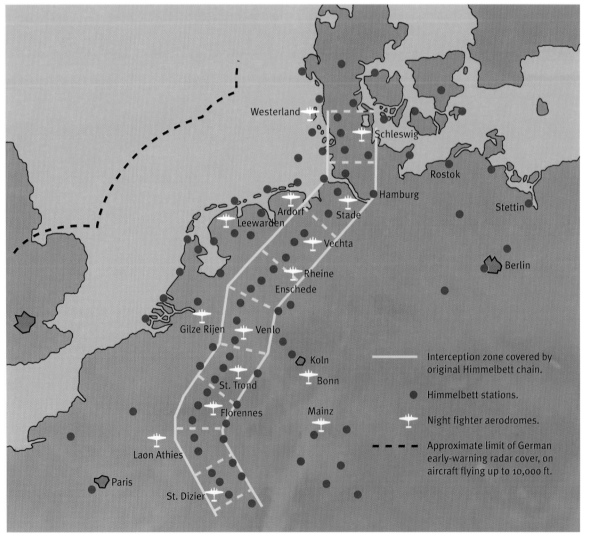

Westerland

Schleswig

Rostok

Hamburg

Stettin

Ardorf

Stade

Leewarden

Vechta

Berlin

Rheine

Enschede

Gilze Rijen

Venlo

Koln

St. Trond

Bonn

Florennes

Mainz

Laon Athies

Paris

St. Dizier

Interception zone covered by original Himmelbett chain.

Himmelbett stations.

Night fighter aerodromes.

Approximate limit of German early-warning radar cover, on aircraft flying up to 10,000 ft.

◄ Some flak towers carried double mountings for the 128 mm gun, the heaviest weapon operated by the Luftwaffe.

▶ As might be expected, the RAF took a keen interest in the development of the German radar system and specially modified aircraft, like this Wellington of No. 1473 (Wireless Investigation) Flight, were sent to find details of new types of radar on the air. This unit scored several major successes, including the discovery of the operating parameters of the Lichtenstein nightfighter radar.

▲ Special equipment operator's position in the rear fuselage of a Wellington of No. 1473 Flight. Note the makeshift nature of the work table. Searches of different parts of the frequency spectrum required different sets of equipment. In this example the black-painted receiver nearest the camera was an American-built Hallicrafters S.27 receiver, popular with radio hams before the war.

against Bremen. On both occasions, however, the attackers found their targets shrouded in cloud and the bombs fell over a wide area. The losses were of the same order as those during the earlier Cologne attack. Soon afterwards, Harris was knighted. He had made his point, that really large scale raids were now within his command's capability. There was no need to hazard his training organisation any further. Bomber Command resumed its attacks on its previous lighter scale, sending out three or four raids of over 100 bombers each week.

In the first few months operational use of GEE it became clear that although the device was an extremely useful aid to navigation, it was not precise enough over Germany to allow blind bombing. The proportion of bomber crews getting their bombs within three miles of the target rose from about a quarter to one third. That increase over what had gone before was worthwhile, though there was still considerable room for improvement.

For its part the *Luftwaffe* quickly realised the reason

for the sudden increase in bombing effectiveness. To counter GEE it ordered the mass-production of the powerful *Heinrich* jamming transmitter, and set these up in ground stations throughout western Europe. As a result, from August 1942, the GEE signals were swamped out and the device was of little further use inland. In coastal areas, however, GEE still provided bomber crews with a final accurate fix as they entered enemy territory. It was, therefore, still useful in assisting bomber crews to stick to their planned routes.

To meet the new tactics of concentration *Generalmajor* Kammhuber buttressed his original defensive line with additional *Himmelbett* stations, in front of it and behind it. In this way he increased the depth of the defences through which the raiders had to pass, and each extra station in a position to engage added its toll to the price the attackers had to pay. To further improve these defences, the *Luftwaffe* and the German Navy erected a chain of the powerful new *Wassermann* and *Mammut* long-range early warning radars along the northern coast of Europe. These could plot the bombers as they rose above the radar horizon, far out to sea.

During the early months of 1942 Bomber Command began to receive two important new types of aircraft: the de Havilland Mosquito and the Avro Lancaster. The Mosquito was a fast twin-engined machine, which in its early forms carried a bomb load of 2,000 pounds at a cruising speed of 260 mph and had the range to attack Berlin. Its high speed and altitude performance enabled it to operate over Germany with comparatively little risk by day, and with virtually none by night. The Lancaster was a four-engined development of the unsuccessful Manchester and could haul a bomb load of 8,000 pounds to Berlin cruising at 210 mph at altitudes around 20,000 feet – a marked improvement over any of the other types then in service. Both aircraft were now coming into large-scale production, but it would be many months before they made up more than a small proportion of Bomber Command's striking power.

With the advent of the bomber stream tactics, there was a clear need in Bomber Command for a means of accurately marking targets for the raiders. Only in this way would attacks achieve the concentration of bombing necessary for the targets to be knocked out. Accordingly, in August 1942, Group Captain Donald Bennett was ordered to set up the Pathfinder Force. In its initial form it comprised four squadrons, one each of Stirlings, Halifaxes, Wellingtons and Lancasters. Their crews had all completed at least one tour of 30

DORNIER Do 215 B-5
Serving with Stab II./NJG 2 at Leeuwarden, Holland, 1942,
this aircraft is painted in RLM 65 (Grauviolet), 74 (Graugrun)
with RLM 76 (Lichtblau) undersurfaces.

operational sorties. The idea of having selected crews to start fires at the target was not new and had been tried before several times, notably during the three 'Thousand Bomber' attacks. The important difference was that the best crews in Bomber Command were to be creamed off, and concentrated in the elite force permanently.

The first raids led by the Pathfinders in the summer of 1942 brought an improvement in bombing concentration, but concentration was not everything. Accuracy was even more important and there the Pathfinder crews, lacking the necessary equipment to locate the targets, were less impressive. A concentrated attack on open fields was of less military value than a scattered attack which fell across fields and built-up areas. Group Captain Hamish Mahaddie, one of those in the force since its inception, told the author:

"With all the fuss made about the formation of the Pathfinder Force, people expected rather more from us than we were physically able to give. We felt rather like the star footballer, purchased at some enormous transfer fee, who fails to score a goal during his first season."

Indeed, the precision radar devices and the distinctive target marking bombs necessary to make the Pathfinder Force effective were all by this time in an advanced state of development, yet during the painful formative period of the force during the summer and autumn of 1942, it seemed that the partially sighted were trying to lead the blind. Clearly RAF Bomber Command had a long way to go before it could present a potent threat to targets in Germany.

By the end of 1942, RAF Intelligence had assembled an almost complete picture of the operation of the *Luftwaffe* night air defence system, except for one important aspect – there was little information on the *Lichtenstein*

interception device fitted to the nightfighters. Since the spring of that year, radio monitoring stations in England had noted a new term in the enemy nightfighter crews' vocabulary – *Emil-Emil*. And from the intercepted conversations, it was clear that *Emil-Emil* was some form of target location device carried in aircraft.

In July, a nightfighter crewman had said "I have the enemy aircraft on Emil-Emil. Please give further vectors." In September a ground station asked a fighter: "I have vectored you to within two kilometres of the enemy aircraft, haven't you picked him up on Emil-Emil?" Also that night, a nightfighter pilot explained why he had broken off radio contact with his ground controller: "I had an enemy aircraft on Emil-Emil, and broke off radio contact with you during that time". The ground controller rebuked him, and said he had to maintain radio contact at all times.

By the autumn of 1942 the number of radio conversations mentioning *Emil-Emil* reached such proportions that it seemed most nightfighters now carried the device. Obviously it was an important system, but what was it? Was it a radar, or was it perhaps an infrared device which homed on a bomber's hot engine exhausts. Before any countermeasures could be taken, that question had to be answered.

To search for an answer, scientists from the

▲ This Do 215 B-5 variant was operated by the Stab II./NJG 2 at Leeuwarden, Holland in 1942. Developed from the Do 17 bomber for the night fighting role, the Do 215 was fitted with more powerful DB 601A engines. Even so its performance fell short of that of the Bf 110, and very few saw front line service.

Telecommunications Research Establishment set up a monitoring station on the Norfolk coast. They sited a radar receiver in a depression in the ground so that it was below the normal horizon and would pick up only transmissions coming from aircraft. Within days the listeners had picked up their first important clue. A ciné camera mounted in front of the cathode-ray tube photographed a series of pulses on a frequency of 490 MHz. The RAF had no equipment operating in that part of the radio spectrum, and the rate at which the sources of the signals moved pointed to it being an airborne system.

That did not mean the aircraft concerned were necessarily nightfighters, however. They might, for example, have been maritime patrol aircraft carrying a quite different type of radar to search for ships. The only way to be certain was to send out specially equipped 'Ferret' aircraft to trail their coats in front of the enemy. If a nightfighter carrying the 490 MHz radar intercepted one of these aircraft, that would constitute clear proof.

The unenviable task of acting as live bait to dangle in front of a *Luftwaffe* nightfighter fell to No. 1473 (Wireless-Investigation) Flight. Lone Wellington Ferret aircraft patrolled over France, Belgium and Holland, their special operators briefed to listen for radar-type transmissions on frequencies around 490 MHz. Then, to be certain the signals came from a nightfighter's radar, they were to allow the enemy to close to short range. Only then were they allowed to make their escape, while the radio operator transmitted a coded message to base with the findings.

On the initial flights the Ferret crews' fears were not realised, for the *Luftwaffe* simply ignored the isolated aircraft. Although the aircraft picked up suspicious signals in the 490 MHz band, the mystery remained. If the *Luftwaffe* refused to react to lone aircraft flying over coastal areas, the next step was to send Ferret aircraft to accompany raiding forces flying to their targets. That made the duty distinctly more dangerous for the Ferret aircraft and its crew, though it must be stressed that the degree of risk was no greater than that experienced by the crews of other aircraft in the force.

On the night of 2/3 December 1942, a Ferret Wellington flew with a force of 113 aircraft attacking Frankfurt. Near Mainz the special radio operator, Pilot Officer Harold Jordan, picked up weak signals on 490 MHz. For the next ten minutes he noted their characteristics – and observed that they gradually increased in strength. Jordan warned the rest of the crew, then drafted a coded signal to the effect that 490 MHz signals had been picked up and almost certainly they

◄ ◄ Staff Sergeant Lusic of the 8th Air Force poses for the cameraman his aircraft in front of the nose of B-17 "MEAT" HOUND. Flying suits needed to be well padded to protect against the cold at high altitude and the life-jacket was also essential in case the aircraft had to ditch in the sea.

◄ Crew members of a B-17 Flying Fortress hitch a ride out to their aircraft on bomb and ammunition trailers at an 8th Air Force base somewhere in England in early 1943. The officer in the foreground is sitting on a 2,000 pound bomb.

came from a nightfighter's radar. Jordan passed the message to the wireless operator, Flight Sergeant Bill Bigoray, to transmit to England.

Any remaining doubts that the signals came from a nightfighter were dispelled when they rose to a level that swamped Jordan's receiver. Shortly afterwards the Wellington shuddered under the impact of exploding cannon-shells. Sergeant Ted Paulton, the pilot, threw the aircraft into a steep diving turn to shake off the assailant. The rear gunner opened fire on the attacker, which he recognised as a Junkers 88. Although he had been hit in the arm, Jordan wrote a second coded message confirming that without doubt the frequency given in the first signal came from a nightfighter's radar. The nightfighter attacked again and the rear-gunner fired another short burst before his turret was put out of action and he was wounded. Also during that attack, Jordan received further wounds in his jaw and eye.

Paulton's manoeuvre shook off the nightfighter, but the encounter had left the Wellington in dire straits. The throttle of the port engine had been shot away, while that to the starboard engine was jammed and both engines were running rough. Both gun turrets had been

knocked out and the hydraulic system was shot to pieces. The starboard aileron no longer worked and both airspeed indicators were useless. Four of the crew of six were wounded.

Despite leg injuries, Bigoray tapped out Jordan's second coded message. Receiving no acknowledgement, he repeated the message many times in the hope that someone might hear it. In fact a ground station in Britain picked up the vital signal and sent a reply, but this went unheard because the Wellington's wireless receiver was wrecked. Doggedly, Bigoray continued tapping at his Morse key as the Wellington struggled home.

It was getting light when the battered aircraft reached the coast of England, and now there was a new problem. The Wellington was too badly damaged to risk a crash landing, so Paulton decided to put it down in the sea close to the shore. Bigoray's legs had stiffened from his wounds, and it was feared that he might not escape from the aircraft before it sank. He was helped to drop by parachute, carrying a copy of the second all-important signal in his pocket. Paulton then ditched the Wellington about 200 yards off the coast at Deal. The aircraft's dinghy was badly holed and useless, so the men climbed on to the wallowing bomber until a small boat picked them up.

Bomber Command showed its appreciation for the crew's selfless devotion to duty in the weeks to follow. Jordan was awarded the Distinguished Service Order, Paulton received a commission and the Distinguished Flying Cross, and Bigoray received the Distinguished Flying Medal.

The gallant mission added the last significant piece to the jigsaw puzzle picture of the *Luftwaffe* night air defence system, and in the months to follow the vulnerabilities of the various radio and radar devices could be exploited to the full.

As 1942 drew to a close, RAF Bomber Command was not the only force flexing its muscles for the struggle against Germany. From the time the USA entered the war, it spared no effort to create a heavy bomber force designed to mount daylight attacks on targets in Europe. That led to a vigorous debate with their British allies. Citing their own bitter experience, RAF leaders tried to convince their ally that to attempt long-range daylight incursions into enemy airspace, far beyond the range of any possible fighter escort, would court disaster. Why not learn from the British experience and attack at night?

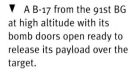
▼ A B-17 from the 91st BG at high altitude with its bomb doors open ready to release its payload over the target.

From their diplomatic, journalistic and business sources in Germany prior to the entry of the USA into the war, US Army Air Force commanders knew that the British night attacks had achieved relatively little. If German industrial targets were to be destroyed from the air, they argued, it would have to be done by means of daylight precision attacks. If heavy losses were suffered in achieving that war-winning aim, so be it. The bombers would be powerfully armed and would fly in tight mutually-defensive formations, so that when the *Luftwaffe* fighter force tried to contest these incursions, it was confidently expected that they would also suffer heavy losses.

In September 1942, Air Vice-Marshal Slessor visited Washington to sense the mood there. In his report to the Chief of the Air Staff, Sir Charles Portal, he wrote: *"They have hung their hats on the day bomber policy and are convinced that they can do it."* He added that in his view, it would be unwise to cast further doubts on the matter since these would *"... only cause irritation and make them very obstinate"*. Air Chief Marshal Portal passed these views on to the Secretary of State for Air, Sir Archibald Sinclair, with the comment:

"My own prophecy of what will actually happen is this: the Americans will eventually be able to get as far as the Ruhr, suffering very much heavier casualties than we

now suffer by night, and going much more rarely. They will in effect do area bombing with the advantage of the absence of decoys. If it can be kept up in the face of the losses (and I don't think it will be) this will of course be a valuable contribution to the war, but it will certainly not result in the elimination of the enemy fighter force ... I do not think that they will ever be able regularly to penetrate further than the Ruhr and perhaps Hamburg without absolutely prohibitive losses, resulting from being run out of ammunition by constant attack or from gunners being killed or wounded."

The US Army Air Force was short of combat experience, but it had the advantage of massive industrial backing. The two heavy bomber types now in large-scale production, the Boeing B-17E Fortress and the Consolidated B-24D Liberator, warranted the title of 'conscripts' aircraft'. They were strongly built, relatively easy to fly and they could be operated and maintained effectively by aircrews and technicians with only a short period of training. To fit them for the expected slogging matches, the bombers carried extensive armour plating and also self-sealing fuel tanks. Their most important defence, however, was from the ten .5 inch machine guns. These weapons delivered twice the weight of fire of the .303 inch calibre guns carried by the RAF bombers, and could engage attackers at ranges of up to 800 yards. Operating their heavy bombers in large formations so each aircraft could provide and receive supporting fire from its neighbours, the US planners believed that it would be possible to inflict severe losses on enemy fighter units attempting to press home attacks. The Flak defences would be an ever-present danger, but by flying at altitudes greater than 20,000 feet, this threat was reduced to within manageable proportions.

The US Eighth Air Force heavy bombers made their first attack on a target in occupied Europe on 17 August 1942, when 12 B-17s bombed the Sotteville marshalling yard near Rouen in France. Nine squadrons of Spitfires escorted this short-range incursion, and there were no US losses. In the months to follow, the Eighth Air Force expanded steadily and its attacks became progressively stronger and more ambitious.

On 9 October US bombers launched their most powerful attack so far, sending 108 B-17s and B-24s with fighter escort to strike at the Fives-Lille steel works in Belgium. At this time the *Luftwaffe* had two fighter *Geschwader* in position to provide the defence of targets in France and Belgium: *JG 2* and *JG 26*. Between them they operated some 330 aircraft, mainly Fw 190s but

also a few Bf 109s. The Fives-Lille attack was one of the first occasions when defending fighters broke through to the bombers and shot down four for the loss of two fighters. One successful German pilot during this engagement was *Oberleutnant* Otto Stammberger of *III./JG 26*. His combat report highlighted the difficulties he and his comrades experienced initially, when trying to engage the big American bombers:

"... At last I got to height and in position. We attacked the enemy bombers in pairs, going in with great bravado, closing in fast from behind with throttles wide open, then letting fly. But at first the attacks were all broken off much too early – as those great barns grew larger and larger our people were afraid of colliding with them. I wondered why I had scored no hits but then I considered the size of the things: 40 metres span! The next time I went in I thought: get in much closer, keep going, keep going. Then I opened up, starting with his motors on the port wing. By the third such firing run the two port engines were burning well, and I had shot the starboard outer engine to smithereens. The enemy kite went down in wide spiralling left-hand turns, and crashed just east of Vendeville; four or five of the crew bailed out."

At this time *Luftwaffe* single-engined fighters were deficient in one important respect: their lack of fire power when it came to engaging the big American bombers. The Focke-Wulf 190 A-4, the most powerfully armed single-seat fighter, carried an armament of four 20 mm cannon and two 7.9 mm machine guns. On average, 20 hits with 20 mm explosive rounds were necessary to bring down a B-17 or a B-24. It is stressed that this was an average figure, for there were occasions when bombers returned with more than 20 hits, and others when less than 20 hits caused lethal damage. The 7.9 mm rounds were ineffective in this type of engagement.

When they analysed air-to-air combat films of the engagements, German armament experts found that of

▲ Oberleutnant Otto 'Stotto' Stammberger of 4./JG 26.

"I wondered why I had scored no hits but then I considered the size of the things: 40 metres span!"

▲ Pilots of 7./JG 2 run to board their Fw 190 A-2s at Théville during the early summer of 1942. In JG 2 there were differing states of readiness which were not laid down according to hard and fast rules, but varied in each Gruppe. In this case the pilots were probably near enough to their aircraft to be able to take off within a few minutes.

the carefully-aimed rounds fired by pilots of average ability at the US heavy bombers, only about 2 per cent scored hits. Thus, to obtain the required 20 hits needed to achieve the bomber's destruction, 1,000 rounds of 20 mm ammunition had to be fired at it whereas the Fw 190 A-4 carried only 510 rounds of this ammunition. The unpalatable conclusion was that, with the present equipment, the average German fighter pilot could not shoot down a US heavy bomber unless he and his comrades made repeated attacks on individual aircraft.

Gradually the defenders began to take the measure of

their new opponent. Yet even seasoned *Luftwaffe* fighter pilots found it disconcerting to have to brave the bombers' massed tracer fire as they moved into firing positions behind their targets. One answer to the problem was to attack the bombers from head-on, where the bombers' defences were far less potent. Not only could fewer guns be brought to bear in that direction, but the 'fire swept' zone could be crossed far more quickly. To exploit this weakness, the commander of *III/JG 2*, *Major* Egon Mayer, experimented with such attacks on the American formations. On 23 November he led his *Gruppe* into action against a force of 36 unescorted B-17s attacking the

► This B-17 named 'TINKER TOY' belonging to the 381st BG, was considered to be a 'jinx ship' as it had returned several times from a mission with dead and wounded on board. It is shown here after a mission on 8 October 1943 showing 20 mm shell damage and the two men point to the hits around the cockpit area which led to the captain being decapitated.

FOCKE-WULF Fw 190 A-3 'WHITE 7'
This aircraft was flown by Oblt. Egon Mayer, Staffelkapitän of
7./JG 2, Théville, June 1942.

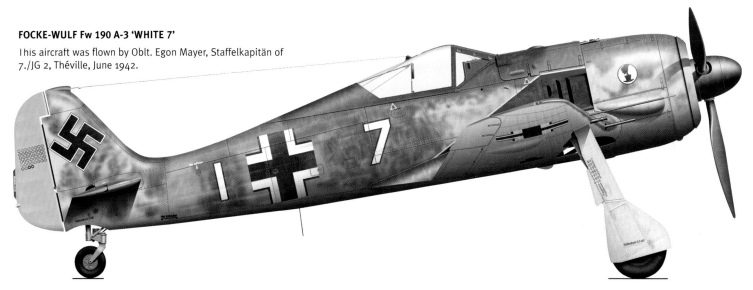

Egon Mayer joined the *Luftwaffe* as a *Fahnenjunker* in the autumn of 1937 and
was commissioned on the outbreak of war in September 1939. His first kill was
a Morane Saulnier 406 fighter, which he claimed on 13 June 1940 when with
6./JG 2, part of the *Richthofen Geschwader*. On 3 September 1940, *Lt.* Mayer
claimed a Spitfire as his second victory and claimed his fourth and fifth victories, both Spitfires, in June 1941. Within the next two months his victory tally
increased to 20. He was awarded the *Ritterkreuz* on 1 August 1941. By June
1942, he had been promoted to *Staffelkapitän* of 7./JG 2 and had increased his
victory tally to 54, as shown on the rudder of his Fw 190 A-3, 'White 7'. At this
time, Meyer had not yet destroyed a US four-engined heavy bomber, but he
later became known among other pilots of 7./JG 2 as the 'Fortress specialist',
eventually credited with 25 B-17s. His aircraft still retains the *Staffel's* top hat
emblem which was replaced in late 1942 by the cockerel's head emblem of
III. *Gruppe* when, *Hptm.* 'Assi' Hahn took over as *Kommandeur*.

The emblem of 7./JG 2.

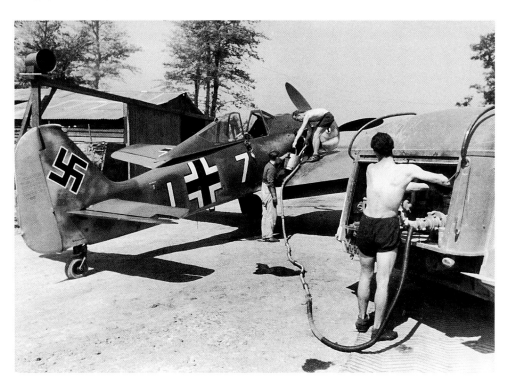

U-boat pens at St. Nazaire. The Focke-Wulfs attacked from head-on in threes, shooting down four bombers and seriously damaging another. It was the most successful defensive effort against the US heavy bombers so far, and other units began employing this method.

Mayer's tactics involved making a rendezvous with the American formation, usually with help from a ground controller, after which the German pilots trailed their quarry for a short time to gauge its course and altitude. That done, the fighters overtook the bombers but kept out of range of the defensive fire. When about two miles ahead of the bombers, the fighters turned through a semicircle and ran in to attack. The US heavy bombers cruised at about 175 mph and the Germans throttled back to a similar speed, to give a closing speed of about 350 mph. That allowed time for a brief firing pass, opening fire at 500 yards and breaking off at 300 yards.

Hauptmann Anton Hackl, who would later command III./JG 11 and who was credited with the destruction of more than 30 US heavy bombers, outlined the alternatives facing *Luftwaffe* fighter leaders during a conversation with this writer:

"If one came in from the rear there was a long period, closing from 1,000 metres to our firing range of 400 metres, when the bombers were firing at us but we could not fire at them. This was a very dangerous time

▲ ► During 1942 the German nightfighter force was considerably strengthened. The majority of fighters now carried the Lichtenstein radar, whose distinctive aerials are seen on the nose of a Bf 110 and a Ju 88.

and we lost a lot of aircraft trying to attack that way.
'An alternative was to attack the bombers from above in
the dive and for that we needed to start from a position
at least 1,000 metres higher and 500 metres in front of
the bombers. Then we could dive with plenty of speed
and the bomber made a nice fat target, but the problem
with this type of attack was that it took time to set up.
The head-on attack was the only way to knock down the
bombers. One accurate half-second burst from head-on
and a kill was guaranteed. Guaranteed!"

Technical Sergeant William Murphy, who flew as
mid-upper gunner on a B-24 Liberator of the 44th
Bomb Group, described the difficulty of hitting the
enemy fighters as they ran in from head-on and flashed
past his turret:

"The only ones we ever got were those who made
a bad pass, and mushed off their speed as they tried
to break away early or pull round on to us; if they
did that we stood a chance, but the experienced
guys knew better than that and they kept going

straight through our formation, giving an extremely
difficult target."

As in the case of the RAF much earlier in the war,
the first half year of operations by the Eighth Air Force
was a time of rapid learning for both the US bomber
crews and their German opponents. Those lessons
would govern both sides' tactics when the US
Eighth Air Force turned its attention to targets in
Germany itself.

The new year, 1943, seemed likely to see the
attacks on Germany itself by American bombers
operating by day. Also, by night, the RAF laid great
store on the introduction of revolutionary new
electronic equipment to locate targets. For those
reasons, December 1942 could be regarded as a
turning point in the war in the air. How apt were
Winston Churchill's words, spoken the previous month
after the victory at El Alamein: "This is not the end. It is
not even the beginning of the end. But it is, perhaps, the end
of the beginning."

▲ Armourers of JG 2
replenish the ammunition
magazines of Fw 190 A-2
W.Nr. 318. The pilot, Klaus-
Heinz Ender of 3./JG 2, was
killed while flying this
aircraft during combat with
120 B-17s near Conches,
France, on 22 September
1943. To make maximum use
of its available fighters, the
Luftwaffe designated several
airfields in the Reich and the
occupied territories where
fighters could be rapidly
refuelled and rearmed to
enable them to fly a second
sortie in the course of a
single action. This second
sortie was made under the
command of the most senior
pilot present.

3

THE NIGHT RAIDERS STRIKE HOME

January-August 1943

"If we must be enemies let us be men and fight it out

as we propose to do, and not deal in hypocritical

appeals to God and humanity."

General Sherman, in a letter to General Hood
before the Battle of Atlanta during the American Civil War, 1864

The first month of 1943 was the most calamitous for German arms in the war so far. At Stalingrad the Red Army had encircled an entire German Army Group comprising more than 300,000 men, and was on the point of annihilating it. Meanwhile, in North Africa, the *Afrika Korps* was falling back after its defeat at El Alamein and had abandoned Libya to the advancing British and Allied forces. Both these events took place a long way from home, and the German people accepted the propaganda line that the setbacks, though serious, would not alter the previous course of the war.

In Germany itself the night bomber attacks were an unpleasantness, but for most people life went on with little interference. As the new year opened *Generaloberst* Hubert Weise, commanding the Air Force Region Centre (*Luftwaffenbefehlshaber Mitte*) which controlled all units operating in the defence of the Reich, prepared to meet the increasingly heavy air attacks that would certainly be mounted from Britain during the months to follow. The nightfighter force had continued to expand throughout 1942 and it now operated some 390 aircraft: Messerschmitt Bf 110s, Junkers Ju 88s and Dornier Do 217s, most of which carried *Lichtenstein* radar. The continual demands of the front-line units in the East and the South had precluded any similar expansion of the day fighter force, however. To ward off the expected American daylight attacks Weise had only about 200 Bf 109 and Fw 190 single-seat fighters.

For the day and night protection of targets there were some 600 four-gun heavy Flak batteries equipped mainly with 88 mm guns, though a few of the heavier 105 mm and 128 mm guns were also in service. There were also about 200 searchlight batteries. The voracious demands for radar and signals equipment for the *Himmelbett* defences had resulted in shortages for many of the other branches of the German armed services. As a result, even at this stage of the war, less than one-third of the heavy Flak batteries possessed fire-control radar sets.

At the beginning of 1943 Bomber Command's operational strength for the night offensive against Germany comprised some 600 Lancaster, Halifax and Stirling heavy bombers, 250 Wellington medium bombers, and 30 Mosquitoes used as light bombers or Pathfinders. By now the obsolete Whitleys, Hampdens and Blenheims, as well as the unsuccessful B-17C Fortresses and Manchesters, had been withdrawn from operations. To compound the effectiveness of this increasingly powerful force, two new airborne blind bombing devices were on the point of entering full operational use in the Pathfinder Force: 'Oboe' and 'H2S'.

Oboe operated in conjunction with a pair of ground stations situated in England, and for this reason its area of effectiveness was limited to

◄◄ From the beginning of 1943 the RAF's Pathfinder Force introduced new systems to enable its aircraft to find and mark the targets for the main force of bombers. This Pathfinder Halifax Mark II of 35 Squadron is seen taking off from its base at Graveley. Under the rear fuselage may be seen the distinctive bulge housing the scanner for the H2S radar. This variant had a maximum speed of 254 mph and cruised at 225 mph. Normal loaded weight was 51,500 pounds. Defensive armament was four Browning .303 inch machine guns in the rear turret, a further four of these weapons in the dorsal turret, and a Vickers K gun on a hand held mounting in the nose. (Daniels, via Garbett/Goulding)

▶ An H2S picture of Wilhelmshaven and the island of Wangerooge, compared with a map of the same area. On the radar, built-up areas gave the best returns, open land the next best, and sea areas the weakest returns.

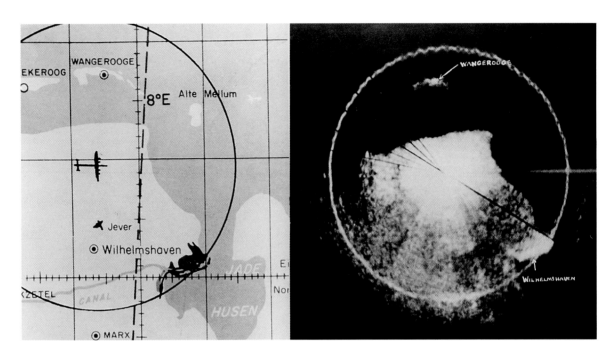

within 280 miles from the more distant ground station; in fact this distance comfortably took in the Ruhr industrial area, and several other important targets besides. Since a pair of ground Oboe stations could control only one bomber at a time, and a bombing run took about ten minutes, a massed attack by aircraft carrying the device was out of the question. Yet in spite of this drawback, Oboe possessed the overriding advantage that it was far more accurate than any comparable device. Releasing on Oboe alone, with no sight of the ground, it was possible to position bombs with a 50 per cent circular error of about 400 yards (The 50 per cent circular error is the radius of the circle into which the best 50 per cent of a number of individually-aimed bombs will fall, when released by a skilled bomb-aimer using a given method of sighting. The plotting of the most accurate half of the bombs discounts gross errors due to malfunctions, and thus provides a quantitative indication of the accuracy of an aiming system).

The airborne Oboe equipment was, moreover, small and light enough to fit into the Mosquito without requiring major modifications or imposing any reduction in its performance. The plan was, therefore, for fast, high-flying Mosquitoes of the Pathfinder Force to provide the initial target marking during the heavy bomber attacks.

H2S was, for its time, an extremely advanced centimetric-wavelength radar which scanned the ground beneath the aircraft. The returning echoes came strongest from built-up areas, less strongly from open countryside, and least strongly from areas of water. By displaying the echo signals on a cathode-ray tube, the radar produced a reasonable representation of the surrounding terrain which could be compared against a map of the area. The size and weight of the initial versions of H2S decreed that the device could be fitted only in heavy bombers. Since it was independent of ground stations, H2S was effective out to the maximum distance that the carrying aircraft could take it.

Depending upon the size and the radar characteristics of the target, the 50 per cent circular error using H2S varied greatly, but it was to the order of three or four times that of Oboe. Even so, this represented a considerable improvement over any previous long-range navigational or bombing system.

To exploit the accuracy of the new electronic target-finding systems becoming available to the Pathfinder Force, special target indicator bombs were put into production. These fell like ordinary bombs until they reached a predetermined height – usually 3,000 feet – where they explosively ejected 60 brilliantly coloured pyrotechnic candles. The candles spread out during their fall to form a distinctive pool of fire some 300 yards in diameter on the ground. The candles from the normal target indicator burned on the ground for about three minutes. A longer burning version was under development, in which the ignition of a proportion of the candles was delayed. This would produce a somewhat less bright fire on the ground, but for up to seven minutes.

The new target indicator bombs were first used during the attack on Berlin on the night of 16/17 January 1943. The presence of their distinctively coloured fires had the important side effect of making it much easier for main force crews to distinguish the real target from any fire decoys that had been ignited in the area.

Accompanying the new target-finding and marking devices into service were no fewer than four separate electronic gadgets intended to ease the bombers' passage through the *Himmelbett* defensive line: 'Monica', 'Boozer', 'Mandrel' and 'Tinsel'.

Monica was a rearward-looking radar set, fitted into bombers to provide warning of an enemy fighter closing in from behind. Within the bomber stream the problem of distinguishing the lone foes from the mass of friends proved insurmountable, however, and the frequent false alarms proved more of a hindrance than a help.

Boozer was a simple radar warning receiver, tuned to the frequencies of the German *Würzburg* and *Lichtenstein* radars. Signals from the former illuminated an orange lamp on the pilot's panel, while those from the latter illuminated a red light. This indicated that a Flak or fighter engagement might be imminent, and the crew should commence a corkscrew evasive manoeuvre. In service, however, Boozer was dogged by similar problems to those afflicting Monica: there were too many false alarms, this time coming from enemy radars tracking other bombers in the stream.

Somewhat more successful were the other two new devices, Mandrel and Tinsel. Mandrel radiated noise jamming on the *Freya* radar frequencies, thereby slowing the process of directing the narrow-beam *Giant Würzburg* radar on to the target bomber. Tinsel was a simple modification to the bombers' communications transmitters, to enable these to radiate noise jamming on the German nightfighter control channels. Working together, these two devices were effective in slowing the working of *Himmelbett*. The time thus bought often made the difference between life and death for bomber crews. Since a defending nightfighter was tied to its ground station, if its crew failed to get the bomber on their short-range *Lichtenstein* before it passed outside the range of the controlling *Giant Würzburg* radars, the interception had to be abandoned.

If any of those at Bomber Command headquarters imagined that the introduction of Oboe and H2S would immediately transform the force from a bludgeon into a rapier, they would be quickly disillusioned. The initial attacks using these systems, during the early months of 1943, were either inconclusive or unsuccessful.

For example, on 3 March a force of 417 aircraft set out to bomb Hamburg, led by 14 H2S-fitted Pathfinders. The new radar had been in service for only two months, however, and its serviceability was poor. Even before they reached the target area, six of the Pathfinders had

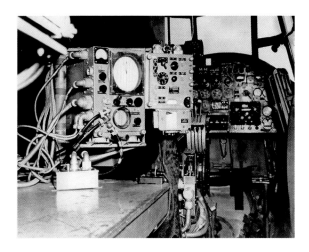

◄ The H2S display unit, to left, in the navigator's position of a Lancaster.

◄ An Oboe ground transmitting station, showing the two sets of aerials which enabled the station to control simultaneous bombing runs by two aircraft.

◄ The Oboe blind bombing equipment mounted in the nose of a Mosquito of the Pathfinder Force.

suffered radar failures. Other H2S aircraft suffered partial failures, including one whose crew decided to press on to the target even though the definition of their equipment had deteriorated greatly. Huddled over his screen, the radar operator saw the line of the Elbe River begin to narrow and from his map he knew the river narrowed at Hamburg. Moreover, on his blurred radar

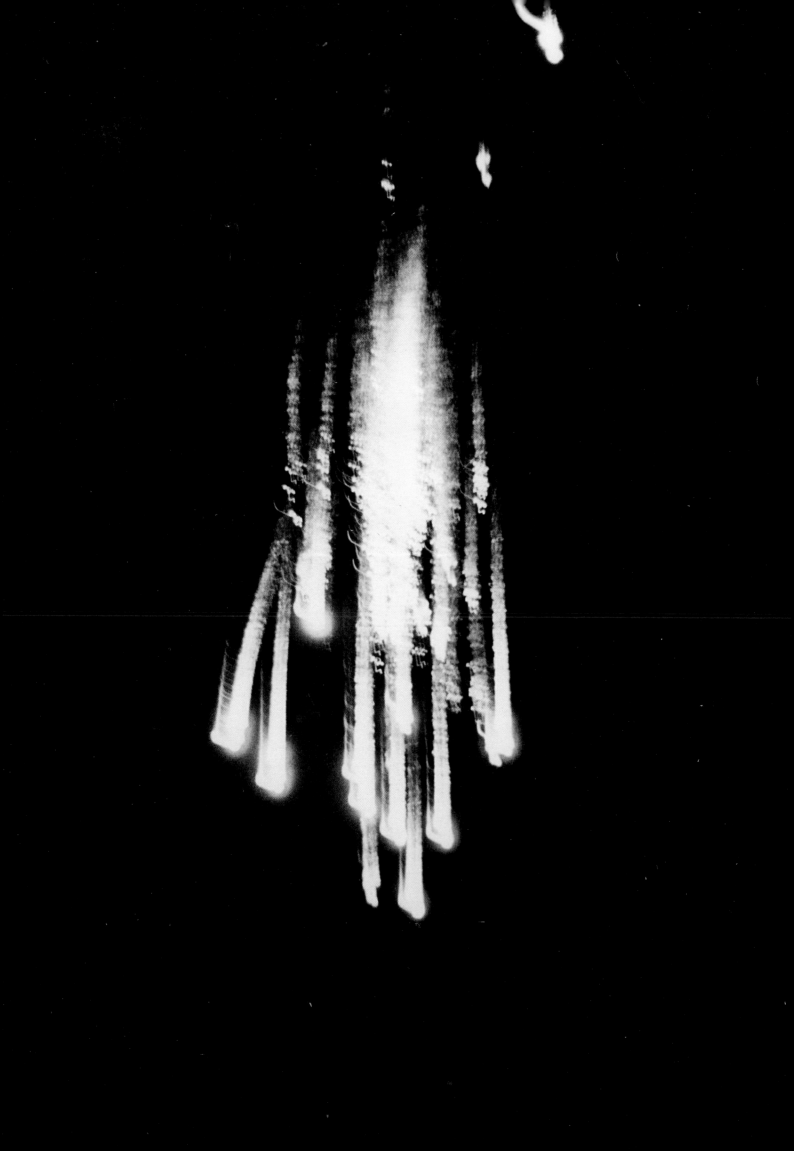

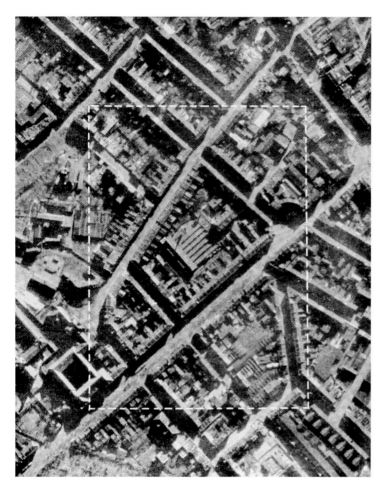

picture he could just make out the shape of Lake Alster, a distinctive feature near the middle of the target city.

Today, radar target prediction – the estimation of how a ground feature will appear on a ground-mapping radar when seen from various angles and under various conditions – is a fairly exact science. In the spring of 1943, however, such sophistication was unknown. It was assumed that a target, especially one at the head of a distinctive river feature such as Hamburg, could be found easily enough using a normal topographical map. During the attack on 3 March, Bomber Command learnt that this was not so.

At the time the raiding force crossed the German coast, the tide was out and the out-flowing waters of the Elbe uncovered extensive sandbanks. Thus, on the H2S radar screens, the river appeared to narrow well downstream of Hamburg. Nor was that all. Near the small town of Wedel, ten miles downstream of Hamburg, there was a fire decoy site with a refinement few others could boast. Engineers had dammed a small mill stream nearby to produce a lake, whose shape resembled the Alster lake in the centre of Hamburg. It was the Wedel Lake the radar operator had seen on his screen. Thus mistaken, he guided the aircraft through its

bombing run and let go the salvo of target markers. Within minutes these markers had been backed-up by markers from other Pathfinders in the stream, and these became the aiming point for a torrent of high-explosive and incendiary bombs. The majority of the raiders released their loads on the decoy, obliterating Wedel itself and several nearby villages. The bomber crews ignored other target markers which had been accurately placed on Hamburg, away to the east, thinking these to be decoys. That night Hamburg went almost unscathed. Later analysis of attack photographs revealed that of 344 crews who reported attacking Hamburg, only 17 had actually done so. The failure cost ten aircraft. Considering the revolutionary nature of the new equipment, such mishaps were inevitable though it gave scant comfort to those involved.

If the defenders drew comfort from the Wedel fiasco, the next major RAF attack brought them back to ugly reality. On the night of 5/6 March the target was Essen. Eight Oboe-fitted Mosquitoes were to mark the target with red target indicators for the 438 heavy Pathfinders and main force aircraft that would follow. During their briefings the crews learnt that the method of placing the red target indicators would be 'a new and

◄▲ A pre-strike photo of Aachen.

▲ A post-strike photo of part of the same area of Aachen, taken after following the Bomber Command attack by 374 aircraft on the night of 13/14 July 1943. In the area depicted there is scarcely a single house with its roof intact.

◄ Ground view of the pyrotechnic candles cascading down from a target indicator bomb. On the ground they produced a distinctive pool of red, green or yellow fire.

FIGHTER UNITS ASSIGNED TO REICH AIR DEFENCE

17 MAY 1943

In May 1943 the front-line strength of the *Luftwaffe* was nearly one-third larger than in the previous July, and close to the peak numerical strength it would ever attain. In each combat theatre it faced numerically far stronger enemy air forces and, overall, the *Luftwaffe* now suffered a serious shortage of single-engined day fighter units. For the daytime defence of the homeland there were only 198 serviceable day fighters available, and to achieve even that meagre figure, three *Gruppen* had been withdrawn from the battle fronts: *I./JG 3* and *III./JG 54* from the Eastern Front, and *I./JG 27* from the Mediterranean.

Unit		Total	Serviceable	Unit		Total	Serviceable
Jagdgeschwader 1				**Nachtjagdgeschwader 3**			
Stab	Fw 190	3	1	Stab	Bf 110	2	2
I. Gruppe	Fw 190	31	27	I. Gruppe	Bf 110	11	11
	Bf 109	7	0		Do 217	11	9
II. Gruppe	Fw 190	39	31	II. Gruppe	Do 217	29	20
				III. Gruppe	Bf 110	23	18
Jagdgeschwader 3				IV. Gruppe	Ju 88	25	22
Stab	Bf 109	3	3				
I. Gruppe	Bf 109	40	17	**Nachtjagdgeschwader 4**			
				Stab	Bf 110	1	1
Jagdgeschwader 11				I. Gruppe	Bf 110	22	19
I. Gruppe	Fw 190	40	27		Do 217	11	8
II. Gruppe	Bf 109	54	27	II. Gruppe	Bf 110	22	20
					Do 217	11	11
Jagdgeschwader 27				III. Gruppe	Bf 110	24	22
I. Gruppe	Bf 109	37	24		Do 217	6	5
				IV. Gruppe	Bf 110	23	23
Jagdgeschwader 54					Do 217	3	3
III. Gruppe	Bf 109	45	41				
				Nachtjagdgeschwader 5			
Nachtjagdgeschwader 1				Stab	Bf 110	2	1
Stab	Bf 110	4	4	I. Gruppe	Bf 110	26	26
I. Gruppe	Bf 110	27	20	II. Gruppe	Bf 110	19	17
	Do 215	1	0		Do 217	2	1
II. Gruppe	Bf 110	26	17	IV. Gruppe	Bf 110	18	18
	Do 217	6	3				
III. Gruppe	Bf 110	23	20				
IV. Gruppe	Bf 110	22	16				
	Do 215	2	2				

► This Bf 110 F-2 coded G9+AA was flown by Major Wolfgang Falck. While still with 2./ZG 26 he carried out nightfighter trials with the Bf 110 and was one of the first officers to join the newly formed NJG 1.

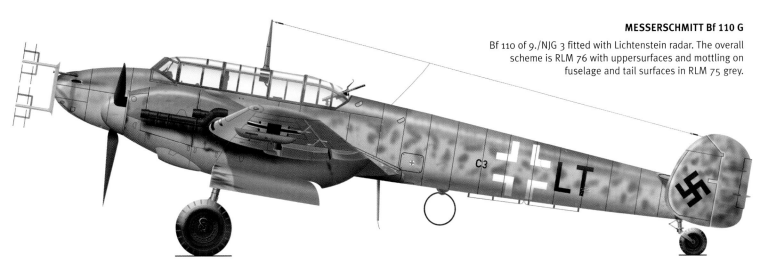

MESSERSCHMITT Bf 110 G
Bf 110 of 9./NJG 3 fitted with Lichtenstein radar. The overall
scheme is RLM 76 with uppersurfaces and mottling on
fuselage and tail surfaces in RLM 75 grey.

very accurate one'. If possible these were to be used as the aiming point, otherwise crews were to bomb the backing-up green markers. At no stage of the attack were bomber crews asked to attempt to identify the target visually.

The first red markers went down on Oboe two minutes early, followed three minutes later by those of the second Mosquito. Two minutes after that, the first green target indicators went down from a backer-up Pathfinder heavy bomber. Thereafter, relays of red or green indicators marked the target throughout the 40-minute duration of the attack. The bombs aimed at these markers laid waste an area of 160 acres, and destroyed three-quarters of the buildings in an area three times that size. That night 14 aircraft failed to return, and a further 38 returned with damage. By the standards of later attacks the damage was modest but, as Sir Arthur Harris later wrote, the Essen raid was *"easily the most important attack so far carried out by Bomber Command"*.

For the first time his force had carried out a raid on a major defended target that was both concentrated and accurate. This had been achieved, moreover, without bomber crews needing to see their target. For those German industrial centres within Oboe range, the writing was on the wall.

The five months that followed the 5 March attack became known as the *'Battle of the Ruhr'*. During its course there were five further attacks on Essen, and the Oboe-aimed target markers pinpointed other targets in north-western Germany for the heavy bombers: Dortmund, Duisberg and Bochum, Gelsenkirchen, Oberhausen and Mulheim, Remscheid, Mönchen-Gladbach and Krefeld, Münster, Aachen, Düsseldorf, Cologne and Wuppertal. All were attacked and in many cases suffered heavy damage.

The devastating raid on Wuppertal on the night of 29 May fitted well into the broad pattern of Bomber

Command attacks during the *'Battle of the Ruhr'*, as did the operation of the German defences to counter it. We shall, therefore, look at both in some detail.

Wuppertal is an extended, oblong town, with a 1943 population of nearly 360,000. It produced ball bearings, chemicals and silk, as well as component parts for weapons and aircraft. It also served as a dormitory area for other Ruhr cities.

Since the attack was to be launched on a moonless night, the use of one or other of the radar blind-marking systems was essential. It was Wuppertal's misfortune that it lay within easy range of the Oboe ground stations in England, making it an ideal target for this system.

For the aiming point, Bomber Command planners chose the centre of the north-eastern end of the town. To get there the raiders were to fly on a north-easterly heading, which would take them over the south-western part. The plan thus exploited the phenomenon known as 'creep-back', which had plagued many previous night attacks. When faced with vigorous Flak defences, the less experienced bomber crews had a natural predisposition to drop their bombs as early as possible, thereby avoiding a long straight-and-level run over the heart of the target area. In consequence, subsequent

▲ A pair of Bf 110 nightfighters of 9./NJG 3 on a daylight sortie against USAAF heavy bombers. By 1943 such daylight missions by nightfighters were a common occurence.

► Warming the engine of a Bf 110 bearing the emblem of the night fighter force on its nose. The absence of radar aerials suggests that the scene may have been photographed at a nightfighter training unit.

reconnaissance photographs had shown swathes of bomb craters extending back into open country several miles from the aiming point. Wuppertal, as a typical Ruhr target, was expected to be well protected by guns and searchlights. By placing the Pathfinder Force's markers on the far end of the town, the usual creep-back would bring devastation to the rest of the built-up area.

Soon after 23.00 hrs, the roar of aero engines shattered the stillness at scores of airfields along the eastern side of England. One by one the heavily-laden bombers rolled out along the dimly-lit taxi tracks, to take their places in the queue stretching back from the runway. The first aircraft off were the Wellingtons and Halifaxes of the Canadian No. 4 Group. Based in the north of Yorkshire, these had furthest to go to reach the force assembly point over the Dutch island of Walcheren. By 23.25 hrs the process was being repeated at all the airfields, as bomber followed bomber into the black night sky at half-minute intervals. In all, 719 aircraft took off to attack Wuppertal: 292 Lancasters, 185 Halifaxes, 118 Stirlings, 113 Wellingtons and 11 Oboe-equipped Mosquitoes. 62 aircraft turned back early with technical or other defects, while the remainder pushed on resolutely towards the Dutch coast.

Even before the first bombers appeared above the radar horizon, the *Luftwaffe* knew that Bomber Command had a major raid laid on for that night. From a painstaking study of the bombers' ground test radio transmissions its monitoring service, the *Horchdienst*, could predict the imminence of raids with confidence. Heavy test traffic in the morning, and very little in the afternoon, indicated that a large scale attack was planned for that night. If no major attack had been planned, the day's test transmissions were spread evenly over both the morning and the afternoon.

Just before 23.30 hrs the inquiring beams of the long-range early warning *Mammut* and *Wassermann* radars on the Dutch and Belgian coasts confirmed the *Horchdienst's* forecast. Over the North Sea, scores of aircraft appeared above the radar horizon heading south-east. The radar plots were immediately flashed up on the darkened situation map at the headquarters bunker of the 3rd Fighter Division, situated at Arnhem-Deelen in Holland. In the operations room there was a flurry of activity, as orders went out to bring the various elements of the defence to readiness. Within minutes the nightfighters were scrambling from their bases in France, Holland, Belgium and Germany, and heading for their allotted *Himmelbett* stations. Simultaneously, Flak sites came to life as men tumbled out of rest-rooms and hastened to prepare their weapons: covers were pulled off, barrels pointed skywards, shells prepared for use and radar sets warmed up.

From all points of the compass between due west and north-west, bombers converged on Walcheren. At midnight, as the leaders crossed the Dutch coast, they funnelled on to an east-south-easterly track and headed inland. From the bombers' new heading it seemed to the watchers at Deelen that yet again the target might be in the Ruhr area. Accordingly, at five minutes past midnight, Air Danger 15 was issued for the region: a restricted warning to hospitals, factories and civil defence headquarters, indicating that an air attack was possible in that area during the next 15 minutes. Nine minutes later a full public *Fliegeralarm* was sounded across the entire Ruhr area: a two-second siren note repeated 15 times, warning that there was now an acute danger of air attack. The sirens sounded in Wuppertal also, but many of its residents chose to ignore the call to take shelter. The town had not come under serious attack before, though there had been numerous false alarms.

As the sirens fell silent at Wuppertal, the town's battle for survival was already in full swing more than

"I attacked the violently evading bomber from behind and below at a range of 80 metres, and my rounds started a bright fire in the left wing."

100 miles away to the west, for the leading bombers were running the gauntlet of the *Himmelbett* boxes covering the approaches to the Ruhr. That night some 50 nightfighters took off, virtually all from *Nachtjagdgeschwader 1*. That small number represented less than one-sixth of the night interceptors available; the rest were positioned to support other parts of the defensive line. It was a wasteful use of resources, but an inevitable outcome of *General* Kammhuber's policy of rigidly tying each nightfighter *Gruppe* to a specific sector in the defensive line.

The first nightfighters to engage were from *II./NJG 1* based at St. Trond in Belgium, which had sent up 13

◄ The ability of the De Havilland Mosquito to fly high enough and fast enough to avoid the German defences made it an ideal vehicle for use by the RAF Pathfinder force to mark targets using the Oboe precision attack system.

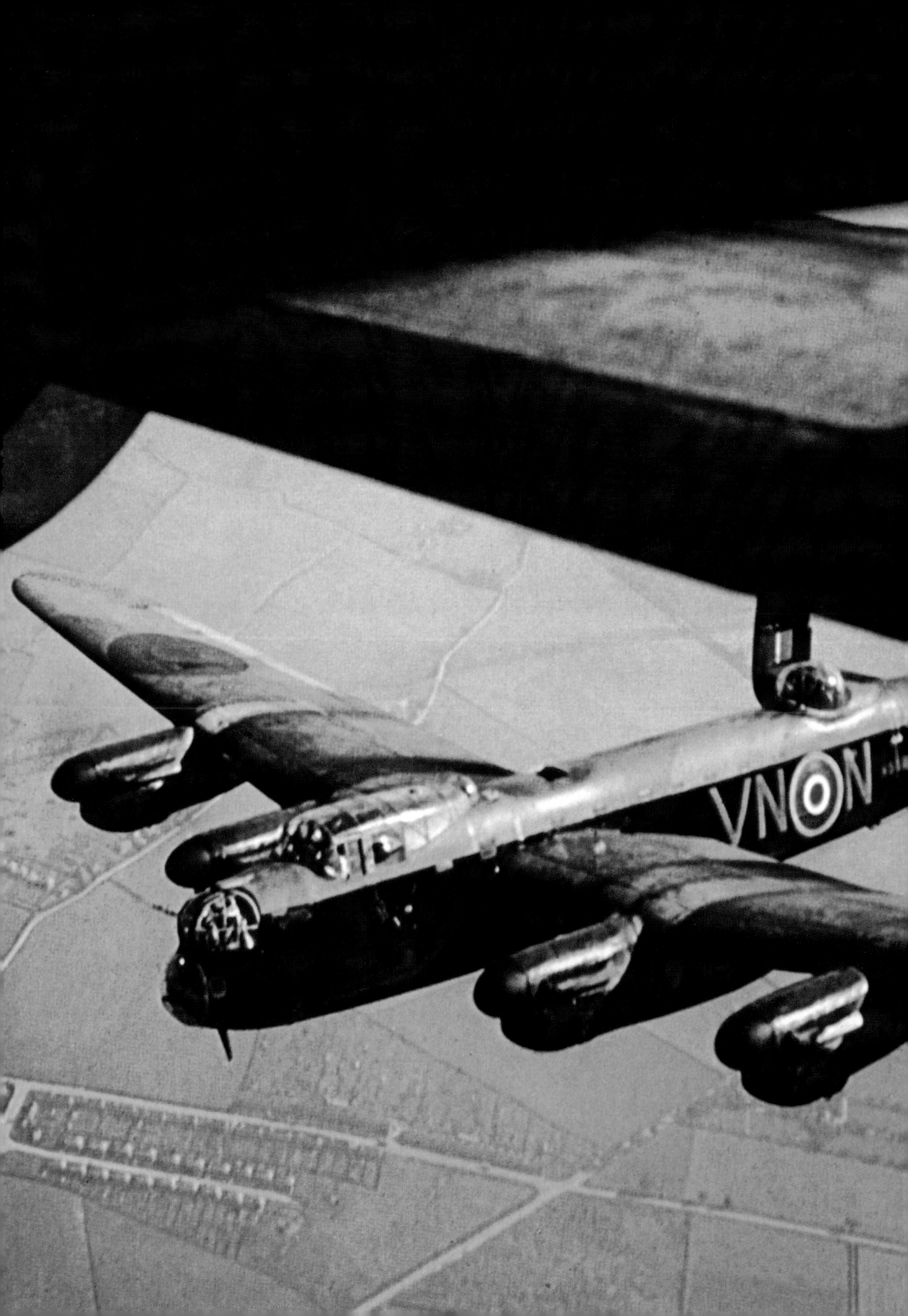
VN O

▲ Ground crew prepare to load a Short Stirling of No. 149 Squadron with its 500 pound bombs during the summer of 1942.

◄◄ Avro Lancaster of No. 50 Squadron on a daytime test flight.

Bf 110s and three Do 217s. Piloting one of the unit's Messerschmitts was a rising star in the nightfighter force, *Leutnant* Heinz-Wolfgang Schnaufer. Later he reported:

"At 23.51 hrs on 29 May I took off for a night operation in the area of Lurch [code-name of the Himmelbett station just to the north of Liege]. At about 00.35 hrs I was directed on to an in-flying enemy aircraft at an altitude of 3,500 metres. It was located on the [Lichtenstein airborne radar] and after further instructions I made out a four-engined bomber at 00.45 hrs, about 200 metres away above and to the right. I attacked the violently evading bomber from behind and below at a range of 80 metres, and my rounds started a bright fire in the left wing. The blazing enemy aircraft turned and dived away steeply, hitting the ground and exploding violently at 00.48 hrs; the position of the crash was 1-5 km to the south of Belven, 5 km north-west of Eupen, map reference 6134."

Before the night was over, Schnaufer and his radar operator, *Leutnant* Baro, would score two more victories. By 00.36 hrs the head of the bomber stream had reached a position 39 miles to the south-west of Wuppertal. This

was the final turning point before the target, and to mark it for the rest of the force one of the H2S-fitted Pathfinders released a pair of yellow target indicators. As the raiders passed over the distinctive fires burning on the ground they turned on to their attack heading; 068 degrees.

Only now did the bomber stream exist as a recognisable entity: some 650 aircraft enclosed within a rectangular-shaped volume of sky 150 miles long, six miles wide and two miles high; as the vanguard passed the final turning point, the rearguard had yet to cross the Dutch coast.

The force was divided into five successive waves each of about 130 aircraft, each wave occupying a 30-mile-long strip of airspace along the track; distributed evenly throughout the stream were the backer-up Pathfinder aircraft carrying further yellow markers to renew those at the turning point, as well as green ones, and high explosive bombs for release at the target. The phalanx of bombers thundered on towards Wuppertal at nearly four miles per minute.

While the raiders curved round the turning point on to their attack heading, and the German nightfighters culled bomber after bomber out of the stream, a drama

▲ Oberleutnant Heinz Wolfgang Schnaufer (right) of NJG 1 at St. Trond in 1943 after having been awarded the Ritterkreuz.

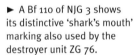

► A Bf 110 of NJG 3 shows its distinctive 'shark's mouth' marking also used by the destroyer unit ZG 76.

of a different sort was in progress. The plan had called for a single Oboe Mosquito to open the marking at the target at zero hour, 00.45 hrs, with further Oboe Mosquitoes renewing this marking at six-minute intervals thereafter. Since an Oboe-controlled bombing run took about ten minutes, and a pair of ground stations could control only one aircraft at a time, it was necessary to employ two pairs of ground stations for this attack, each operating on separate frequencies: two Cat stations near Cromer in Norfolk, and two Mouse stations near Dover. The leading Mosquito had been two minutes late in beginning its bombing run, while the second aircraft had begun its run some four minutes early; thus, instead of aircraft being spaced evenly at six-minute intervals, the first two were running in to drop their target indicators almost simultaneously. Inevitably, there was going to be a hiatus in the Oboe marking when the first target indicators burnt themselves out; errors smaller than this had wrecked attacks in the past.

The two primary-marker Mosquitoes darted towards Wuppertal at nearly five miles per minute, rapidly overhauling the stream of heavy bombers. In his earphones, the pilot in each Oboe aircraft heard the signals to keep him on the correct path during the bombing run. Morse dots indicated he was to port of the correct track; Morse dashes indicated he was to starboard.

If he was on the correct track, an arc of radius of precisely 262 miles centred on Cromer, he heard a steady note. Their tracking arcs took the two Pathfinders high over the darkened city of Cologne where the gunners, ignorant of the aircraft's true purpose, opened fire with an inaccurate and less than vigorous cannonade. After all, how could the two fast, high-flying machines be of any great significance compared with the veritable swarm of heavy bombers now heading inexorably towards the Ruhr.

For its close defence, the Ruhr industrial area came under the aegis of *Generalmajor* Hintz's 4. Flak Division. The attack heading of 068 degrees for Wuppertal took the raiders through the narrow gap between Solingen and Düsseldorf, and within range of the powerful gun defences of both. The gunners' accurate predicted salvoes destroyed at least four raiders and caused serious damage to 22 others, before the stream of bombers cleared the hazard.

At 00.40 hrs the *Luftwaffe* raid warning organisation issued its latest assessment of the air situation: *"The first waves are flying over the Rhine between Düsseldorf and Cologne, heading eastwards."* Perceptively, the announcement continued, *"A real danger exists of an attack on Wuppertal."*

It did indeed. In the two pathfinder Mosquitoes now closing rapidly on the town, the navigators listened assiduously for the final transmission from their Mouse station near Dover. Just after 00.46 hrs it came: five Morse dots followed by a three-and-a-half-second dash. The end of the dash indicated that the aircraft was at its bomb-release point, exactly 250 miles from the ground transmitter at Dover. In succession, the navigators pressed their bomb-release '*tits*' and each Mosquito disgorged its load of four target indicators. About 40 seconds later, some 3,000 feet above the still disbelieving residents, the barometric fuse in each bomb set off the small bursting charges which blew away the tail. From each marker the 60 pyrotechnic candles spilled out and ignited. Burning bright pink, the showers of candles cascaded to the ground where they lay in clusters about 100 yards across. Two minutes late, the battle of Wuppertal had opened.

Although the Flak defences of the Ruhr area as a whole were powerful, there were insufficient heavy guns for every town to enjoy their protection. One of the towns that had to go without was Wuppertal itself, having lost its heavy batteries during a defensive re-shuffle the previous April.

All it had left were two batteries belonging to the 750th Light Flak Battalion, each with nine 20 mm guns and three or four searchlights. The unit's commander, *Oberleutnant* Herminghausen, watched with horror as the burning target indicators silhouetted the surrounding buildings against their unnatural glow. There remained just one slim chance of saving the town: the industrial haze had concealed Ruhr targets from raiders in the past, provided the defenders did not give the game away by opening fire and exposing searchlights. Accordingly, Herminghausen ordered his men to hold their fire.

Following their violent reception a few minutes earlier when they brushed against the defences of Düsseldorf and Solingen, the crews at the head of the bomber stream found the tranquillity at the target almost unbelievable. The usual industrial haze shrouded the ground features, but its translucent mists did no more than give a dull tinge to the distinctive marker fires. With such beacons to beckon the raiders, Herminghausen's plan had no chance of success.

Wuppertal was naked, exposed and vulnerable. The delay in the initial marking, coupled with the punctuality of the Main Force, resulted in an almost immediate concentration of high explosive and incendiary bombs round the first target indicators. The Oboe Mosquitoes had demonstrated poor time keeping, but they atoned for this fault with their accuracy. Their burning markers all lay within half a mile of the aiming

SCARECROWS

At this point it is appropriate to mention the so-called 'Scarecrows' that night bomber crews reported seeing from time to time. One wartime RAF report described them as 'An explosion releasing a quantity of smoke, coloured stars and flaming debris, resembling an aircraft which has been destroyed. Distinguishable from the real thing, and apparently not lethal at close range.'

The point of the exercise, apparently, was to attack the morale of night bomber crews rather than themselves or their aircraft. Yet to produce such an effect would require a pyrotechnic feat of a high order, not to mention an extra large calibre gun or rocket to transport the material to the required position in space. The author questioned several ex-members of the Flak arm on this subject, from a General down to humble gunners. Not one of them had heard of such a stratagem.

It is extremely difficult to prove a negative: that in the entire war nobody ever attempted such a thing. Nevertheless, in the absence of any supporting evidence from the German side, this author is certain that gunners never fired anything into the sky intended to produce the Scarecrow effect. Militarily, the concept was flawed. For less effort, and using the guns they already had, the gunners could produce explosions in the vicinity of bombers which were 'lethal at close range' and which would produce a more spine-chilling reaction. And if the Scarecrows were 'distinguishable from the real thing', what was the point of launching them anyway?

From RAF night bomber crews, on the other hand, there is powerful, if one-sided, evidence of the existence of the Scarecrows. If the gunners did not fire such a device into the sky, what gave the impression that they did? In all probability, different effects on different occasions were described as Scarecrows by different people. Almost certainly some explosions casually dismissed as Scarecrows were caused by real bombers that had been blown to pieces. When it suffers catastrophic damage an aircraft can break up in many different ways, and even an experienced observer might be misled. Another possibility was the detonation of the 57 pound shells from the largest of the anti-aircraft gun, the 128 mm. These rounds produced a much larger and brighter explosion than that from smaller weapons, and because comparatively few 128 mm guns were deployed, the effect never became commonplace. If the detonations were seen from a distance, it is possible that some of these were taken for Scarecrows. A third possibility centres on the rocket-fired spoof markers, launched above fire decoy sites in an effort to imitate the Pathfinders' target indicators. In their initial form these spoof markers had cardboard casings which on occasion broke up and burned prematurely, giving rise to unusual pyrotechnic effects. Perhaps the truth of the matter will never be known with certainty, and the phenomenon of the Scarecrows will remain one of the minor mysteries of the Second World War.

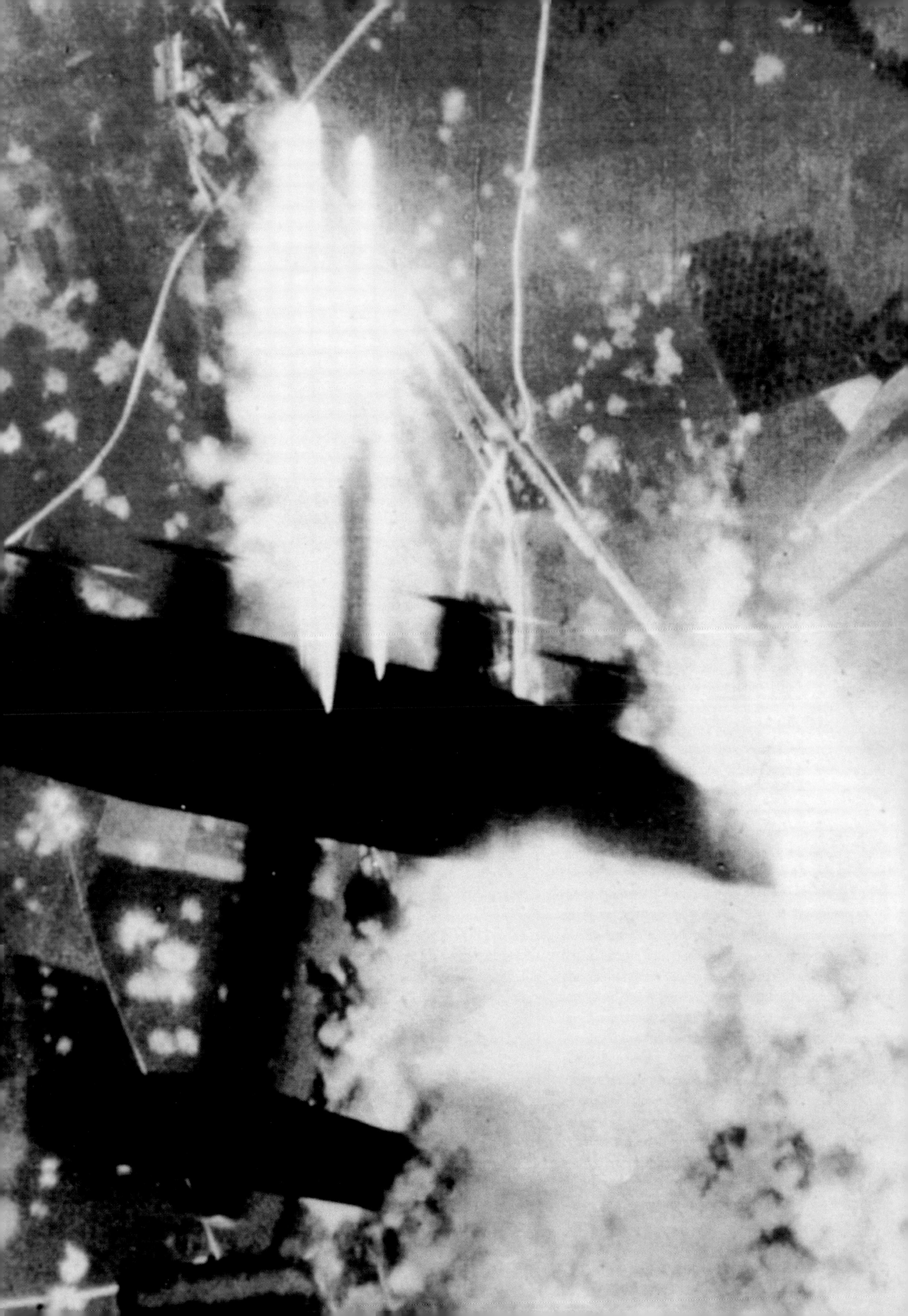

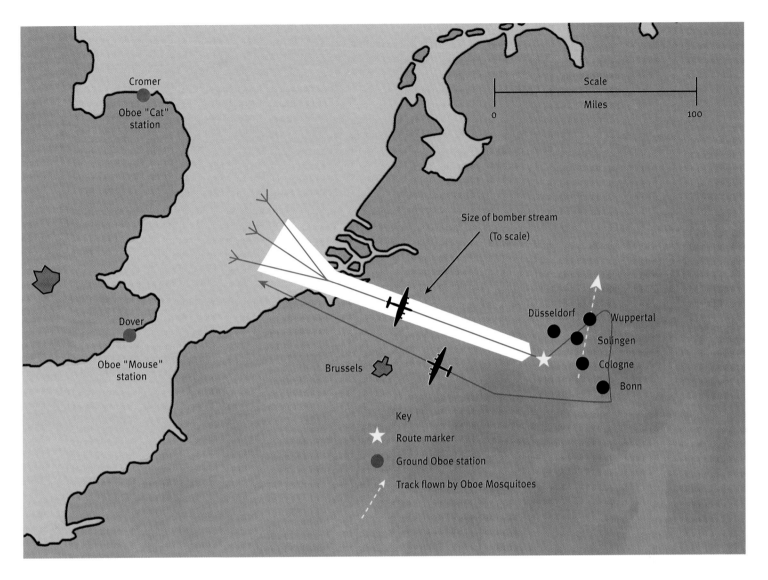

Cromer

Oboe "Cat"
station

Scale

Miles

0   100

Size of bomber stream

(To scale)

Düsseldorf   Wuppertal

Solingen

Dover

Cologne

Oboe "Mouse"
station

Brussels

Bonn

Key

★ Route marker

● Ground Oboe station

⇡ Track flown by Oboe Mosquitoes

point straddling the centre of the north-east district of the town, and there bomb-aimer after bomb-aimer directed his load.

Two minutes after the release of the first markers, at 00.49 hrs, the first backer-up Pathfinder arrived; still unhampered by any ground defences, its crew laid their salvo of green target indicators hard against the initial red ones.

One minute later two aircraft repeated this process, one minute after that two more, and two minutes after that two more still. Thus, at 00.54 hrs, when the last of the original red markers flickered and died, there existed a solid core of green fires dotted around the aiming point. Moreover the hundreds of 30 and 40 pound incendiary bombs had begun to have their effect, and as their fires took hold the flames were clearly visible to those above. These unmistakable conflagrations became the focus of the attack, rendering futile the German attempt to draw the attackers on to a hastily-lit decoy in the countryside nearby. Belatedly Herminghausen

ordered his men to open fire, but he knew there was little they could do to influence events. Afterwards bomber crews described the Flak over Wuppertal as 'inaccurate' and 'ineffective'. That was hardly surprising, for the light shells from the 20 mm guns could hardly reach even the 12,000-feet altitude of the Stirlings scattered along the base of the bomber stream.

The interval with no Oboe marking lasted until 01.05 hrs, 18 minutes after the first red target indicators had ignited and eleven since the last had gone out. Then came another lack of co-ordination, which again resulted in two of the Pathfinder Mosquitoes bombing almost simultaneously. Their two salvoes of markers dropped through the stream of heavy bombers making their attack runs, and again landed close to the aiming point. Within minutes, further salvoes of green target indicators were burning alongside them. Those backer-up markers would be needed, for there would be no more Oboe-aimed markers for a further 24 minutes. Meanwhile the Lancasters, Halifaxes, Stirlings and

▲ The attack on Wuppertal on the night of 29/30 May 1943. The bomber stream is shown in its position at 00.36 hrs on the 30th.

◄ ◄ A Halifax of Bomber Command is silhouetted by the flares, fires and anti-aircraft fire of a full-scale night attack on a German city.

Wellingtons of the main force streamed across Wuppertal, with an average of ten bombers per minute releasing their loads. The green target indicators guided the attackers until 01.29 hrs when, at last, there were further red markers to draw in the final wave of raiders.

After release, the heavy bombers held their attack heading for a further minute and a half to take them clear of the target. Then they turned almost due south, on to a track which took them just out of range of the Ruhr, Cologne and Bonn defended areas. Carefully the raiders skirted round Bonn, before curving on to their north-westerly withdrawal heading. As they cleared the gun-defended areas, however, the bombers had once more to pass through the belt of *Himmelbett* stations and their attendant nightfighters. There, again, the raiders suffered losses.

Behind them, the raiders left Wuppertal fighting its battle for survival. The large numbers of high-explosive bombs released with the incendiaries had made it extremely difficult for civil defence workers to contain the initial fires. As a result the flames took hold in many places, and soon whole blocks of houses were blazing fiercely. The intense heat caused the air above the fires to rise and drew in winds strong enough to topple the walls of already gutted buildings. Moreover, the turbulent air, carrying sparks and burning debris, spread the conflagration. The Wuppertal fire department, with 150 professional firemen augmented by about 1,000 volunteers, was soon overwhelmed by the size and extent of the fires. Yet help was close at hand. Within minutes of the release of the first target indicators, fire brigades and civil defence units were on their way to the stricken town from all directions. As the raid ended, it was particularly important to get the survivors in the burning area out of the apparent safety of their basement air-raid shelters. Otherwise the fires would draw the oxygen out of the shelters, and the occupants would die silently and painlessly from carbon monoxide poisoning.

Soon after 03.15 hrs a reinforcing fire-fighting unit from Bochum got through to the heavily bombed area round the town hall. Playing their hoses on the buildings to either side, they cleared an escape route through which more than 2,000 people scrambled to safety. Simultaneously, other firemen battled with the scores of conflagrations, large and small. The rubble-blocked roads and the ruptured water mains made their task all the more difficult. Moreover, since the previous month had been dry, the level of water in the Wupper River was low. Initially, the fire-fighting teams had to depend on supplies from the emergency static water tanks positioned around the town. When these were exhausted, the men connected their serpentine hose lengths together for distances of up to four miles to draw up the necessary water. By such methods they eventually brought the fires under control, after a battle lasting nearly eight hours.

Against Wuppertal, Bomber Command had delivered an unusually discriminate attack: from photographic evidence it was later ascertained that nearly 500 aircraft had planted their loads within three miles of the aiming point. This unprecedented concentration of bombs had fallen on the north-east end of the town. The high-explosive bombs and fires produced an area of severe damage that covered nearly 700 acres. In the absence of any appreciable creep-back, the south-western end of the town escaped with little more than superficial glass and roof damage.

The main railway station, two power stations, two gasworks, a waterworks and five out of the six major factories all suffered serious damage. The loss of life was no less crushing: an estimated 3,350 people were killed; a further 2,000 suffered injuries, and more than 100,000 people lost their homes.

Thirty-three bombers failed to return from the raid, and two more crashed on landing. That represented nearly five per cent of the raiding force, about average for attacks on targets in the Ruhr area at this time.

After correlating the debriefing reports from returning crews, British intelligence officers concluded that at least 22 bombers had fallen to nightfighters; it is interesting to note that this figure agreed exactly with the *Luftwaffe* nightfighter force's claim after the battle. Of the remaining losses, seven were attributed to Flak, and the other four to causes unknown. Sixty bombers returned with serious damage from Flak, and two after being hit by nightfighters. The well-concentrated bomber stream played an important part in keeping down losses due to enemy action, but there was a price to pay for this protection: six aircraft returned with damage caused by incendiary bombs falling on them from above.

By the standards of a raid on an area target, this had been an extremely successful attack. The force's ability to focus such a withering deluge of high explosive and incendiary bombs into such a small area was due in the main to one factor: Wuppertal's lack of heavy Flak protection. For bombers flying at high level, Flak was a discomforting hazard which often caused damage, though it did not bring down many aircraft. Yet anti-aircraft fire, coupled with the blinding beams of massed searchlight batteries, greatly increased bombing errors and spread attacks over a much wider area. The lack of heavy Flak protection at Wuppertal made clear its significance at all

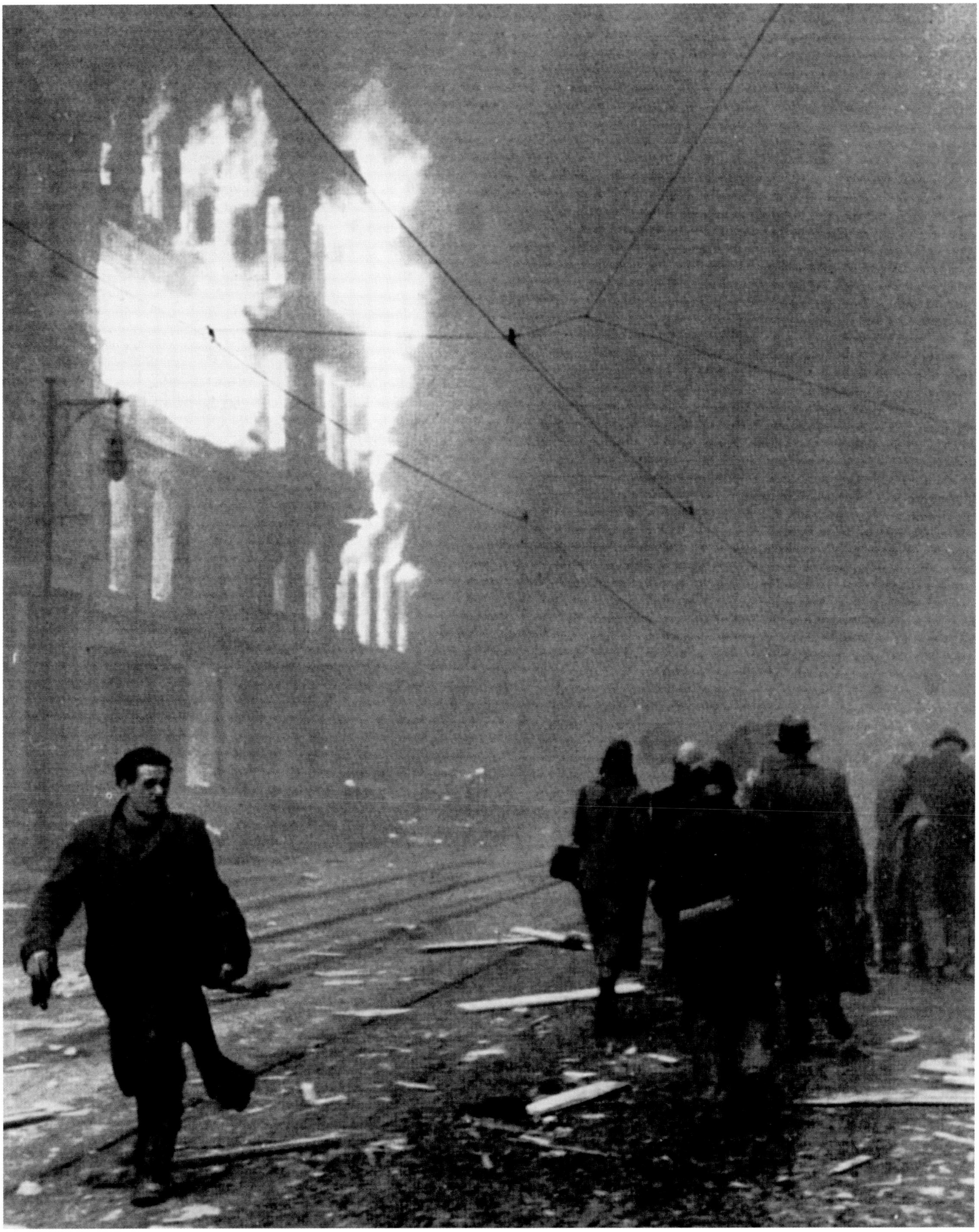

▲ A Lancaster of No. 617 Squadron on a flight prior to the raid on Wuppertal on 29 May, is seen here without the bomb attached.

the other targets. When they did not have to face this hindrance, Bomber Command crews could and would bring concentrated destruction to their targets.

Within the limited range of Oboe, the Pathfinder Force could mark targets for the main force with a high degree of precision. During the spring of 1943, however, Bomber Command did not confine its attentions to this small segment of Germany. But when the bombers ranged further, and were forced to rely on H2S for the target marking, the raids had somewhat less effect. Stuttgart, Mannheim and Frankfurt, Kiel, Rostock and Stettin, Berlin, Pilsen, Nuremburg and

Munich, all were raided, but none of them suffered a blow comparable to those dealt against the targets in the Ruhr valley. As well as the less accurate marking at these targets, the bomber crews had other problems to contend with. The longer flights over enemy territory made accurate tracking and time-keeping much more difficult. During the Stuttgart attack on 11 March, for example, the initial marking was accurate but the main force arrived after the target indicators had burnt themselves out. Similarly, the weather was much harder to predict over the more distant targets. During the attack on Frankfurt on 10 April, unexpectedly thick cloud over the target swallowed up the target markers and the subsequent attack was ineffectual.

One other RAF night attack on Germany during the spring of 1943 deserves a special mention at this point, namely that against the dams. The features of Barnes Wallis' special bomb for use against these massive structures have been described elsewhere, but they still

AVRO LANCASTER B.Mk.III SPECIAL
Serving with 617 Squadron from RAF Conningsby, Lincolnshire during Operation 'Chastise', May 1943. Overall standard finish of Dark Earth and Dark Green over Night (black) undersurfaces. Codes in Dull Red. Note the modified fuselage to mount the 'Upkeep' mine and the pulley to the motor that spun the bomb before release.

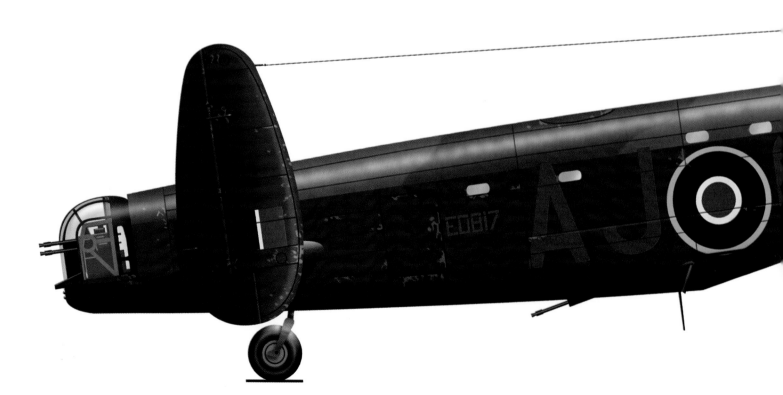

deserve mention here. The weapon, code-named 'Upkeep', was shaped like a large dustbin. It was 50 inches in diameter, 60 inches long, and weighed 9,250 pounds of which 6,600 pounds was powerful RDX explosive. The bomb was mounted across the bomb bay of the extensively modified Lancasters: it was held between two V-shaped arms which gripped it firmly at each end and, at the same time, acted as pivots to allow it to rotate about its axis. Via a simple belt drive a small hydraulic motor spun the weapon up to its release speed of 500 rpm. When the bomb-aimer pressed his release 'tit' the V-shaped supporting arms, pivoted at the top, sprung apart and allowed the weapon to fall clear. Hitting the water with a high forward speed, the bomb bounded across the lake until it slammed into the wall of the dam. It rebounded off the structure, but the spinning of the cylinder forced it back into contact with the wall. It then wound its way down the vertical face, until the water pressure actuated the hydrostatic fuse at a depth of 30 feet. In this position, and only in this position, did this special bomb stand a good chance of rupturing the massive masonry wall.

For the attack on the dams, Bomber Command took the unprecedented step of forming a special unit: No. 617 Squadron. Its already distinguished leader, Wing Commander Guy Gibson, was allowed the privilege of selecting his crews. The candidates all had to have completed, or nearly completed, two tours of bomber operations. Since it was rare at this time for anyone to survive the 60 operational sorties necessary for two such tours, it is clear that the men Gibson received were amongst the most skilful, the most experienced, and also the most lucky in Bomber Command. As soon as No. 617 Squadron received its quota of crews, the men began intensive training under conditions of great secrecy.

To place Upkeep with the necessary accuracy demanded a degree of flying precision never called for in war either before or since. The crew had to release it at a speed of exactly 220 mph and at a height of exactly 60 feet above the surface. Moreover, the bomb had to leave the aircraft at a range of 425 yards from the dam, plus or minus 25 yards. At 220 mph, an aircraft takes a

► The air attack on the German dams, mounted by No. 617 Squadron on the night of 16 May 1943, was the most precise to be made before the advent of guided missiles. Here, one of the dustbin-shaped 'Upkeep' bombs is seen on its special mounting under the Lancaster. The belt drive, to spin the weapon to its release speed of 500 rpm, is clearly visible.

►► The Möhne Dam pictured on the morning after the raid, with the waters still gushing out of the breach. In the foreground are the torpedo nets which should have protected the structure, after they had been carried away by the outgoing waters.

quarter of a second to cover 25 yards. As if all this was not enough, the aircraft had to have its wings level at the time of release or the bomb would strike the water at an angle and spin off to one side.

The aircraft carried simple but effective systems for height and range measurement, to enable crews to release their bombs with the required precision. For height estimation each Lancaster carried a pair of spotlights, one in the nose and one in the tail. The beams were set at such an angle that when they were switched on and the aircraft was at precisely 60 feet, the discs of light merged on the water to form a figure of eight shape. Range estimation was by means of a home-made sight comprising a triangular piece of plywood, with a peephole at one corner and a nail at each of the other two. The bomb-aimer squinted through the peephole and when the nails lined up with the towers on the dams, as they would when the range was 425 yards, he released the bomb. Airborne trials with this laughably crude method gave a release accuracy to the order of four yards.

To achieve the necessary precision of attack called for a very high degree of crew co-operation, however. The engineer watched the discs of light on the water and directed the pilot to keep to the correct height; the pilot aimed the aircraft straight for the dam, ensuring that his wings were level by the time of bomb release; and the bomb aimer watched the approaching towers through his special sight and released the weapon. By such

means, a practised crew was able to plant their weapon with an accuracy similar to that achieved by army demolition engineers.

Once the men had been trained and the aircraft modified, two further conditions had to be satisfied before the attack could take place: for maximum disruptive effect the lakes behind the dams had to be full of water, and to see their target the crews needed clear skies and the light of a full moon. On 16 May conditions were favourable and that night the attack, codenamed Operation 'Chastise', was launched. Nineteen Lancasters took off from their base at Scampton in three separate waves. The first nine were briefed to attack the Möhne Dam and then, if it had been breached and there were bombs remaining, they were to attack first the Eder and then the Sorpe Dam. The second wave, with five aircraft, was to go for the Sorpe Dam. The third wave, also with five aircraft, would serve as an airborne reserve and either reinforce the other two waves as needed, or else attack as secondary targets the Lister and Eneppe Dams.

The first wave, led by Gibson himself, lost one aircraft on the way to the target; but the remainder carried on according to plan and breached the Möhne Dam shortly after midnight. Gibson then took the three aircraft still with bombs to the Eder Dam, and less than an hour later that one was broken also. The success of the first wave was equalled only by the bad luck that dogged the second and reserve waves. Two of the five

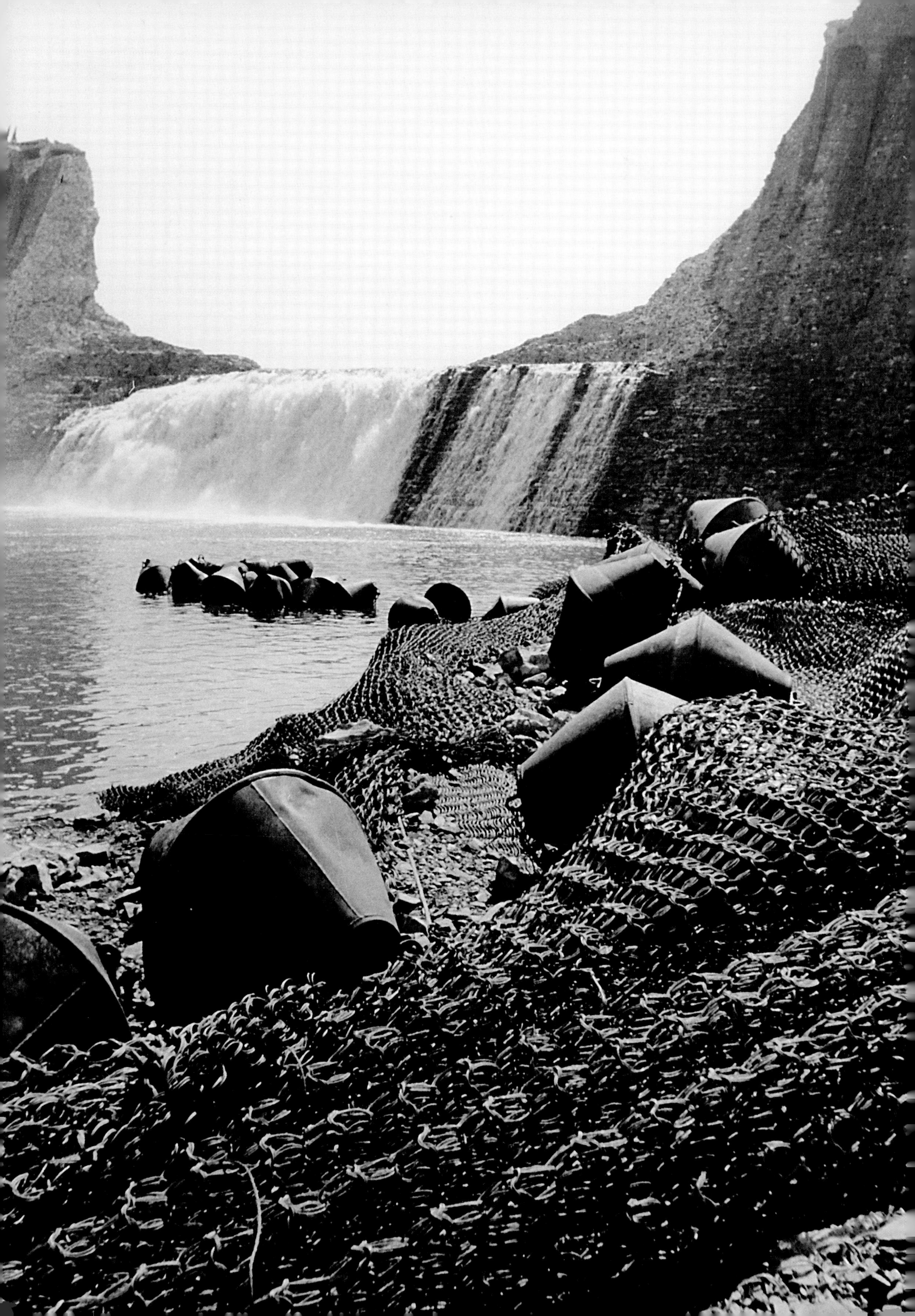

► Waters flowing out of the Eder Dam, after the attack.

►► The waters from the Eder Dam reached the Unter Neustadt district of Kassel, where they caused widespread flooding.

▲ Dellwig, a village 27 kilometres along the Ruhr valley from the Möhne Dam, was partially flooded. The waters breached the embankment of the road crossing the valley in several places (arrowed).

aircraft making for the Sorpe Dam were shot down, and two more suffered damage en route and had to turn back. Thus only one aircraft in the second wave reached its target. The Sorpe Dam was constructed of hard-packed earth around a concrete core, giving a somewhat more resilient structure than either the Möhne or Eder Dams. For this reason the Sorpe Dam was not really a suitable target for the special bomb, but the importance of its waters decreed that it too should be attacked. Alone, Flight Lieutenant McCarthy's Lancaster arrived at the dam to find a thickening mist rising off the water. He pressed home his attack, however, and his bomb scored a hit which crumbled away part of the crest of the wall. Three aircraft of the reserve force then received orders to follow up this partial success, but one was shot down before it got there.

By the time Flight Sergeant Brown reached the area the mist had thickened appreciably. Undaunted, he coolly made ten successive attack runs low over the water until, finally, his bomb-aimer let the bomb go. The weapon bounded across the water and hit the dam, but still the damaged structure remained standing. When the third of the reserve aircraft arrived at the Sorpe Dam, the blanket of mist was so thick that no further attack was possible.

The two remaining aircraft in the reserve wave received instructions to make for the secondary targets, the Ennepe and Lister Dams. The attack on the former was without apparent effect, while the aircraft sent to the latter was shot down or crashed on its way there.

So it was that No. 617 Squadron, by a brilliant feat of arms, breached the Möhne and Eder Dams and caused serious damage to the Sorpe Dam. There could be no question of further attacks with the bouncing bomb on other dams in Germany, however, for within hours the *Luftwaffe* had erected strong light Flak defences around these targets.

Nor was there any doubt in the minds of *Luftwaffe* armament experts of the nature of the weapon that had caused such destruction. One of the Lancasters had crashed in Holland on its way to the target, either after being hit by Flak or flying into high tension cables. The aircraft broke up on hitting the ground, but the Upkeep weapon broke away and came to rest on the ground undamaged. A bouncing weapon was already under development for the *Luftwaffe*, using the same principle, intended for use against armoured warships. So what had been Bomber Command's most secret weapon, was no secret any more.

Of the 19 aircraft and 133 men who had set out to attack the dams, nine bombers and 56 crewmen failed to return. Five of the Lancasters had crashed, or been shot down, on their way to the targets. Two were destroyed while delivering their attacks, one by the Flak defences and one whose bomb crashed into the parapet of the Eder Dam exploding when the bomber was directly overhead. The ninth Lancaster was shot down on its return flight. Two bombers had suffered damage on their way in, and been forced to abandon the mission.

For leading the operation and repeatedly accompanying other aircraft during their bombing runs in order to draw away enemy fire, Wing Commander Guy Gibson received the Victoria Cross; 33 other members of his squadron were also decorated for their parts in the attack.

The swirling waters from the Möhne Lake caused severe flooding along the valleys of the Möhne and Ruhr Rivers. About 1,200 people were killed, half of them women workers from the east in a forced labour camp near Neheim. About 100 houses and six small electrical stations were washed away, and one of the main railway lines passing through the area was disrupted for a considerable time. Sixty miles away the flood waters from the broken Eder Dam caused similar damage, inundating the Bettenhausen suburb of Kassel. In neither area was there any long-term effect on production, however.

Throughout the operation the Sorpe Dam had borne a charmed life. Eight aircraft had been sent against it, a

▲ On the way to the Sorpe Dam, Flight Lieutenant R. Barlow's aircraft was believed to have been hit by Flak and then struck high-tension cables. The aircraft crashed near the border between Holland and Germany, leaving no survivors. When the Lancaster hit the ground it broke up, and the 'Upkeep' weapon tore loose, ending up in a small wood where eager Luftwaffe armaments experts examined it the next day. The weapon presented few surprises, for the Luftwaffe had experimented with a similar device for use against warships.

◄ After the attack on the dams the King visited No. 617 Squadron at Scampton to congratulate the crews. He is seen here talking to Flight Lieutenant Harold 'Micky' Martin (later Air Marshal Sir Harold), while Wing Commander Guy Gibson is nearest the camera. (IWM)

▶ To mark the aiming points for raids, Pathfinder aircraft dropped salvoes of the special Target Indicator bombs. One of these weapons is seen here soon after release during a daylight raid. Note the barometric fuse protruding from the nose. When the bomb reached a pre-set altitude in its fall, an explosive charge blew off the tail and ignited then released the pyrotechnic candles. (Lees via Garbett/Goulding)

▶ ▶ An RAF Beaufighter nightfighter with an 'arrowhead' airborne interception radar aerial on the nose. In the late spring of 1943, No. 141 Squadron sent its Beaufighters over Holland and Belgium to hunt down enemy nightfighters.

number that had been sufficient to smash the other two dams. Had the Sorpe Dam burst in addition to the Möhne Dam the German armament industry would have been in serious trouble, since between them these two lakes held a large proportion of the water necessary for the industries in the area. As *Reichsminister* Albert Speer later commented, without these supplies *"...Ruhr production would have suffered the heaviest possible blow"*. In the event, the Sorpe Dam was able to supply the water required until the autumn rains came, by which time the other two dams had been repaired.

Thus, although it had been an exemplary piece of night precision bombing, the attack on the dams failed to bring about the hoped-for collapse in production in the Ruhr industrial area. The most important tangible effect of the raid was the diversion of labour from the construction of fortifications along the French Channel coast, Hitler's pet Atlantic Wall project. Within days more than 20,000 labourers had been pulled back to repair the dams. Before their work was finished, RAF and the USAAF heavy bombers would ensure that there would be plenty of additional work to prevent the workers returning to France.

Following the destructive raids on targets in the Ruhr industrial area, and its spectacular attack on the dams, RAF Bomber Command entered the summer of 1943 on a new wave of confidence. Furthermore, amongst those party to the force's innermost secrets, there was a well-founded belief that this run of success would continue. Mandrel and Tinsel, Monica and Boozer were now in large-scale use and helped to protect the night bombers from the attentions of the defenders.

One further idea that had been mooted for a considerable time was to send RAF nightfighters with the bomber streams, to harass their enemy counterparts. Previously this concept had foundered on the problem of identification: how were the crews to pick their quarry out in large areas of darkened sky which contained numerous friendly bombers? Now the problem was solved by 'Serrate', a small receiver produced by the Telecommunications Research Establishment which picked up signals from the *Lichtenstein* radar carried by *Luftwaffe* nightfighters, and displayed them in such a way that the RAF fighters could home on to their source. During the late spring of 1943 the Beaufighters of No. 141 Squadron were modified to carry Serrate in addition to their normal airborne interception radar. When the unit began flying night operations, crews evolved a new tactic that proved effective. Crews found that their airborne interception radar showed when a would-be attacker closed in from behind, thinking their aircraft was a bomber. It became a standard tactic for the Beaufighter crew to act as a wolf in sheep's clothing, holding steady course like a bomber while their unsuspecting enemy closed on them. When the would-be attacker was within about one mile, the RAF nightfighter swung rapidly through a full circle and engaged it from behind. These tactical methods were well demonstrated by the commander of No. 141 Squadron Wing Commander 'Bob' Braham, during a Serrate sortie over Holland on the night of 16/17 June 1943. Afterwards Braham reported:

"... At 02.10 hrs, when we were over Staveren, my navigator saw an enemy aircraft coming up from behind to attack us from our port side. I orbited hard to port to get behind him but as I did so the enemy aircraft also turned to port. A dogfight followed and I finally manoeuvred until I was on his port beam at 400 yards

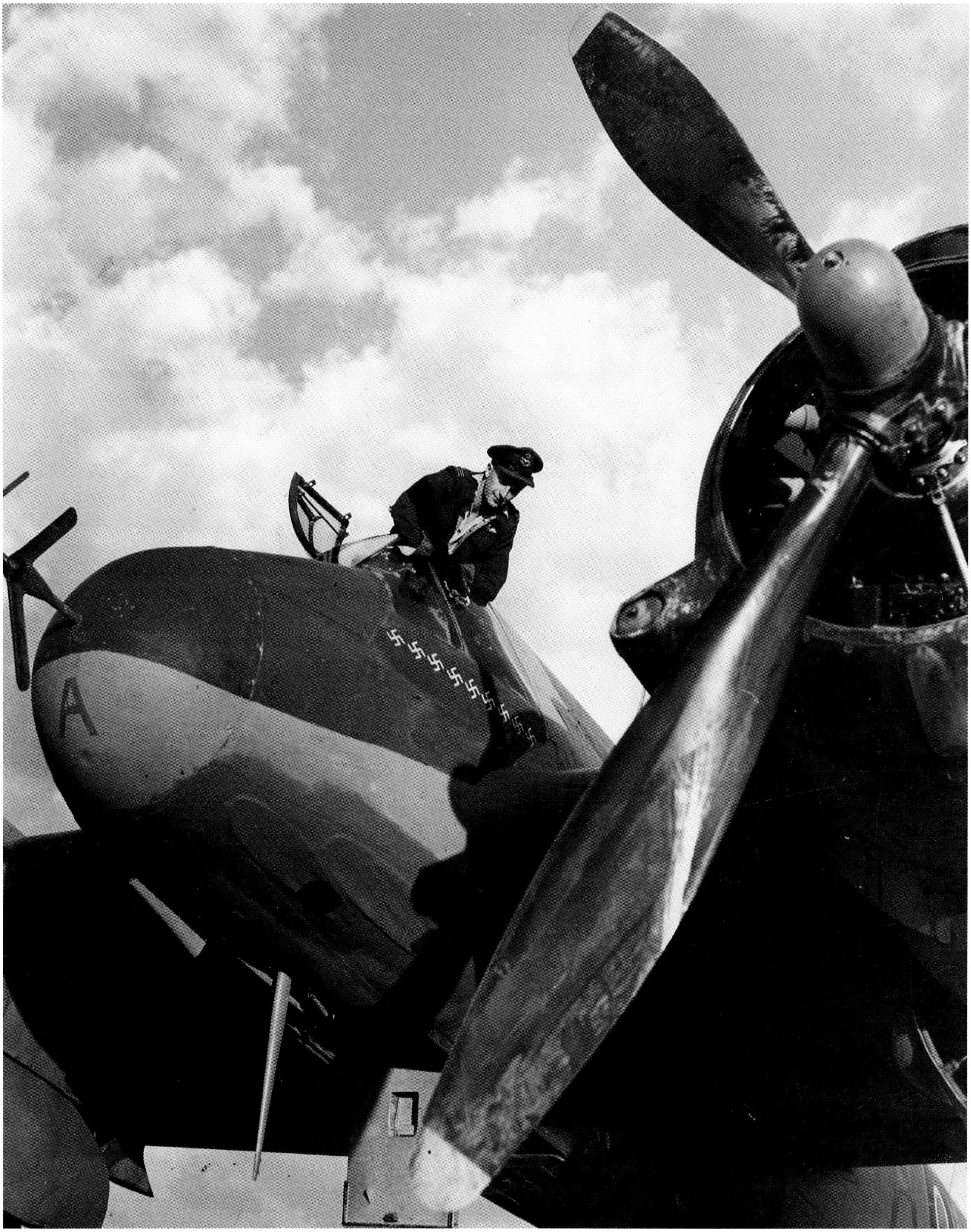

▲ The 'business end' of a
Bf 110 Nachtjäger showing
its formidable armament of
four MG 17 machine guns in
the nose with two MG FF,
20 mm cannon fitted in a
gondola under the fuselage.

*range. I opened fire with cannon and machine guns and
finished a 5 seconds' burst 20° astern at 200 yards
range, raking his fuselage from tail to cockpit and setting
his port engine on fire. As I throttled back to attack
again, the enemy aircraft went into a vertical dive and
crashed in flames 8 miles north of Staveren. The combat
took place at 10,000 feet in clear moonlight above cloud;
we saw no return fire."*

In the *Luftwaffe*, too, there were new tactics in the offing.
Several senior officers considered that *Generalleutnant*
Kammhuber's *Himmelbett* system was altogether too
rigid and disciplined. It was also wasteful in resources,
since only a relatively small proportion of the available
nightfighters went into action on any one night.
Moreover, as the destructive attack on Wuppertal had
shown, if the Flak defences were ineffective the current
deployment of nightfighters provided little or no direct
protection at the target itself.

Bomber ace *Major* Hajo Herrmann, then serving at
the *Luftwaffe* staff college at Potsdam, submitted a
proposal to use single-engined fighters to engage
enemy bombers over their target. There, bombers were

often illuminated by searchlights, or silhouetted
against fires on the ground or the Pathfinders' target
indicators, making them vulnerable to fighters
attacking visually.

If the local Flak commander would agree to restrict the
ceiling of the bursting shells to a certain altitude, Herrmann
suggested, then the single-engined fighters would be able to
operate over the target without hindrance. When
Kammhuber heard of the suggestion he rejected it out of
hand. He had had to fight a long-running battle to bring his
system into being and to defend his methods. The idea of
sending fighters into action over Flak-defended areas at
night had already been tried, and its weaknesses were clear.

Hajo Herrmann was a determined character who
refused to accept 'no' for an answer, however. Ignoring
the chain of command, he went over the head of
Kammhuber and submitted his proposal to
Generaloberst Weise, head of the Reich air defence
organisation, requesting permission to conduct an
experiment along the lines he suggested. Weise agreed
to give the idea a try, ignoring Kammhuber's objections.

One of the beauties of Herrmann's scheme was that
initially it would not require aircraft of its own: he
asked to borrow single-seat Bf 109s and Fw 190s from

operational day fighter units which would be sitting on the ground at night. For his experiment Herrmann assembled some twelve volunteer bomber pilots, all with considerable night flying experience. Herrmann assembled his small force at Mönchen-Gladbach near the Ruhr, to await the next British attack. The commander of the 4th Flak Division, *General* Hintze, agreed to limit the Flak ceiling to 20,000 feet over Essen and Duisburg, and above that altitude Herrmann's single-seat fighters would be free to engage the bombers.

As luck would have it, the next big RAF attack, on the night of 3/4 July, was on Cologne which lay outside the area Hintze controlled. Unaware of the problem, Herrmann and his pilots scrambled in five Focke-Wulf 190s and seven Bf 109s and fought a running fight with the bombers as they streamed over the target. However, the Cologne Flak batteries knew nothing of Herrmann's experiment, and hurled their wrath at friend and foe alike. Several of the defending fighters came under attack, and the cannonade became so severe that Herrmann and his volunteers were forced to break-off the engagement. Before they did so, however, they had claimed the destruction of twelve of the 30 bombers lost to the raiding force that night.

The following morning brought a swift congratulatory telegram from *Generaloberst* Weise. An hour or so later Herrmann was summoned from his bed to take a telephone call from *Reichsmarschall* Göring in person. Herrmann was ordered to fly to Karinhall, Göring's country retreat near Berlin, to report on the night's action to his commander-in-chief. That evening Herrmann expounded his theory in detail. When the raiders approached, his fighters would assemble over one or more strategically placed beacons, and wait until the bombers' target was known. The single-seaters would then be directed en masse to the target, where they would engage the bombers as they passed overhead. The fighters were then to pursue the bombers until fuel ran short, and they could then land at the nearest airfield. The tactic was given the apt code-name 'Wild Boar' (*Wilde Sau*). Göring endorsed the scheme whole-heartedly, and ordered Herrmann to assemble a full *Geschwader* with 90 Messerschmitt and Focke-Wulf single-seaters to exploit the new tactic.

Hajo Herrmann enthusiastically outlined his new tactical method when he addressed a top-level conference in Berlin, on 6 July:

"I opened fire at one bomber, which immediately caught fire but it carried on flying for about four minutes. I let

him have it once more, firing right into the cockpit, and it went down like a stone – the pilot must have been hit."

At times Herrmann had seen as many as 15 bombers, clearly recognisable by their exhaust flames. They were sitting targets for a fast single-seat fighter. If for a time he did not see any bombers, he had only to wait only a minute or so for the next salvo of target indicators to blossom, and more bombers would be illuminated in their glare. Herrmann continued:

"I would like to stress the following. In the area of one Flak division in the Ruhr, where the weather is moderately clear, one can reckon that an average of 80 to 140 enemy bombers are picked up and held by searchlights for longer than two minutes, during an air raid. The demand I make of my crews is that every aircraft held for more than two minutes is shot down. I would go so far as to say that if the British continue their attacks in weather conditions like these, they can lose an extra 80 aircraft every night, if I am provided with the necessary personnel."

Generalfeldmarschall Milch expressed wholehearted agreement for this view. How often had he seen an enemy bomber coned by searchlights, and wished that a German fighter could be up there moving in for the kill. Now it looked as if this was going to come true. Milch asked Herrmann if he had enough pilots. Herrmann replied: *"Jawohl! There are 120 crews!" "And how many aircraft do you have?" "In my experimental unit I have 15 aircraft, and 15 more have just been allocated to me."* Milch ordered that Herrmann was immediately to receive all the fighters he needed.

▲ Oberst Wolfgang Falck on the telephone at a ground control centre directing nightfighter operations.

▲ Generalleutnant Wolfgang Martini, commanding General of Luftwaffe air signals, was responsible for devising measures to counter or exploit the various Allied electronic systems.

► A German poster telling the population to take cover during air raids in order to avoid splinters falling from exploding Flak shells.

Herrmann stressed that he did not advocate single-seater or two-seater night-fighting as such, but that he wanted to introduce a new concept. His aim was to launch a massed attack by using all available forces, as soon as the bombers' target became known. Herrmann had promised Göring that his *Geschwader* could be ready for operations in three months time, or early in October. In fact, it would be needed much earlier than that.

"Every week a city is being smashed, so we must act fast".

Significantly, Herrmann's scheme did not rely on electronic systems other than early-warning radar, radio beacons and VHF radio. In consequence (although nobody in the *Luftwaffe* realised the importance of it at the time) the *Wilde Sau* tactics were impervious to radar jamming.

Meanwhile, *Generalleutnant* Kammhuber continued to press for yet more equipment to buttress his system of

boxes. A few days later, at a further Berlin air conference on 16 July, he drew attention to a serious recurring problem:

"Where the bomber stream enters on a narrow front, for example in the Ruhr and over the Heligoland Bight where there is very little early warning, it is vital that the few boxes that are affected are 100 per cent operational. Most unfortunately, it keeps happening that the most important boxes break down, like No.5 box for instance. The loss of one box during one night brings the number of kills right down."

Backed by *Generalmajor* Martini, he urgently requested that the production of *Freya* radars be doubled or even trebled. The request was noted, though it would never be acted upon.

Also at that meeting an experienced nightfighter controller, *Major* Günthner, described a new system under development which would make it possible to funnel nightfighters into the bomber stream, using radio beams similar to those used over Britain in 1941. He requested the provision within the next two months of about 30 nightfighters to exploit the new system, code-named 'Y-control'. Günthner commented: *"Every week a city is being smashed, so we must act fast"*. In his view the key to the problem was to shoot down many more of the night bombers. *"I think if we can add 80 kills to the 20 we are scoring now, that will mean they will drop their attacks altogether."*

Major Werner Streib, a leading nightfighter ace, proposed that the new method be used to feed nightfighters into the RAF bomber stream as it came over the estuary of the River Scheldt. The nightfighters could pick off bombers one after another along their route to and from the target. *Generalfeldmarschall* Milch warmed to the idea: *"So they can keep up with them, shoot down one after another and keep asking: "And the next please!"*

To overcome the problem of identifying targets in the bomber stream, *Luftwaffe* pilots should be instructed to attack only those aircraft with four-engines. *"Those are the worst ones anyway,"* Günthner added.

Oberst von Lossberg then mentioned that a new nightfighter device was being developed at the signals establishment at Werneuchen. Code-named 'Monica', this was a passive receiver to enable nightfighters to home on emissions from the tail warning radar fitted to RAF bombers.

Together with *Major* Herrmann's proposed new system of target defence night fighting, the assembled officers felt sure they could achieve even higher night victory scores. It was left to *Generalfeldmarschall* Milch to end the meeting on a serious note:

"The best that can be achieved by us is that the enemy ceases to operate against us altogether. Until we can get things in order, however, the best we can hope for is to make the business a messy one. In that case, there is only one worry for us and that is that in some way he again catches us on the hop with some radar trickery, and we have to start trotting after him again."

As the raid on Wuppertal had shown, if the Flak defences at the target were ineffective while the bombers made their attack runs, and the marking was accurate, there was a good chance of laying a devastating concentration of bombs. But if the defence were present in the target area in strength, how could the Flak and searchlight defences be neutralised? In fact, for effective operation against high-flying night bombers, both of these systems were dependent upon their Würzburg control radar. And technically the answer to the radar problem was simple enough: strips of aluminium foil. Known by the cover-name 'Window', these strips measured 30 cm in length and 1.5 cm in width; a single bundle comprised 2,000 of these strips held together by an elastic band, and weighed 765 g.

◄ Generalmajor Adolf Galland (left) served as Inspector General of Luftwaffe day and night fighters and Generalfeldmarschall Milch who wholeheartedly supported Major Hajo Herrmann's proposal to use single-engined fighters to engage enemy bombers over their target at night.

◄ A 'Window' cloud photographed from an RAF bomber. This countermeasure was used to devastating effect against the Luftwaffe air defence system, during the series of attacks on Hamburg during July and August 1943.

When tossed from an aircraft, the bundle broke up and blossomed into a cloud of fluttering strips which produced a radar response similar to that from a large aircraft. By releasing one such bundle per minute from every aircraft in a large attacking force, it was possible to fill the sky with so many responses that radar tracking would become impossible.

During 1942 scientists in both Britain and Germany had experimented with the use of metallic strips to jam radar, both working quite independently and under conditions of great secrecy. In both countries the experts reached the same conclusion: if the strips were released in large quantities, either side's precision radars would be neutralised. At first both sides felt they had more to lose than to gain by using the countermeasure, with the almost certain risk of provoking retaliation in kind.

By the summer of 1943, however, the military balance had changed considerably. RAF Bomber Command was powerful and expanding, while the much smaller *Luftwaffe* bomber force was firmly tied down on the Eastern Front and quite unable to mount any effective retaliatory strike. Moreover, while Allied radar experts had striven to build new sets that were less vulnerable to this form of countermeasure, the German

position remained unchanged.

The metal strips had to be cut to approximately one half the wavelength of the radar to be countered, and strips of a certain length were effective against radars working on a fairly narrow band of radio frequencies. Fortunately for Bomber Command, and unfortunately for the *Luftwaffe*, the Flak control *Würzburg* radar worked on exactly the same frequency as the *Giant Würzburg* used for nightfighter control, and both of these were close to the frequency of the *Lichtenstein* nightfighter radar. Since these radars were all close together in the frequency spectrum, the same sized strip was effective against the three most important *Luftwaffe* air defence precision radars. The failure to rectify this weakness, which was known to several senior *Luftwaffe* officers, was a major sin of omission. It would not go unpunished.

On 15 July, just over a week after Hajo Herrmann expounded on his tactical concept during the conference in Berlin, Winston Churchill authorised the use of Window over enemy territory.

Ten nights later, on 24 July, each of the 746 bombers attacking Hamburg released one bundle of strips every minute as it passed through the target area. As predicted, the effect was devastating. After release, the millions of fluttering metal strips remained effective for about 15 minutes, until they fell far below the bombers altitude and started to disperse. Thus the *Luftwaffe* radar operators were treated to the horrifying spectacle of a raiding force that appeared to comprise more than 11,000 aircraft!

Straddling the approaches to Hamburg, the nightfighters orbited patiently over their assigned *Himmelbett* stations, awaiting intercept instructions from the ground, but none came, and soon the radio channels were in a state of complete and utter chaos. Confused appeals and exclamations flashed through the ether:

"Try without your ground control..."
"It is impossible, too many hostiles..."
"I am searching without your control..."
"The enemy are reproducing themselves!"

In the nightfighters themselves, the scenes of confusion were repeated as they came within *Lichtenstein* range of the drifting clouds of foil. As one *Luftwaffe* pilot airborne that night later wrote (Wilhelm Johnen in *'Duel Under the Stars'*, William Kimber Ltd):

"At 5,000 metres my radio operator announced the first enemy on his Lichtenstein. I was delighted. I swung

▼ The effect of Window is shown on this Würzburg radar screen and clearly shows the interference caused on the viewing screen which made guidance for interception by Luftwaffe nightfighters virtually impossible.

round on to the bearing, in the direction of the Ruhr, for in this way I was bound to approach the stream. Facius proceeded to report three or four targets on his screens. I hoped that I should have enough ammunition to deal with them all.

'Then Facius shouted: 'Tommy flying towards us at a great speed. Distance decreasing ... 2,000 metres ... 1,500 ... 1,000 ... 500 ...' I was speechless. Facius already had a new target. 'Perhaps it was a German nightfighter on a westerly course,' I said to myself, and made for the next bomber. It was not long before Facius shouted: 'Tommy flying towards us at a great speed'. It was not long before Facius shouted again: 'Bomber coming for us at a hell of a speed. 2,000 ... 1,000 ... 500 ... he's gone!' 'You're crackers, Facius,' I said jokingly. But soon I lost my sense of humour, for this crazy performance was repeated a score of times."

As the first waves of bombers arrived over Hamburg itself, their crews were struck by the air of unreality. This city was protected by 54 heavy Flak and 22 searchlight batteries; it was amongst the most heavily defended targets in Germany. In the past, as raiders approached, the beams of the radar-directed master searchlights had stood bolt upright, before tilting swiftly over to mark some unfortunate bomber; then four or five other lights would switch on and grasp the prey in their lucid mesh.

Tonight, it was different. It seemed that all the searchlights were on, swinging this way and that as they groped blindly for the raiders. Where the beams crossed, others would quickly join them. Sometimes as many as 30 or 40 beams formed a gigantic cone in the sky – on a cloud of Window.

As it was with the searchlights, so it was with the Flak. During previous attacks on such heavily defended targets, bomber crews had expected to be bracketed from time to time by accurate salvoes from the ground. On this occasion the Flak gunners were forced to abandon predicted fire, however. Now they loosed off round after unaimed round ineffectually into the sky above. If the staccato bark of their guns did little else, it gave the sheltering citizens the comforting if mistaken impression that the raiders above were having an equally harrowing time as those in the shelters.

Hamburg was now almost defenceless, but before it could be hit the Pathfinders had to mark it accurately, and keep it marked. As the city lay far outside the range of Oboe, the crews had only the less precise H2S equipment with which to do it. Since the Wedel fiasco earlier in the year, however, Bomber Command had learnt much about the limitations of its new radar, and crews were aware of the potential problem of the exposed sandbanks. This time there was no difficulty from that source, and the wide Elbe River pointed straight towards Hamburg.

On this occasion 74 radar-equipped bombers took part in the attack, and the serviceability of H2S had

▲ A Bf 110 nightfighter of NJG 4 fitted with long-range drop tanks.

"...a fire typhoon such as was never before witnessed, against which every human resistance was quite useless..."

improved greatly since the previous March. Also, Pathfinder navigators had strict orders not to release their target markers, if they were not satisfied that their radar was working properly.

The plan called for 20 H2S aircraft to open the attack by releasing yellow target indicators and strings of flares, solely on radar indications. Following them were eight visual markers which were to attempt to identify the target visually in the light of the flares, and drop red target indicators at the aiming points. Finally, the 53 backers-up distributed throughout the bomber stream were to aim their green target indicators at, in order of preference, the red markers, just beyond the centre of the green markers already down (a measure to counter possible creep-back) or, failing all else, the centre of the yellow markers. The bombers of the main force had orders to bomb the red markers if they were visible, or else the centre of the green markers; they were told to ignore the yellow markers.

During the first 15 minutes of the attack the green markers followed each other accurately into the area round the aiming point, but after that a marked creep-back developed. That process continued until the end of the attack, by which time there was a seven-mile-long carpet of burning incendiary bombs extending back from the aiming point.

That night Bomber Command lost twelve aircraft, probably half to Flak and half to nightfighters. Most of the aircraft lost had been coned by searchlights before they were hit, in itself a testimony to the effectiveness of the Window against the various radars. This loss rate, 1.5 per cent of the force which had set out, contrasted with the six per cent loss rate which had been normal during previous attacks on this target. Twenty aircraft returned with Flak damage, and two having been hit by nightfighters. One Pathfinder suffered damage when a target indicator blew up shortly after release, almost certainly having been hit by an anti-aircraft shell; two aircraft were damaged by falling incendiary bombs.

Without doubt, Window had been an outstanding success during this first action. Had the raid cost the six

per cent normal for an attack on Hamburg, some 50 bombers would have been shot down out of the large attacking force. So there is reason to believe that more than 35 aircraft were saved by the 40 tons of Window dropped that night – 92 million strips of aluminium foil.

For its part Hamburg had been hit harder than ever before although, as might be expected when a less accurate marking system was used, the bombing was not as concentrated as was now usual in the Ruhr. Nevertheless the previous month had been particularly hot and dry, and for this and other reasons the city was unusually vulnerable to the torrent of incendiary bombs which rained upon it. As the city's police chief later reported:

"Coal and coke supplies stored for the winter in many houses caught fire and could be extinguished only weeks later. Essential services were severely damaged and telephone services were cut early in the attack. Dockyards and industrial installations were severely hit. At noon the next day there was still a gigantic, dense cloud of smoke and dust hovering over the city which, despite the clear sky, prevented the sun from penetrating... Despite the deployment of all available forces, it was impossible to prevent large fires flaring up again and again."

Yet Hamburg's ordeal had only just begun. With its defences still reeling under the shock of Window, its roads barricaded with rubble, much of its telephone system out of order and water supplies disrupted over a wide area, the city was almost helpless when Sir Arthur Harris launched a repeat attack two nights later on the 27th.

During the second attack, the force of more than 700 bombers crossed Hamburg from north-east to south-west. This time there was little to stop the fires from taking hold, and soon much of the north-eastern quarter of the city was engulfed in a sea of flame.

The fate Wuppertal had narrowly missed now struck Hamburg: a firestorm. In principle, a firestorm is a

◄ The fires started in Hamburg continued to burn for several days, as this Allied reconnaissance photograph shows.

▲ The aftermath of the devastating raid on Hamburg. More than 40,000 people lost their lives in the firestorm caused by the concentration of burning buildings.

►► A Bf 110 E-2 nightfighter being re-fuelled at Schleswig in July 1942 for a forthcoming mission against Allied bombers. The aircraft in the foreground is a Junkers Ju 88 nightfighter. The Luftwaffe nightfighters were unable to stop the deadly Allied bombing and destruction on the cities

comparatively simple exercise in applied physics. A concentration of burning buildings heats the air above them and, as the hot air rises, cold air rushes in to take its place. The incoming air fans the flames before itself becoming heated and rising, and during this continuing process the fires blaze hotter and hotter. This was what now happened in Hamburg. The mighty convection currents caused winds of up to 150 mph – twice hurricane force – and temperatures exceeding 1,000 degrees Centigrade. Again in the words of the police chief:

"In a built-up area the suction could not follow its shortest course, but the overheated air stormed through the streets with immense force taking with it not only sparks but burning timber and roof beams, so spreading

the fire further and further, developing in a short time a fire typhoon such as was never before witnessed, against which every human resistance was quite useless."

The fires developed so fast that in the firestorm areas escape was almost impossible. Many died quietly of carbon monoxide poisoning in their cellar shelters while others, trying to avoid this fate, left cover to run clear and were lifted bodily by the storm winds and hurled into the flames. The loss of life in Hamburg that night transcended anything previously seen as a result of an air attack, with well over 40,000 dead.

Two nights later the bombers returned to Hamburg in force, as they did yet again on 2 August, but although these two attacks created further swathes of damage in the battered city, the loss of life was comparatively light. By then more than a million people had fled the city, leaving behind only those employed in the fire-fighting and defence services.

Throughout the Hamburg battle, the Window had effectively neutralised the *Luftwaffe* systems for close-controlled nightfighting and radar gunlaying. In doing so, the countermeasure had cut losses from the former and reduced the harassing effect of the latter.

During the first six attacks in which the foil had been used – two on the Ruhr in addition to the four on Hamburg – Bomber Command flew more than 4,000 sorties; out of this total 124 aircraft, just over three per cent of the total, failed to return. Towards the end of this series the defenders recovered from their initial surprise, but although RAF losses climbed a little they remained well below the rates suffered prior to the introduction of the countermeasure. The general in charge of *Luftwaffe* signals, *Generalmajor* Wolfgang Martini, later commented on the operational debut of Window: *"The technical success of this action must be assessed as absolute."*

Before we look at the steps taken by the *Luftwaffe* to retrieve the situation after the Hamburg catastrophe, it is necessary to examine the emerging threat to German industry that had taken shape during the spring and early summer of 1943: that mounted by the United States Eighth Air Force.

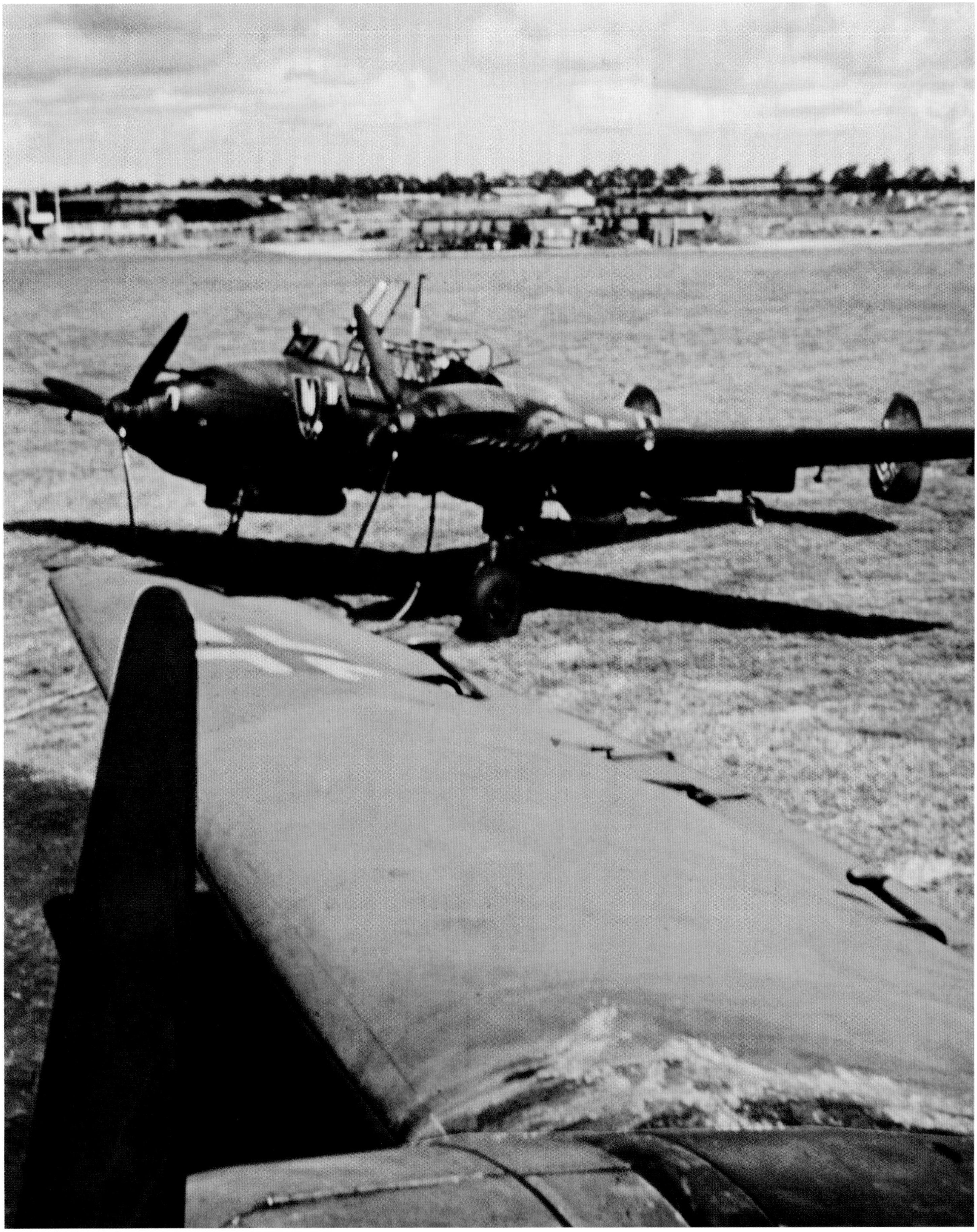

4

THE COMING OF THE YANKS

January to July 1943

"War means fighting, and fighting means killing"

General Nathan Bedford Forrest

The US Eighth Air Force mounted its first heavy bomber attack on a target in Germany on 27 January 1943, when it sent 91 B-17s and B-24s against the port of Wilhelmshaven and the nearby naval munitions depot at Mariensiel. Due to a layer of thin cloud at the target, and a smoke-screen which obscured part of it, many of the units failed to find their targets. Nevertheless, 55 Flying Fortresses found the Mariensiel depot and delivered a concentrated attack which caused considerable damage and set off several secondary explosions. The *Luftwaffe* fighter units in the area, newcomers to the business of attacking the tough US heavy bombers, shot down only three raiders for the loss of seven fighters.

There followed nearly a month of attacks on targets in France and Belgium before the Eighth Air Force returned to Germany in force. When it did, on 26 February, the 93 raiders found their primary target at Bremen obscured by cloud. The secondary target, at Wilhelmshaven, was, however, clear of cloud and 65 aircraft bombed the harbour. On this occasion the defending fighter force, though still cautious, reacted more strongly and shot down six bombers. Flak accounted for a seventh.

An innovation during this action was *Luftwaffe* use of twin-engined nightfighters against the American bomber formations. With their longer endurance and heavier ammunition loads, the nightfighters could maintain the pressure on the raiders long after their single-engined counterparts were forced to break off the action to refuel and rearm. Moreover, the nightfighters could operate at greater distances from their bases, thus effectively increasing the depth of the defences.

These advantages were not gained cheaply, however. The nightfighter's usual tactic was to fly alone, stalk its prey and close to within 100 yards before opening fire. Using similar methods during the day against the US heavy bombers proved extremely dangerous, for the bomber formation amassed considerably more fire power than the nightfighters sent against them in ones and twos. To be effective a nightfighter crew required a long training and considerable combat experience, so any lost in action were difficult to replace. One of the first to be lost in this way was ace *Hauptmann* Ludwig Becker, credited with 46 night kills, who had been one of the pioneers in the use of radar to assist night interceptions. Becker and his crewman were shot down and killed during the action against US bombers on 26 February.

Three weeks elapsed before the next major US attack on Germany, on 18 March. One hundred and three B-17s and B-24s set out, 97 of which delivered an accurate concentration of bombs on the U-boat construction yards at Vegesack near Bremen. Despite attacks from more than 50 enemy fighters, only two bombers were lost. This heartening result seemed to vindicate the US Army Air Force's theories regarding the effectiveness of the bombers' defensive crossfire to ward off enemy fighters.

◄◄ B-24D Liberators of the 44th Bomb Group taxiing out from their base at Shipdham in Suffolk. This variant of the bomber had a maximum speed of 303 mph and cruised at 180 mph at 25,000 feet. Maximum take-off weight was 64,000 pounds. Defensive armament comprised two Browning .5 inch guns in the dorsal, ventral and rear turrets, one of these weapons on a hand-held mounting in the waist positions on either side of the fuselage and in the nose.

► Early in 1943 the USAAF mounted its attacks on targets in Germany. Here B-17F Flying Fortresses of the 305th Bomb Group are seen on their way to a target. This variant of the aircraft had a maximum speed of 325 mph at 25,000 feet, and a cruising speed of 175 mph. Maximum take-off weight was 48,720 pounds. Defensive armament comprised two Browning .5 inch guns in the dorsal, ventral and rear turrets. In addition there was one of these weapons on a hand-held mounting in the waist position on either side of the fuselage, and the radio operator's position. As a local modification there might be as many as six hand-held Browning .3 inch guns on mountings positioned around the nose. (USAF)

► The important munitions depot at Mariensiel near Wilhelmshaven holding stores for the German Navy, pictured before the attack mounted in late January 1943.

►► On 27 January 1943 the US Eighth Air Force delivered its first attack on German territory, when 55 Boeing B-17s struck the Mariensiel depot. Post-strike photographs revealed that the bombs had detonated large quantities of munitions and flattened several storage bunkers at 'A'. The blast from the powerful explosions caused considerable damage throughout the area outlined with a dashed line 'B'. On the far left, at 'C', the fuel storage tanks on the opposite side of the basin had also suffered damage.

◄ B-17 Flying Fortresses of the 96th Bomb Group unload their bombs over a target.

Until now US bombers raiding Germany had flown in 18-aircraft group combat box formations, with succeeding boxes following each other at intervals of one and a half miles. Despite the success of the Vegesack attack, it was clear that in the future *Luftwaffe* fighters were likely to attack in far greater numbers. To meet such a move, Eighth Air Force planners devised a new formation intended to concentrate the bombers' defensive fire-power still further. From now on the bombers were to fly in a tighter Wing formation, comprising three 18-aircraft groups. Instead of trailing behind the Lead Bomb Group, one Group in each Wing flew above the Lead Group, and the remaining Bomb Group flew below it. This produced a huge formation of 54 aircraft providing powerful mutual fire support, occupying a volume of sky 600 yards long, over a mile wide and half a mile deep. Succeeding combat wings followed each other at six-mile intervals.

The Combat Wing formation was tested in action for the first time on 17 April, when 115 heavy bombers attempted to repeat the Vegesack success against the nearby Focke-Wulf assembly works. As the formations assembled over East Anglia they came under the watchful eyes of the German early warning radar chain, however, and long before the leading bombers approached the Friesian Islands the defending fighter units had been brought to readiness to meet the incursion. Even so, the *Luftwaffe* controllers had no wish to scramble the short-endurance day fighters until they were reasonably certain of the raiders' intended target. As a result, the raiders had nearly reached their target before the fighters engaged.

Then, nearly two full *Gruppen* of Fw 190s from *JG 1* hurled themselves at the leading Wing of bombers, whose bomb groups had moved into line-astern as they began their bombing runs. Wave after wave of fighters stormed head-on through the formation, ignoring the bursting salvoes from the Bremen Flak batteries below. The fighter attacks continued with unabated ferocity until the bombers were well out to sea on their way home.

At the end of the hard-fought battle the US losses were the heaviest suffered so far: 15 bombers destroyed by fighters and one by Flak. Forty-eight bombers returned with battle damage. The raiders' return fire claimed five *Luftwaffe* fighters destroyed and five damaged.

The operation neither proved nor disproved the value of the new Combat Wing formation. In action the 54 aircraft formation was unwieldy and difficult to hold, and as a result the leading Wing formation was rather

BOEING B-17F

'Paddy Gremlin' of 524th Bombardment Squadron,
379th Bombardment Group, Kimbolton, Huntingdonshire, late 1943.
Standard finish of Olive Drab over Neutral Gray undersurfaces. Note
the red surround to the national markings.

ragged by the time it arrived over the target; all 16 bombers lost had come from its ranks. The second Wing, on the other hand, maintained its cohesion and suffered no losses.

———

At this stage, with the British and US bombers mounting a round-the-clock offensive against targets in Germany, it is appropriate to discuss the characteristics of each form of attack. We shall look at these from the standpoints of the two most important aircraft types used at this time, the B-17F Flying Fortress and the Avro Lancaster Mark I, the accuracy of their bombing and their ability to penetrate enemy defences.

Fully loaded the B-17F weighed just under 49,000 pounds, while the Lancaster grossed out somewhat heavier at 65,000 pounds. Flying Fortresses cruised in formation at about 175 mph at altitudes between about 20,000 feet and 26,000 feet, each carrying 3,500 pounds of bombs to a distant target. About 12 per cent of the aircraft's all-up-weight was devoted to defensive armament.

Lancasters cruised singly at 220 mph at altitudes of between 20,000 and 22,000 feet, each carrying about

◄▼ During the darkest days of the US 8th Air Force's bombing offensive on Germany some individual aircraft were considered lucky machines. One of these was 'Paddy Gremlin' of the 524th BS, 379th BG at Kimbolton, Huntingdonshire. By the end of 1943 the aircraft had survived several hazardous missions but was eventually lost on 30 January 1944 when it was hit by a bomb dropped from an aircraft flying higher in the formation. With the No. 3 engine damaged the aircraft gradually fell back from the formation and was eventually forced down near the Belgian border. After crash-landing the crew were attacked by a Luftwaffe fighter and several were injured. The surviving crew members believed the reason for the attack was to stop them from setting fire to their aircraft.

▲ General Hap Arnold, Commanding General of the US Army Air Forces, discussing a point with RAF Air Chief Marshal Sir Charles Portal, Chief of the Air Staff.

▶ Armourers loading a 1,000 pound bomb into a Liberator of the 93rd Bomb Group at Hardwick. Note the minimal ground clearance available for this operation.

square pattern of bombs on the ground, with sides some 500 yards long. Given clear skies, the average 50 per cent circular error of the leader's bombs was about 450 yards, and the pattern from the combat box formation centred on this. If there was partial cloud cover or poor visibility, the 50 per cent circular error would rise to about 1,200 yards.

The RAF night bombers aimed their bomb loads individually, and the accuracy depended to a large extent on the quality of the Pathfinders' marking. By the summer of 1943 the 50 per cent circular error during night attacks on targets in Germany was about 700 yards when Oboe marking was used. With H2S marking the error was between two and six times that figure, depending on the targets distinctive signature on radar.

From these figures, two important points emerge. First, that even under clear daylight conditions, the so-called 'pinpoint' bombing from 20,000 feet or above meant that in reality only half the bombs landed within a quarter of a mile of the aiming point. Secondly, that by night or by day under poor conditions, unless the target was approximately circular and had a radius of three miles or greater, at least half of the bombs aimed at it would do no more than plough up the surrounding fields (sometimes termed 'agricultural bombing').

During this period every US daylight incursion into Germany was met by defending fighters, and the fighters were the most dangerous adversary. From a survey carried out at the close of 1943, we know that out of every 100

8,900 pounds of bombs to a distant target. About six per cent of the bomber's all-up-weight was devoted to defensive armament.

Provided the skies were clear, daylight bombing was far more accurate than night bombing. Each US combat box formation now comprised about 18 aircraft, and the bomb-aimers released their bombs when they saw those of the formation leader fall away. This produced a more or less

US heavy bombers lost, 48 had been in formation immediately before being brought down. Of these, 28 had fallen to fighter attack, 16 to Flak, and four to other causes (collision, mechanical failure, etc.). The remaining aircraft had left the formation before being shot down, in 16 cases because of Flak damage, 14 due to damage inflicted by fighters and 21 for other reasons. Of these stragglers, 46 were finally despatched by fighters, five by Flak and one after further mechanical failure. In fact, few straggling US bombers survived over Germany, unless they were fortunate enough to receive protection from escorting fighters.

In the case of night bombers, between 80 and 90 per cent flew each mission without ever encountering a defending fighter. Of those that were intercepted by nightfighters, about half were shot down. The majority of bombers shot down by nightfighters were taken by surprise, and did not open fire on their assailant. That fact is important: much has been said about the relative ineffectiveness of the rifle-calibre .303 inch machine guns fitted to the RAF bombers, yet if so many of the gunners failed to detect the attacker before it delivered the death blow, would heavier calibre machine guns have made any difference?

If an enemy nightfighter was detected before it opened its attack, the bomber's best course was to enter a corkscrew manoeuvre, and the more violent the better. If this was done early enough, the aircraft made an extremely difficult target. The more experienced *Luftwaffe* pilots usually would not attempt to follow a cork-screwing bomber whose gunners were fully alerted. Instead, they would resume their search hoping to find a bomber that they could take by surprise.

To sum up: the daylight bombers fought their way through the defences because they could not evade them; and the night bombers evaded the defences because they could not fight their way through them.

During the spring of 1943 the day fighter force in Germany underwent a steady expansion. A new home defence *Geschwader, JG 11*, was formed and another three experienced fighter *Gruppen* were withdrawn from the Mediterranean and Eastern fronts. During the first six months of 1943 the number of single-engined fighters defending the Reich nearly doubled.

To make the maximum use of the available fighters, the *Luftwaffe* made sweeping changes to its home defence fighter control and support organisations. Previously, individual *Gruppen* had scrambled in forces of 15 or 20 fighters on receiving local warning of the

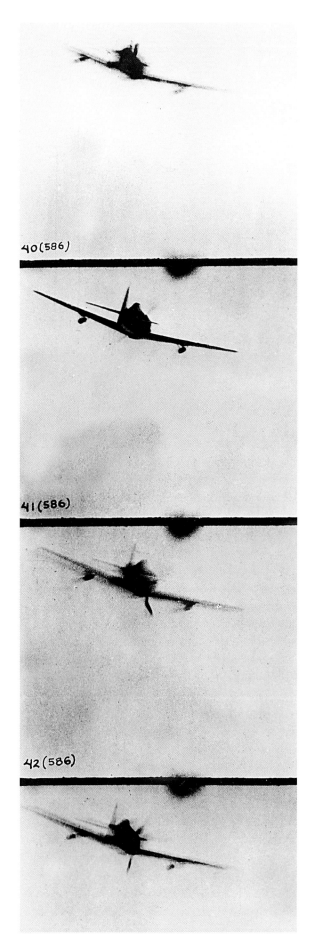

40(586)

41(586)

42(586)

◄ During a mission to Kassel and Oschersleben on 28 July 1943, American bombers were attacked by Bf 109s and Fw 190s fitted with 21 cm mortars. These camera gun frames show an Fw 190 with underwing mortars under attack from a US escort fighter.

◄▲ The 88 mm anti-aircraft Flak batteries initially formed the core of the defence of the Reich and were progressively increased in number and calibre as the Allied bombing increased in intensity both by day and by night.

HEAVY FLAK WEAPONS AVAILABLE IN 1943

For the purpose of this section the term 'heavy Flak' includes all weapons of calibre 75 mm and larger. These guns employed predictor control when engaging aircraft at long range and high altitude, in contrast to the lighter automatic weapons which were fired over open sights and which were ineffective above about 6,000 feet.

The smallest-calibre heavy Flak weapon produced in quantity in Germany was the 88 mm Flak 18, which entered service in 1933. Fitted with a semi-automatic breech mechanism, this weapon had a practical rate of fire of 15 rounds per minute and had a maximum engagement altitude of 26,000 feet. The firing crew numbered ten, later reduced to seven. The 88 mm Flak 37 was fitted with an improved mounting, and it had an electrical data transmission system to carry the fire control information directly from the predictor. The 88 mm Flak 41 was the first major redesign of the gun itself, with a longer and stronger barrel and a powered ramming system. This version entered service in 1943.

The 105 mm Flak 37 entered service just before the outbreak of war. It had a practical rate of fire of 15 rounds per minute and had a maximum engagement altitude of 35,000 feet. It had a powered ramming system and power-assisted laying, and normally employed a crew of nine. The Flak 38 was similar, but incorporated an electrical data transmission system and other detailed improvements.

The heaviest Flak weapon employed by the *Luftwaffe* was the 128 mm Flak 40. This weapon had a practical rate of fire of ten rounds per minute and had a maximum engagement altitude of 35,000 feet. It featured powered ramming, elevation and traverse. The 128 mm *Flakzwilling* 40 comprised two barrels mounted on a common traversing and elevating mounting. The use of this ultra-heavy paired weapon was confined to the giant Flak towers erected in the principal German cities.

As the war progressed, the Flak arm made increasing use of captured foreign weapons. These included the British Vickers 3 inch and 3.7 inch guns, the French 75 mm, the Italian 90 mm and 102 mm, the Czech 76.5 mm and the Soviet 76.2 mm and 85 mm weapons. These weapons fired captured ammunition while supplies lasted, after which those captured guns which were suitable, notably the Soviet 85 mm weapon, were re-bored to fire the standard German 88 mm round.

◄ A B-17 under attack over Oschersleben by an Fw 190. The Fortress has already been set on fire and separated from its formation.

▲ A gun camera still showing another B-17 under attack by an Fw 190. This gives a good impression of the view an attacking German pilot might have seen as he opened fire.

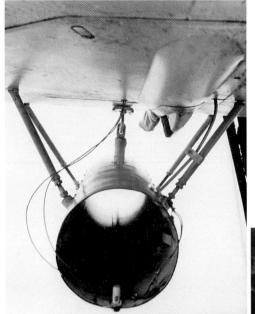

◄ A rear view of a 21 cm, Wgr 21 mortar tube as fitted to an Fw 190.

▼ During the summer of 1943, many Luftwaffe single and twin-engined fighters were modified to carry underwing Wgr 21 mortars. These unguided missiles were fired from outside the range of the US bombers' defensive fire with the intention of breaking up the formations. The missiles were fused to explode some 1,000 metres in front of the launching aircraft. Some of the Fw 190 A-5s and A-6s of I./JG 1 were equipped with the 21 cm mortars from early June and although early results were encouraging, they were removed a few weeks later when the Allied escort fighters began to appear over Europe.

FOCKE-WULF Fw 190 A-5/R6

Yellow 8' of 3./JG 1, Deelen, Holland, July 1943. With its tactical number, Tatzelwurm and spinner in yellow, the 3. Staffel colour features prominently on this machine, although the yellow nose panel is a recognition aid common to all German fighters of the period.

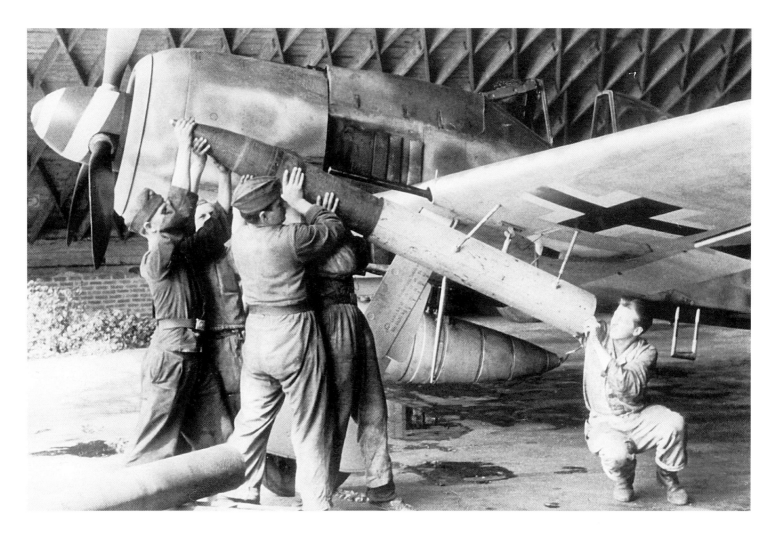

▲ Ground crew installing a Wgr 21 mortar under the wing of an Fw 190.

◄ This B-17 is one which returned from the raid to Kassel and Oschersleben on 28 July 1943 and shows damage caused by fragments from a German air-to-air mortar. The aircraft, belonging to the 379th Bomb Group, was named 'The Sack'. It was struck below the top turret and large fragments exploded the aircraft's oxygen bottles which blasted a large hole in the forward fuselage. Parts of the mortar round were later removed and examined by USAAF Technical Intelligence personnel who obtained valuable information on the weapon.

► Major Karl Borris commanded I./ JG 26 from June 1943 until the end of the war, and was credited with 43 aerial victories. He is seen here with Franz, the unit's red setter mascot.

► Major Anton Hackl seated in the cockpit of his Fw 190. Anton Hackl commanded III./JG 11 in the autumn of 1943 and became one of the leading fighter aces in the West. At the end of the war his victory score stood at 192, including 32 four-engined bombers.

approach of enemy formations, and engaged the bombers piecemeal. Now the various Fighter Divisions began to co-ordinate the operations of fighters in their areas, bringing together formations of 50 or more fighters and then directing them to launch a concerted attack on the bombers. To enable the short-range single-engined fighters to fly second sorties against an attacking force, the *Luftwaffe* stocked designated airfields with fuel and ammunition, and provided each with sufficient ground crew to service, refuel and rearm visiting fighters.

Also during the spring of 1943, *Jagdgeschwader 1* began experimenting with air-to-air bombing attacks,

releasing time-fused 250 kg bombs from its Bf 109s. The intention was to destroy the American bombers directly, or damage them sufficiently to force them to leave their protective formations so that they became easier prey for other fighters. Although the tactic destroyed or damaged a few bombers, it did not find favour. Since the bomb exploded after a pre-set distance of fall, the fighter had to be flying straight and level at the correct distance above the US bomber at the moment of bomb release, although this also meant that the target aircraft was out of sight of the fighter pilot, at the time he released the weapon. Had it been possible to fit the weapon with some form of proximity fuse, to detonate it as it fell past the target aircraft, the tactic would have been far more successful. As it was, the *Luftwaffe* was never able to perfect such a device and the air-to-air bombing tactic was soon discarded.

Despite the hurried improvements made to the defences, and the losses inflicted on the daylight raiding forces, the *Luftwaffe* found itself facing ever larger, more ambitious and more frequent attacks from the Eighth Air Force.

During the spring of 1943 the expansion of the Eighth Air Force continued apace, allowing progressive increases in the size of its attacking forces and a greater

AIRCRAFT VULNERABILITY AND REPAIR

The ability to withstand battle damage was an important factor common to all types of bomber. The three main causes of losses due to enemy action were, in order of lethality: fire, loss of motive power, or loss of control.

Fire was by far the greatest danger to an aircraft: once a blaze took hold it was only a matter of time before something important, like a wing, burned through and fell off. A heavy bomber loaded with around 2,000 gallons of high-octane fuel, and carrying explosive stores such as bombs, ammunition and flares, was a highly inflammable craft. The fitting of self-sealing fuel tanks and armour reduced the fire risk, yet it was always present to a dangerous degree.

Loss of motive power was the next most common cause of losses. After examining the evidence of aircraft losses at the end of the war, British operational research scientists concluded that more aircraft and crews would have returned safely had the armour plate installed for crew protection been positioned instead to protect the engines. In general terms, liquid-cooled engines were twice as

vulnerable to battle damage as their air-cooled counterparts.

Loss of control was the next most common cause of losses, although it fell somewhat below the other two.

Ease of maintenance and repair was an important if often overlooked factor if a bomber force was to launch repeated operations against enemy targets. Without it the B-17s and Lancasters, no matter how brilliantly they performed in the air, would not have achieved much in the long term. After each large-scale attack a proportion of the bombers returned with battle damage, and the number available for the next raid depended upon the speed with which that damage could be repaired. About 1,000 pounds of the Lancaster's weight was taken up with bolts and flanges to allow for rapid dismantling to fit replacement components. Had the Lancaster been constructed in one piece it could have carried a further 1,000 pounds or more bombs over a given range, or flown faster or higher, yet such extra lifting capacity or performance would have been dearly bought in terms of the greater number of aircraft on the ground and unserviceable.

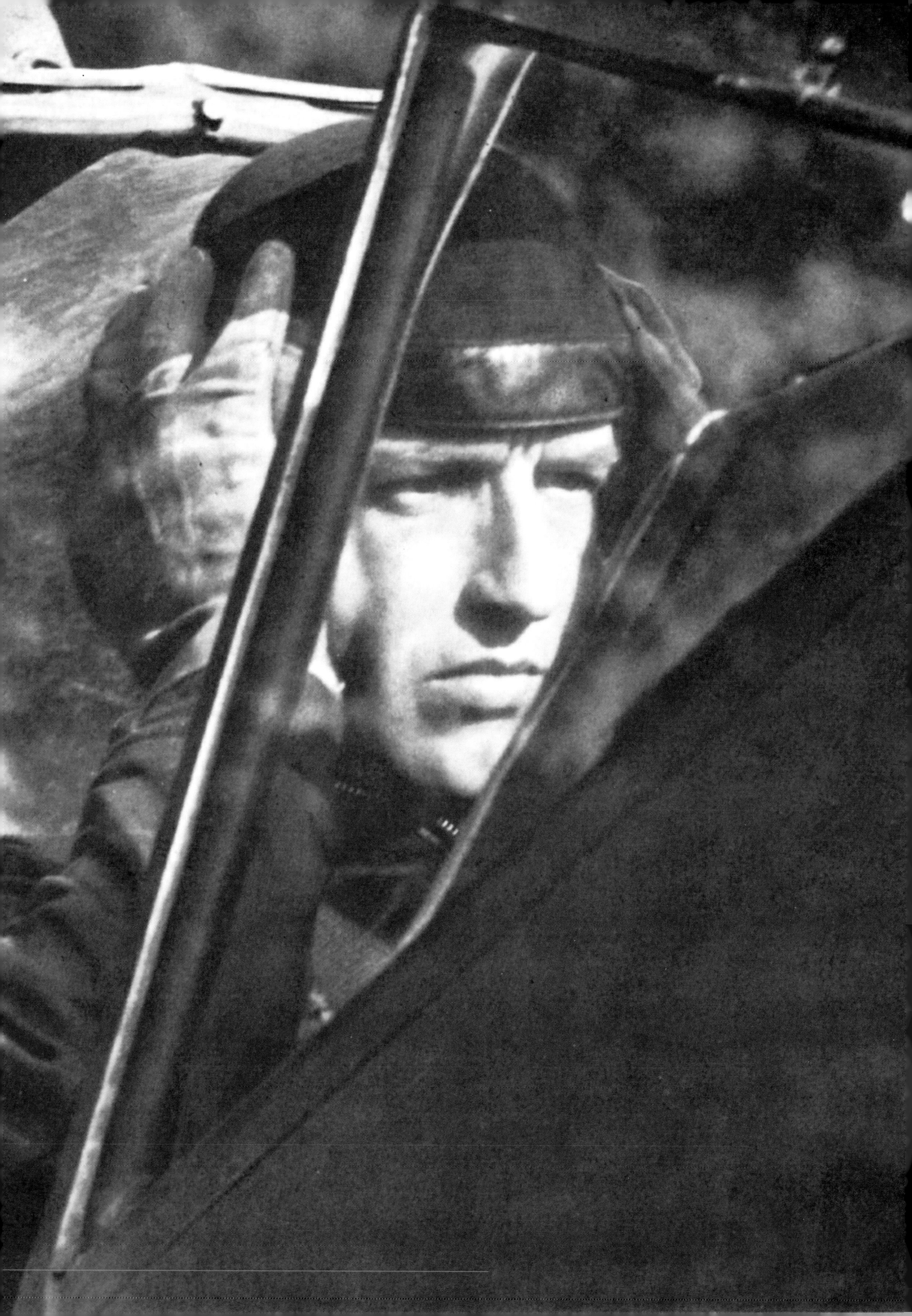

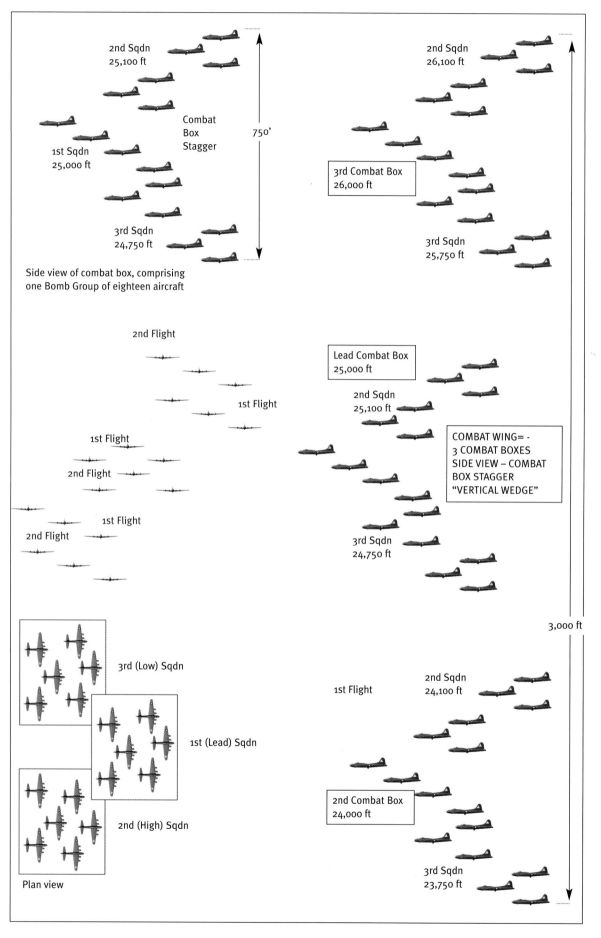

2nd Sqdn
25,100 ft

Combat
Box
Stagger

750'

1st Sqdn
25,000 ft

3rd Sqdn
24,750 ft

Side view of combat box, comprising
one Bomb Group of eighteen aircraft

2nd Flight

1st Flight

1st Flight

2nd Flight

1st Flight

2nd Flight

3rd (Low) Sqdn

1st (Lead) Sqdn

2nd (High) Sqdn

Plan view

2nd Sqdn
26,100 ft

3rd Combat Box
26,000 ft

3rd Sqdn
25,750 ft

Lead Combat Box
25,000 ft

2nd Sqdn
25,100 ft

COMBAT WING= -
3 COMBAT BOXES
SIDE VIEW – COMBAT
BOX STAGGER
"VERTICAL WEDGE"

3rd Sqdn
24,750 ft

3,000 ft

1st Flight

2nd Sqdn
24,100 ft

2nd Combat Box
24,000 ft

3rd Sqdn
23,750 ft

◄ **The Combat Wing Formation**
Throughout the course of its strategic bomber offensive the US 8th Air Force made several alterations to its attack formations, to meet tactical requirements. This diagram shows the 54-aircraft Combat Wing Formation, employed during the early unescorted raids in March and April 1943. It enabled individual bombers to give a high degree of mutual fire support to those around them, although the formation was rather unwieldy. Three Bomb Group formations as shown (left) combined to form a Combat Wing Formation (right). In a Wing the Groups were drawn up in a stepped 'V', in a manner similar to that of the squadrons. The entire Wing formation occupied a volume of sky six hundred yards long, over a mile wide and half a mile deep. At the Initial Point before the target, the individual combat box formations moved into line astern behind the lead box, so that each could concentrate on its bomb run.

◄ Combat Wing Formations followed each other at six-mile intervals.

frequency of attacks. On 14 May, 136 US bombers set out to attack the port of Kiel and eight failed to return. Five days later there was another attack on the same target by 123 bombers, of which six were lost. On 11 June, 252 B-17s set out to attack Wilhelmshaven and Cuxhaven and eight were lost.

During this period the US attacks were becoming more effective, but so were the re-organised defences. On 13 June the Eighth Air Force launched a twin attack on Bremen and Kiel, involving 227 heavy bombers, but the raiders suffered their heaviest loss so far when 26 bombers failed to return. Nine days later, on 22 June, a force of 235 B-17s made the deepest penetration yet into Germany, with an attack on the important synthetic rubber plant at Hüls in the Ruhr. The bombing was both accurate and destructive, and halted production for a month before the plant resumed partial production. The attack cost 16 heavy bombers.

During the final week of July the Eighth Air Force joined its British comrades in the crescendo of bombing, sending large formations on the 25th to attack Hamburg (still burning after its visit by the RAF the previous night) and Kiel; Hamburg again and Hannover on the 26th; Kassel and Oschersleben in the deepest-yet penetration on the 28th; Kiel and Warnemünde on the 29th; and Kassel again on the 30th. The series of attacks cost 87 bombers shot down, but their targets also suffered heavily.

The attacks on Kassel and Oschersleben on 28 July presented the *Luftwaffe* day fighter units operating over the homeland with a new problem: a force of 123 P-47 Thunderbolts, many of them carrying the new 100-gallon drop tanks, met the returning bombers as they crossed the German-Dutch frontier and covered their withdrawal.

The US fighters' appearance so far inside German-held territory surprised *Luftwaffe* fighters in the act of hunting down damaged bombers, and during the ensuing melee the P-47s claimed nine enemy fighters for the loss of one of their number. In itself the action was barely significant, though it would be a grim portent for the defending fighter force.

The first week of August 1943 saw *Luftwaffe* leaders numbed by the blows of the previous ten days. Overshadowing all else was the destruction and fearful loss of life inflicted upon Germany's second largest city, which the defenders had been powerless to prevent. As Göring's deputy, *Generalfeldmarschall* Erhard Milch, stated during a conference at the Reich Air Ministry in Berlin on 3 August:

"Give us another five or six attacks like those on Hamburg, and the German people will just give up, no matter how strong-willed they are. The people will say: 'We've had enough, we simply cannot take any more ...' All those fancy ideas about nightfighters for the Eastern Front or air cover for Sicily; now they are all quite out of the question. The man at the front will have to dig himself a hole and stay in it until the attackers have gone away. What the homeland is having to suffer, that is appalling."

In the next Chapter we shall look at the steps taken by the *Luftwaffe* to retrieve the situation after the Hamburg catastrophe and the emerging threat to German industry from the daylight attacks.

5

THE DEFENDERS
HIT BACK HARD

August 1943

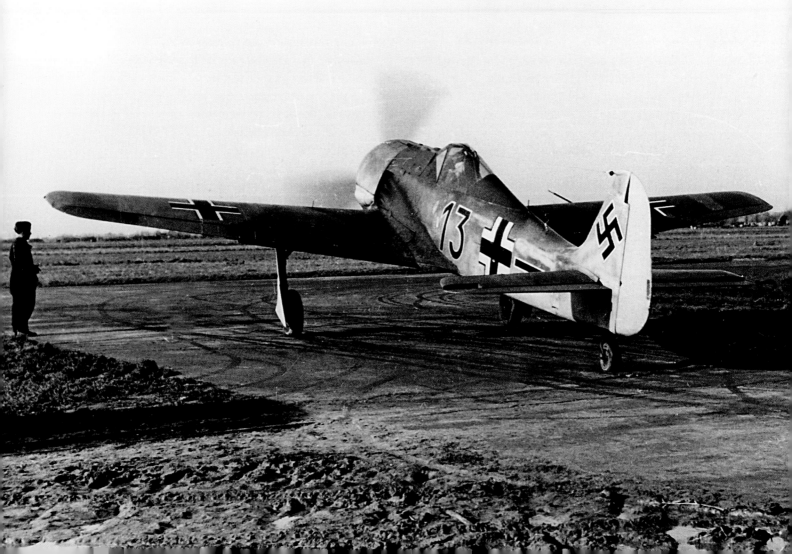

"The enemy cannot withstand losses of 25 or 30 per cent. This means that, if we can inflict such losses at regular intervals, he will be forced to desist from his attacks."

Generalfeldmarschall Erhard Milch,
speaking on 24 August 1943

By the summer of 1943 the *Luftwaffe* was seriously over-extended, and at each crisis point it had been unable to prevent its enemies from gaining their objectives. The time had passed when the *Luftwaffe* could be strong at every point where its services were needed. From now on it could be effective only by concentrating the bulk of its forces at a single vital point – and the defence of the Reich itself would soon assume that position.

There can be no doubting the resolve of its senior commanders to protect the homeland. The Inspector of Fighters, *Generalmajor* Adolf Galland, later commented:

"Never before and never again did I witness such determination and agreement among the circle of those responsible for the leadership of the Luftwaffe. It was as though under the impact of the Hamburg catastrophe everyone had put aside either personal or departmental ambitions. There was no conflict between the General Staff and war industry, no rivalry between bombers and fighters; only the one common will to do everything in this critical hour for the defence of the Reich and to leave nothing undone to prevent a second national misfortune of this dimension."

Following the Hamburg debacle, the first major change was the replacement of *Generalmajor* Kammhuber himself. Josef Kammhuber had built up the nightfighter force from scratch, but throughout that time his relations with Göring had always been difficult. The latter regarded him, not without reason, as a technical perfectionist who demanded an unreasonably large share of the available aircraft and electronic systems for his force.

So long as Kammhuber's methods were seen to be successful, Göring could not easily oust him. But in August 1943, following the neutralisation of the *Himmelbett* system and the success of tactics that Kammhuber had previously eschewed, the *Reichsmarschall* had the justification he needed. Kammhuber was shunted off to a backwater in Norway, and in his place Göring appointed a newcomer to the business of air defence and one more compliant with his views, *Generalmajor* 'Beppo' Schmid.

Schmid's first priority was to improvise some form of defence against the devastating RAF night attacks. In this he was fortunate, for Hajo Herrmann's alternative method of nightfighter operation was already being introduced. Since the scheme did not depend upon the use of precision radar, either on the ground or in the air, it was invulnerable to the Window countermeasure. In great haste the first *Wilde Sau Geschwader, JG 300*, was being readied for operations with a strength of some 60 Bf 109s and Fw 190s. Herrmann had never advocated his new tactic as anything other than to complement the existing nightfighter methods, but now it would have to bear the brunt of the defence against the night bombers, until something better was devised.

◀◀ Lt. Sternberg taxies to his take-off point in his Fw 190 A1, 'Black 13' at Wevelgem, Belgium. By 3 January 1943 he had attained 10 victories and was promoted to Staffelkapitän of the 5. Staffel. He was eventually shot down and killed by a P-47 on 22 February 1944.

▲ Hermann Göring inspecting Wilde Sau pilots. Beside him stands Major Hajo Herrmann, architect of the new tactical method.

▲ Generalmajor Adolf Galland shaking hands with Adolf Hitler during a meeting at Berchtesgaden in 1943 to discuss Luftwaffe matters. Generalfeldmarschall Erhard Milch, responsible for aircraft development and production, is just visible behind Hitler. On the far right, nearest the camera, is Generalmajor Hans Jeschonnek, Chief of Staff of the Luftwaffe. He committed suicide after the German air defences failed to prevent the USAAF's deep penetration attack on the Messerschmitt plant at Regensburg on 17 August 1943.

Since its system of ground radar control was no longer effective, the force of twin-engined nightfighters had to change its tactics completely. To overcome this problem *Oberst* Viktor von Lossberg, an ex-bomber pilot serving on the General Staff of the nightfighter force, devised the *Zahme Sau* (Tame Boar) method of control. On the bombers' approach the twin-engined nightfighters were to take off and, on broadcast instructions from the ground, make their way from one radio beacon to another gradually closing on the stream. Finally the fighter controller would direct the nightfighters to the area where the precision radars had reported the greatest concentrations of Window, and a visual search for the prey could begin. By such means von Lossberg hoped to establish the conditions for long-running battles all the way to and from the targets. If the twin-engined fighter crews found bombers illuminated or silhouetted in the target area, there was no reason why

they too should not adopt the *Wilde Sau* methods.

The introduction of the *Wilde Sau* and *Zahme Sau* tactics affected almost every aspect of the German home defences. As *Generaloberst* Weise informed his men:

"The present enormous difficulties of defence against the heavy night attacks demand extraordinary measures everywhere. All crews must understand that success can come only through the most self-sacrificing operations ..."

At the target, every possible means was to be used to assist the fighters to find their prey. If there was a thin layer of cloud, the searchlights were to play slowly across its underside to produce a soft glow on the top that would silhouette the bombers and point them out for the fighters cruising above. Window could not shield the raiders from a tactic like that. To reduce the risk to fighters operating over the Flak-defended areas, Weise decreed that his gunners were to set their shells to explode below a previously decided altitude, initially 15,000 feet. Above that level, the fighters would be free to engage the bombers.

The new tactics would, of course, require a period of readjustment for the established nightfighter crews. Under the *Himmelbett* system they invariably stayed within about 50 miles of their home bases, operating under the watchful eye of the same group of ground radar stations. Then, navigation had been a simple matter, using the familiar local radio beacons. Now all of that was changed: the nightfighter crews would have to

► During the late summer and early autumn of 1943, the Luftwaffe night air defence system made a dramatic recovery following the devastating attacks on Hamburg. Generalmajor 'Beppo' Schmid (wearing summer uniform) had replaced Josef Kammhuber as head of the nightfighter force that August.

▲ Oberst Viktor von Lossberg devised the loose control Zahme Sau method for use by twin-engined nightfighters, which made it possible to direct nightfighters into the bomber stream from great distances.

◄ Following the success of Window over Hamburg, the Luftwaffe nightfighter force underwent a sweeping reorganisation. Under the Wilde Sau tactic single-engined fighters, like the Bf 109 F shown here were used to engage raiding bombers over the target. This photograph with the aircraft carrying spurious markings, is in fact a posed propaganda scene to impress the German public and was used on a Messerschmitt company 1943 calendar.

navigate their own way across the length and breadth of Germany in pursuit of their prey, landing at whatever airfield happened to be nearest when fuel ran short.

The new tactics also required a new system of ground control. Under the *Himmelbett* system, the headquarters bunkers of the fighter divisions had served merely as clearing-houses for information on the battle, which was directed from the individual radar stations. Now the direction of the main flow of information was to be reversed, with the radar stations providing their divisional headquarters with plots on the progress of the enemy bombers. The divisional controllers ordered the nightfighters to scramble, then broadcast orders for units

to move from radio beacon to radio beacon before 'stepping off' to join the bomber stream. Each fighter division held domain over a set area, and controlled both the day and the nightfighters operating from its area. The 1st Fighter Division covered north-east of Germany, from its headquarters in Berlin. The 2nd covered the north, from Stade near Hamburg. The 3rd covered the north-western approaches, from Arnhem-Deelen in Holland. The 4th covered the western approaches, from Metz in France, and the 7th Fighter Division covered southern Germany, from its headquarters at Schleissheim near Munich.

The German nightfighter force first employed its

MESSERERSCHMITT Bf 109 F

Demonstrating Wilde Sau defence markings, this colour profile shows the aircraft painted in spurious unit markings for propaganda purposes.

The spurious emblem painted under the cockpit of the Bf 109 F.

LUFTWAFFE FIGHTER CONTROL CENTRE

The *Luftwaffe* day fighter units, and from August 1943 the nightfighter units as well, were directed into action from massive concrete bunkers like this one situated at Grove in Denmark (right). The bunkers were some 200 feet long, 100 feet wide and 60 feet high. The roof of reinforced concrete was 12 feet thick, and there were airtight doors and an air conditioning system to protect the occupants from possible gas attack. The inner core of the building comprised a large operations room, along one side of which was a huge vertical translucent screen on which was painted a gridded map of the area. Plots on the movements of friendly and hostile aircraft were projected on to the rear of the screen by women *Luftwaffe* auxiliaries. In front of the screen sat the fighter divisional operations officer, his fighter controllers and liaison officers.

Generalmajor Adolf Galland later described what it was like inside one of the so-called 'Battlefield Opera Houses' during an action:

"On entering one was immediately infected by the nervous atmosphere reigning there. The artificial light made faces appear even more haggard than they really were. Bad air, cigarette smoke, the hum of ventilators, the ticking of the teletypes and the subdued murmur of countless telephone operators gave one a headache. The magic centre of attraction in this room was a huge frosted-glass panel on which were projected the position, altitude, strength and course of the enemy as well as of our own formations. The whole was reminiscent of a huge aquarium lit up, with a multitude of water fleas scuttling madly behind the glass walls. Each single dot and each change to be seen here was the result of reports and observations from radar sets, aircraft-spotters, listening posts, reconnaissance and contact aircraft, or from units in action. They all merged together by telephone or wireless in the centre to be received, sorted and within a few minutes transposed into transmittable messages. What was represented here on a giant map was a picture of the air situation in the sector of a fighter division, with about one minute's delay."

From 'The First and the Last' by Adolf Galland, Methuen and Co London.

▲ From massive concrete bunkers, such as this carefully camouflaged example near Grove in Denmark, the Luftwaffe directed its fighter units during the day battles, and after the summer of 1943, also those at night. The bunker was more than 60 feet high and was topped with a 15 feet thick concrete bomb-proof roof.

▲ The picture of the air situation was flashed on to the rear of the translucent map by some 40 Luftwaffenhelferinnen (Luftwaffe women auxiliaries) using small light projectors. By inserting a covering plate in these projectors it was possible to mark with distinctive symbols the head and tail of the bomber stream, with plots on jamming sources, H2S bearings and the known positions of fighter units.

◄ No photograph can adequately convey the sense of bustle and high drama in the operations room while the battles were in progress, though this artist's impression comes close. The layout varied slightly from bunker to bunker, but all were similar to a cinema with the main situation map in place of the screen. In this example the Chief Operations Officer (1) sat near the rear of the 'stalls', with his broadcast officer to his right. In front of them sat the fighter liaison officers in telephone contact with the airfields.

new *Zahme Sau* tactics on a large scale on 17 August 1943. That night 597 RAF bombers set out to attack the V-weapons research establishment at Peenemünde on the Baltic. After their raid briefings, crews were read a letter from the Commander-in-Chief of Bomber Command. This said that the target was so important that if the bombers failed to destroy it on the first attack, they would return each night until its destruction was complete. The emphasis was on accurate bombing, and to that end the attack was launched on a night when the moon was full. Also, because the target's Flak defences were weak, the raiders were ordered to attack from an altitude of around 8,000 feet. Thus, conditions would be ideal for the RAF bomb-aimers.

That night, the first aircraft shot down did not belong to the raiding force. Five *Bf 110s of IV./NJG 1* had been ordered to investigate a suspicious-looking gaggle of aircraft flying over the Friesian Islands. The strangers turned out to be Serrate Beaufighters of No. 141 Squadron, and the *Luftwaffe* crews ran straight into the trap set for them. In the rough-and-tumble that followed Wing Commander Braham shot down two Messerschmitts and another Beaufighter accounted for another.

Meanwhile, the vanguard of the bomber stream pushed across Denmark on its way to the target. After the series of attacks that had devastated large parts of Hamburg, *Luftwaffe* commanders fully expected Sir Arthur Harris to follow up that success with a similar blow against Berlin. The night's events opened with a cleverly executed diversion attack on the capital, by eight Mosquitoes of the Pathfinder force. That led the commander of the 1st Fighter Division to assume that this was the beginning of the expected attack on Berlin. He scrambled 55 of *Major* Hajo Herrmann's *Wilde Sau* single-engined fighters, and 158 twin-engined fighters. Soon there were more than 100 fighters milling round over the city, thirsting for action. Thinking the roar of so many aero engines could only mean that the enemy had already arrived, a few Flak batteries opened fire; gradually, the rest of Berlin's 89 heavy batteries joined in. Overhead, harassed nightfighter crews dodged uncomfortably accurate shell bursts, firing off recognition signals in vain attempts to get the gunners to aim at someone else. Yet the nightfighters remained over the city, continuing to search for the bombers. Surely the guns would not be firing, unless the enemy was close at hand?

Only when they saw the first target indicators falling on Peenemünde, 100 miles to the north, did the nightfighter crews realise they had been duped. By then no single-engined fighters, and few twin-engined

▲ Wing Commander J.R.D. 'Bob' Braham, the commander of No. 141 Squadron, whose Beaufighters achieved some success using the Serrate homing device against German nightfighters over their home territory. (IWM)

◄ Target indicators, searchlights and fires silhouette a Lancaster over Berlin. Under these conditions the bombers were vulnerable to attack from single-seat Wilde Sau nightfighters.

▲ The tail of a Lancaster which broke up in mid-air over Berlin, during the attack on 31 August 1943.

◄ The aerial system of a Korfu ground direction-finding station, used to track the movements of the H2S fitted Pathfinder aircraft of RAF Bomber Command.

▲ A Fieseler Fi 103 (v-1) sits ready on in its launch ramp. This photograph was taken at the Peenemünde test facility.

fighters, had fuel left to go chasing off after the raiders. Those with sufficient fuel remaining ignored their orders to remain over the capital, and headed with all speed towards the brightening glow on the horizon. Some of them reached Peenemünde in time to engage the final two waves of the attack, and exacted some retribution.

With the dawning realisation that the target for the night was not Berlin, the 'battle' over that city quickly ended. Only the generally observed Flak 'ceiling' of 15,000 feet prevented the fighter force from suffering serious losses, for a later count revealed that the gunners had loosed off more than 11,000 rounds.

Meanwhile, at bases in northern Germany and Denmark, other fighters were getting airborne and moving out to catch the bombers on their return flight. One of those ordered off for this purpose was *Oberleutnant* Hans Meissner of II./NJG 3, flying a Bf 110. Shortly after 02.00 hrs on the 18th he was directed to radar station Ameise in south-eastern

Denmark. On that bright, moonlit night he had little difficulty in finding targets, as he later related:

"Unfortunately the R/T was so badly jammed that we could make no contact with Ameise, and could get no information. Meanwhile we were at 2,500 metres as we approached the Apenrader Bight. My radar operator picked up several contacts on the Lichtenstein which passed across the tubes very quickly, so at first we took it to be Window. As the contacts were below I went into a descent, and picked up speed.

"At 02.54 hrs I saw the first Lancaster at about 2,000 metres, flying directly in front of me on a westerly heading. I closed in and opened fire from about 150 metres, somewhat to the right and 50 metres below. The No. 3 engine caught fire. As I broke away below him, return fire from the rear gunner passed to my left. From the beginning of the engagement both aircraft were illuminated from time to time by our searchlights. The Lancaster pilot attempted to escape in a diving turn to the left, but as he did so he came into my sights and I was able to give him a short burst. He went down at 02.56 hrs, crashing a few hundred yards from Ufer.

"I immediately set off eastwards, obtained another contact from my radar operator, descended, and saw a Lancaster flying directly above me on a westerly heading. I fired from more or less the same position, again at No. 3 engine. He went into a dive and crashed at 03.01 hrs, on the shore of the Apenrader Bight.

"After that I headed north, and my radar operator soon picked up yet another contact. I was able to make

► (Left) The launching pad at the V-2 test facility at Peenemünde photographed by an RAF reconnaissance Mosquito before the raid on the research station. (Right) The severely damaged test facility pictured after the raid.

▲ A Lichtenstein-equipped Bf 110 G nightfighter seen in flight while on a daylight operation.

out the aircraft about 1,200 metres away. My first attack was the same as the others, from 150 metres range, a little to the right and 50 metres below. As the No. 3 engine caught fire we were held by a searchlight, and in spite of the moonlight the effect was dazzling. The Lancaster pilot pulled his aircraft up (perhaps he was also dazzled, or maybe he wanted to reduce speed quickly so that I would overshoot or the crew could abandon). The enemy aircraft now filled my horizon; I pulled up to within 20 metres and with a few rounds set the No. 2 engine and the fuselage on fire. The aircraft broke up and crashed at 03.11 hrs, two kilometres to the west of Ustrup."

Oil from the exploding bomber spattered the Messerschmitt's canopy, forcing Meissner to break off the action.

That night Bomber Command lost 41 aircraft. Although they were large, the losses were somewhat lower than had been feared. The importance of the target had decreed that crews were to sacrifice safety in exchange for bombing accuracy: the attack had been made on a moonlit night, and the crews had been briefed to fly at 8,000 feet instead of their usual attack altitudes of more than double this. Also, as we have seen, the losses were small compared with what they might have been had the defending fighters not been lured to Berlin.

That first action in which the *Luftwaffe* employed its new freelance tactics highlighted the serious weakness of the system. The defending fighter force could now be likened to a blindfolded heavyweight boxer swinging a lead-lined glove at a similarly blindfolded but moving opponent. If the glove struck home with its full or near-full force, the recipient would be floored, but unless he was careless or unlucky, the chances were he would escape serious damage from most of the punches aimed at him.

The truth of this became clear six nights later, when the same tactics that had failed to protect Peenemünde

enjoyed triumphant success.

On the night of 23 August Bomber Command despatched 727 heavy bombers to the German capital, with zero hour set for a quarter to midnight. Quite apart from the strong circumstantial evidence available to the Germans, it was extremely difficult to conceal the raiders' objective: even by the shortest possible route the bombers had to cross more than 240 miles of

> *"The enemy aircraft now filled my horizon; I pulled up to within 20 metres and with a few rounds set the No. 2 engine and the fuselage on fire."*

hostile territory – over one hour's flying time. For more than an hour before the raiders reached the city, the nightfighter broadcasts on the bombers' progress gave Berlin as the possible target. Soon after 23.00 hrs that possibility became a probability in the minds of the fighter divisional controllers and they ordered all

◄ In the morning following a heavy raid, the remains of RAF bombers often littered the German countryside. Here a Lancaster of Bomber Command lies smouldering from destruction the night before.

► The searchlight batteries played an important role in illuminating bombers as they passed over the target, so they could be engaged by 'Wilde Sau' nightfighters.

available fighters to make for the capital. Although there was not the same brilliant moonlight of the previous week, the skies were clear. The 'lead-lined glove' was drawn back ready for the strike, and the bomber stream was running straight along the line of the punch.

Over the capital the raiders received a fiery reception. Returning bomber crews reported nearly 80 fighter interceptions and 31 attack runs by fighters – 15 of them over the target itself. This last was a most unpleasant innovation for the bomber crews, who had come to expect to be spared this hazard over the Flak-defended areas. During the post-raid debriefings, many

crews reported that the *Luftwaffe* had sent up '*scores of fighters*' and that searchlights '*were used to assist the nightfighters more than the anti-aircraft guns*'. All in all those were the sort of comments to be expected, considering the nature of the recent changes the *Luftwaffe* had made to its night flying tactics.

The outcome of the attack was the heaviest beating so far, both for Berlin and for Bomber Command. The capital city suffered widespread damage to its south-western suburbs, though the death toll did not exceed 300. Bomber Command, for its part, mourned its highest loss to date: 56 bombers failed to return.

The 'lead-lined glove' had landed a glancing blow, for at the last moment the punch was pulled: gathering fog at airfields in the Berlin area had forced many fighters to break off the action early. Nevertheless, the defenders' new tactics were reflected in the wounds borne by returning bombers. Previously, the main cause of non-lethal damage had been anti-aircraft fire, but on this occasion, of the 31 aircraft which returned with battle damage, 20 had been hit by enemy fighters. Without the *Himmelbett* stations to reposition them for the coup de grâce, the nightfighter crews were more likely to lose contact with their damaged prey if the bombers evaded violently.

► A ventral gun turret was fitted to a small number of Halifax bombers. The periscopic sight protruding through the bottom of the turret was for searching and sighting, but this was difficult at night. The turret occupied the same position in the aircraft as the scanner for the H2S radar, and when the latter became available in quantity the ventral gun turrets were removed.

▲ **The effective corkscrew evasive manoeuvre, employed by RAF bombers to shake off an attacking nightfighter.**
On detecting an enemy fighter, the bomber entered a steep diving turn to port or starboard into the direction of the attack (to port in this example), angle of bank 45 degrees, (**1**). This enabled the bomber to build up speed quickly, and made visual sighting from the fighter difficult since it placed the bomber beneath its level. After a descent through about 1,000 feet in seconds, the bomber reached a speed of around 300 mph. Then, maintaining its turn to port, it pulled up and climbed (**2**) for 4 seconds. It then rolled to starboard, and turned in that direction continued climbing (**3**) for 4 seconds

gaining 200 feet in altitude during which its speed fell to about 250 mph. The bomber then rolled into a climbing turn to starboard and speed continued to fall to about 225 mph. If the enemy fighter was still behind, there was a good chance it would now overshoot the bomber. At the top of the climb the nose was pushed down again (**4**), and after a descent of 1,000 feet the turn was reversed (**5**). The bomber continued its descent through a further 1,000 feet (**6**). It then repeated the procedure from (**2**), if there was evidence that the fighter remained a threat. As a tactical evasive manoeuvre, the corkscrew had three outstanding features: first, it gave a good chance of throwing off the night-fighter; secondly, even if it did not throw off the

nightfighter, the latter was left with a difficult target with almost continual and changing deflection with fully alerted gunners; and thirdly, since the manoeuvre could be flown along a mean heading and height, it combined the maximum possible evasion with the minimum deviation from the bomber's intended track and altitude. Luftwaffe nightfighter pilots stated that the corkscrew manoeuvre, if executed in time and to the bomber's full capability, left them with an extremely difficult target. Most German Experten (fighter aces) would abandon the chase at that point and go in search of another bomber in the stream in the hope that its crew would be less vigilant.

After the battle the *Luftwaffe* nightfighter force confirmed a total of 48 kills during the action. In all probability that was an underclaim since it is unlikely that the Flak batteries, restricted over the target to a burst height of 15,000 feet, shot down as many as six. Of the fighters' total, the majority of the claims, 44, went to 'old guard' nightfighter crews flying twin-engined aircraft fitted with radar.

After their initial baptism of Window, the more experienced airborne radar operators discovered that it was still possible to engage bombers despite its presence, as aircraft at the head or the edge of the stream received less protection from the countermeasure. Since the Window clouds were stationary in the sky, they appeared on the fighters' radar screens as rapidly closing targets, whereas the bombers, when flying in approximately the same direction as the nightfighters and at about the same

◄ A captured RAF Sergeant, a survivor from a shot down Wellington bomber is interrogated by a Luftwaffe officer after capture.

▲ A Bf 110 of III./ZG 76 fitted with two Wgr 21 rocket mortars under each wing. Supervising the loading of the mortar shells in their launch tubes is (at left) Hptm. Johannes Kiel, the Gruppenkommandeur of III./ZG 76. Kiel had been awarded the Ritterkreuz in March 1942 while serving with 3./ZG 26. In May 1942, he was appointed Kapitän of 6./ZG 2 and later flew the Me 163 interceptor with Erprobungskommando 16. He was shot down and killed by US fighters on 29 January 1944. At his death, he had been credited with around 25-30 victories.

speed, maintained their relative position in front of the fighters.

Sir Arthur Harris was not the sort of man to be diverted from his purpose by the setback of his first raid in the new series on the German capital. Since it was a good deal larger than Hamburg, he knew that Berlin would require several attacks if he was to inflict major damage. Accordingly eight nights later, on 31 August, he dispatched another large force against the enemy capital. The raid added further swathes of destruction in the city, but in the face of an alerted defensive system the raiders also suffered heavily. Together, the two raids cost the Royal Air Force 103 bombers and their crews. The losses amounted to 7.6 per cent of the forces committed, a figure close to the limit of what the force could sustain indefinitely. The defenders had recovered from the initial shock of Window with disconcerting swiftness.

Also during August 1943, the US Eighth Air Force made its first attempt to conduct a series of deep-penetration attacks on targets deep inside Germany. As in the case of the night raiders, however, the defenders were ready to meet them.

In the *Luftwaffe* the withdrawal of units from the battlefronts, coupled with a reorganisation of the fighter control system, resulted in steady improvements in the daylight home defence system during August 1943. By now the single-engined fighter units available for this purpose had reached a strength of more than 400

combat-ready aircraft. In addition there was a twin-engined fighter unit, *Zerstörergeschwader 26*, with 80 Bf 110s specially modified for operations against the American day bombers.

To provide the necessary firepower to allow day fighters to engage the US heavy bombers effectively, the *Luftwaffe* introduced two important new weapons. The first was a 30 mm MK 108 heavy cannon developed by the Rheinmetall Company. This weapon fired eleven-ounce high-explosive rounds at a rate of over 600 per minute, and on average only three hits were sufficient to bring down a large bomber. The second new weapon was the 210 mm rocket mortar, adapted from a weapon already in large-scale use by the German Army. The tube-launched spin-stabilised projectile weighed 248 pounds, and a time fuze detonated the 90 pound warhead at a preset range of between 600 and 1,200 yards from the launch point. Both new weapons were immediately included in the armament of the home defence fighters. The Bf 109 G was modified to carry one 30 mm cannon firing through the propeller boss and two 13 mm machine guns. Others retained the 20 mm weapon firing through the propeller boss, and carried either two 20 mm cannon or two 210 mm mortar launchers under the wings. Some examples of the Focke-Wulf 190 A carried two 20 mm cannon, two 13 mm machine guns, and either 20 mm cannon or two mortar launchers under the wings. The specially modified Bf 110 G 'bomber destroyers' carried the heaviest forward firing armament of all, with four 20 mm cannon, two 30 mm cannon and four 210 mm mortar launchers.

To ensure a continuous flow of information on the movements of enemy formations, the *Luftwaffe* employed the so-called *Fühlungshalter* technique under which Bf 110, Me 410 or Ju 88 aircraft followed the bombers at a safe distance. The crews of these aircraft reported to their divisional headquarters details of the composition, position, altitude and heading of the enemy force, as well as the weather and the progress of the German fighter attacks. However they did not, as some accounts have suggested, provide direct control to fighters engaging the bombers.

The other essential for effective ground control was a method of keeping track of the German fighter formations, even when they were flying above cloud. This was achieved by means of the Y-System, a modification to the standard fighter VHF radio which enabled the set to reply automatically to interrogating signals from ground stations.

When fighters landed away from their base, at an

◀ This Bf 109 G-6/R6 'Black 7' photographed at Leeuwarden in the summer of 1943, was flown by Fw. Josef Kehrle of 8./JG 1. He was one of the pilots who took off on 3 November 1943 to intercept a formation of Allied bombers attacking Wilhelmshaven. The Allied escort fighters bounced the Bf 109s and Kehrle was wounded. After returning to the Staffel, he ended the war with a total of 14 victories.

The personal emblem of Fw. Josef Kehrle's Rotte.

Emblem of 8./JG 1.

airfield designated with facilities for rapid re-fuelling, re-arming and servicing, a quick turn-around was essential. Aircraft from several different units would arrive at such an airfield and when they were again combat ready, the senior officer present was to lead the fighters into action on their second sorties.

These tactics enabled single-engined fighters to make successful interceptions at long distances from base. Moreover, sectors that had committed all their forces were reinforced by switching units from areas that were not under immediate threat. As many as 100 nightfighters, Bf 110s, Ju 88s and Do 217s might be sent into action to meet a raid, their main role being that of finishing off stragglers rather than engaging the bomber formations directly.

One may get an insight into the working of the German day fighter defences at this time from the experiences of *Unteroffizier* Hans Seyringer, who joined *II./JG 27* from training in the summer of 1943. When he arrived at the unit he had only about 200 flying hours in his logbook. The *Gruppe* had recently been withdrawn from the Mediterranean theatre to bolster the defence of the homeland, and was commanded by the successful ace Major Werner Schroer. Most of the unit's Bf 109 Gs were armed with one 20 mm cannon firing through the propeller boss, two 13 mm machine guns, and two 20 mm cannon, one being mounted in a gondola beneath each wing. With its heavy armament and the fuselage-mounted drop tank which was usually carried during interception missions, the aircraft required careful handling especially during take-off. Some aircraft in

MESSERSCHMITT Bf 109 G-6/R6,
'Black 7' flown by Fw. Josef Kehrle of 8./JG 1, summer 1943.

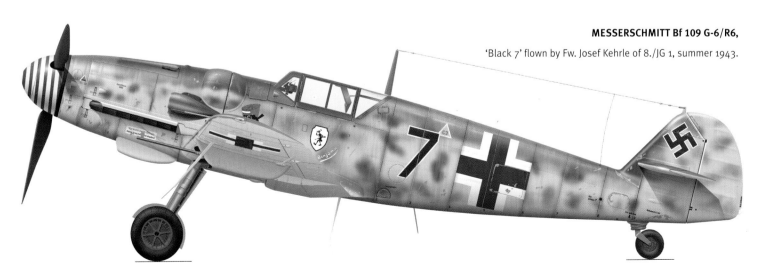

▲ Uffz. Franz Seyringer of 4./JG 27 poses on the wing of Bf 109 G-6, W.Nr. 410 300, 'White 5' at Wiesbaden-Erbenheim in January 1944. The aircraft has a prominent spiral pattern on its spinner and is fitted with a 300 ltr drop tank. Note also the protective covers pulled over the barrels of the underwing MG 151/20 cannon. Seyringer was wounded in this aircraft during an air battle with Allied fighters over Holland on 30 January 1944. Seyringer bailed out, but the aircraft was destroyed. (Seyringer)

the *Gruppe* carried 210 mm mortar launchers, but Seyringer never flew one of those.

The normal method of take-off for the *Gruppe* is described in the box below, but these take-offs were not always accomplished without incident. Seyringer described one nerve-racking scramble when, due to incorrect fitting, the jolting of the take-off run caused the inadvertent launching of some rocket mortars fitted to aircraft of a *Staffel* taking off towards his own. The missiles came scorching past the Messerschmitts of Seyringer's *Staffel*, causing no damage but considerable consternation until everyone was clear of the airfield!

During his early missions Seyringer was paired with an experienced pilot, and told to stay with him closely in combat, 'like a faithful dog'. Once the *Gruppe* had the enemy bombers in sight, the formation leader decided on the type of attack. Seyringer took part in head-on attacks on a few occasions, but he felt that the time spent manoeuvring into position was out of all proportion to the short firing pass which resulted. More often the *Gruppe* engaged the bombers from the rear, usually in a series of four-aircraft *Schwarm* attacks flying either in line abreast or in line astern. After the initial attack, the *Schwarm* would usually split into two pairs, or *Rotten*, for further firing runs until the fighters had exhausted their ammunition.

While other units certainly operated differently in points of detail from *III./JG 27*, on the whole, Seyringer's

RAPID TAKE-OFF AND ASSEMBLY OF A LUFTWAFFE FIGHTER GROUP

The battles fought by the US heavy bombers over Germany in 1943 and 1944 have been likened to those during the Battle of Britain in 1940. Both were major air actions taking place by day, in which numerically inferior defenders strove to protect their homeland against devastating attacks by the enemy. But tactically, the differences between the two campaigns were greater than the similarities. In 1940, the nearest *Luftwaffe* bases had been within 100 miles of the targets in southern England.

During 1943, US bombers often flew four times that distance to reach their targets in Germany. Thus, in contrast to the hectic British fighter scrambles of 1940, the German fighter controllers had ample time to prepare their counterattack. Fighter units therefore received their first warning of the approaching enemy more than an hour before they were ordered to take off, and went through the range of readiness states until the pilots were at cockpit readiness.

Even when they carried auxiliary fuel tanks, the relatively short range of the Bf 109s and Fw 190s was often a problem. Units frequently intercepted enemy formations at points more than 100 miles from the fighters' bases, then engaged in a running fight that used a lot of fuel. For that reason it was important that once the *Gruppe* had been ordered to take off, it assembled into battle formation and commenced its climb to fighting altitude as rapidly as possible.

The technique employed was as follows. The three *Staffeln* and the *Stab* unit of the *Gruppe* were drawn up by *Staffeln* in line abreast, at four points spaced evenly around the perimeter of the airfield. When the scramble order was given by firing a green Verey light, the first two *Staffeln* took off in opposite directions but on parallel headings. As the first two Staffeln passed each other at the middle of the airfield, the other two *Staffeln* began their take off runs repeating the procedure. As soon as the *Gruppe* leader was airborne he made a slow orbit of the airfield, to allow the remaining three *Staffeln* to form up behind him. He then turned on to his initial intercept vector, and began climbing to attack altitude. This method enabled a *Gruppe* to take off and assemble into its formation rapidly and with minimum expenditure of precious fuel.

THE DANGEROUS SKY

A factor common to both sides, during the day and night battles, was the intensely hostile environment in which the participants had to live and fight. Over northern Europe the outside air temperature at 25,000 feet is often below minus 30 degrees Celsius, which meant that unless the men were well protected, frostbite was inevitable when bare flesh was exposed.

Moreover, in the rarefied air at this altitude, the air pressure is less than half that at sea level. Without extra oxygen to breathe, a man had only about two minutes of full consciousness. Battle damage or equipment failure or misuse could cause the loss or reduction of this vital extra oxygen supply. For a time, shortage of oxygen placed the victim in a twilight world of semi-consciousness, producing symptoms akin to those of drunkenness. For example, after an attack the crew of a Halifax reported:

'The captain became very talkative and resented any suggestion that he was behaving abnormally. On seeing the marker flares over the target he found that he could not take his eyes off them and forced the aircraft into a steep dive. Afterwards he said that he could read only the large figures on the instrument panel and these appeared far away. When we realised that the aircraft was out of control, the engineer retrimmed the machine. The pilot resented this and assaulted the engineer. He then gave the order to bail out, which we cancelled. He opened the window to look out and was prevented from falling out only by the engineer, who pulled him back in. He said he felt very happy and had no feeling of fear even when he tried to force-land on a cloud, thinking he was near the ground. After being forced to take oxygen from the spare helmet and mask he gradually recovered his senses and was able to fly the required course to base, although he suffered from a headache which persisted after landing.'

The sky is merciless to those who fail to pay due regard to its physical laws. Similar mishaps occurred from time to time in high-flying aircraft of all nations, often with fatal results.

---

experiences can be regarded as typical for the *Luftwaffe* fighter force at this time.

These improvements in the defences were well advanced by August 1943, when the Eighth Air Force felt strong enough to launch even more ambitious deep-penetration attacks into Germany. On the 17th, the anniversary of the first US heavy bomber operation over Europe, 376 heavy bombers took off to attack the Messerschmitt fighter assembly plant at Regensburg and the ball-bearing production centre at Schweinfurt. To reach the more southerly target, Regensburg, involved a flight over enemy territory of some 300 miles beyond the cover of American escort fighters. Then, to save the raiders from having to run the gauntlet of the defences a second time during their withdrawal, after hitting their target the bombers were to continue south and land at designated airfields in Algeria.

The 147 Fortresses making for Regensburg were first off, flying in three combat wing formations. The powerful escort of Thunderbolts deterred large-scale

◄ Hauptmann Egon Mayer tries to enjoy a book while waiting at readiness. Appointed Kommodore of JG 2 in July 1943, he pioneered the tactic of attacking US heavy bombers from head-on. At the time of his death in action in March 1944 his victory score stood at 102, including 25 heavy bombers.

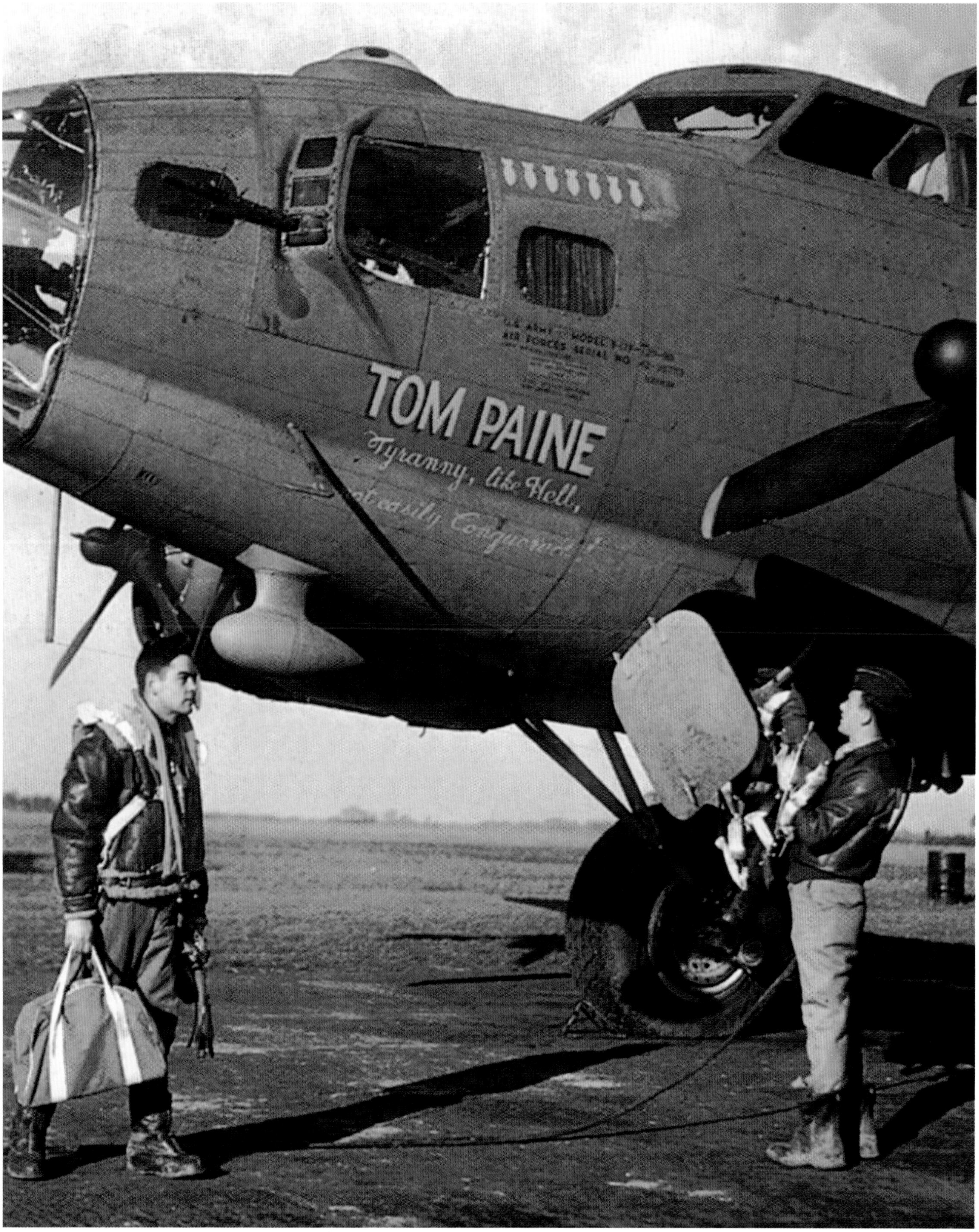
TOM PAINE
Tyranny, like Hell,

FOCKE-WULF Fw 190 A-6

'Yellow 2', W.Nr. 530314, flown by Oblt. Josef Wurmheller, Staffelkapitän of 9./JG 2, Vannes, August 1943.
Josef Wurmheller was one of the Luftwaffe's most successful fighter pilots as the victory markings on the
rudder of his aircraft show, together with the Knight's Cross and Oak Leaves, complete with ribbon enclosing
the number 60 in a partial RAF roundel. His tally is a total of 78 victories including eight B-17s.

◄ The photograph is believed to
have been taken shortly after a
mission against Spitfires and
shows Wurmheller with Lt. Jung,
one of III./JG 2's senior technical
officers.

fighter attacks until the raiders reached the German
frontier, where shortage of fuel forced the escorts to turn
back. That was the cue for the *Luftwaffe* to pounce. For
the next hour and a half, relays of single-engined fighters
tore into the bomber formations, attacking with cannon
and rockets. Several nightfighters followed the raiding
force like so many vultures, to finish off bombers that
had been forced to leave the protection of their
formations. The B-17s at the low group in the rear
combat wing suffered the fiercest and most prolonged
fighter attacks, and incurred the heaviest losses.

It lost seven B-17s in rapid succession during this
phase of the action. Two more suffered damage and were
forced to leave their formation, to be finished off soon
afterwards by *Luftwaffe* fighters. Of those nine bombers,

six were from the beleaguered 100th Bomb Group.

By the time the raiding formations passed
Mannheim, most of the single-engined fighters had
exhausted their ammunition. One by one they broke
away from the fight and the action fizzled out. Of the
139 Flying Fortresses that crossed the Dutch coast,
14 had been shot down and several others had suffered
damage and struggled to maintain position
in formation.

Few of those in the raiding force now realised it, but
the defending fighters had shot their bolt. The B-17s,
now deeper inside Germany than they had ever been
before, had entered an area where no regular *Luftwaffe*
day fighter units were based. For the final 25 minutes of
their run to the target, the bombers enjoyed virtually no

◄◄ This B-17F was named
after Thomas Paine who
served in the American Army
during the War of
Independence. The
personnel of the 388th
Bomb Group discovered that
Knettishall where they were
stationed was only a few
miles from the town of
Thetford where he was born
and gave the name to this
replacement aircraft in his
honour.

▲ B-24 'Geronimo' nosed over during take-off after a nose wheel collapse in bad weather on 12 December 1942 with Lt W. Williams at the controls. The ground crew debate how best to remove the aircraft, although it was eventually decided to scrap her.

▶ ▶ A strike photograph of B-24s of the 44th BG over Kiel taken from a B-17 of the 306th BG high above.

molestation. The only enemy presence was the shadowing Bf 110 nightfighters which hovered on either flank and behind the raiders.

Because its position so far inside Germany had safeguarded Regensburg from daylight attack, the town and its aircraft factories were weakly defended. About a dozen newly-built Bf 109s were kept armed on combat standby at the works airfield, to be flown by factory test pilots. Also there were three batteries of 88 mm anti-aircraft guns.

As they neared the target, the raiders found perfect weather conditions for their attack; cloud-free skies and horizontal visibility of about 30 miles. Some 25 miles to the west of the target the raiders passed their Initial Point, and the leading combat wing moved into attack formation. The low and high bomb groups slid into trail behind the lead squadron, thereby reducing the width of the formation to that required for the bomb run. The leading unit, the 96th Bomb Group, reached the IP unscathed with all 21 of its B-17s.

The bomber crews had been briefed to attack the factory complex from altitudes of between 17,000 and 20,000 feet, depending on their position in the formation. That was less than the B-17's maximum attack altitude, but was intended to give improved bombing accuracy against this important but weakly defended target.

Captain John Latham was lead bombardier for the 96th Bomb Group at the head of the raiding force, and his aiming point was on the near side of the target complex. When the B-17 was established on its bomb

run, the pilot engaged the autopilot which was linked electrically to the aircraft's Norden bombsight. From then until bomb release, Latham 'flew' the aircraft. Each time he adjusted his sight to keep the aiming cross over the target, corrections were fed into the autopilot to steer the aircraft on the correct path for an accurate attack.

When Latham's bombsight computed that his B-17 was at the bomb release point, a pair of electrical contacts closed and the load of ten 500 pound high explosive bombs was released automatically. During the bomb run the rest of the aircraft in the group had held tight formation on the lead aircraft. When the leader's bombs were seen to fall away, the other B-17s in the formation released theirs so that the entire bomb group placed its bombs in a dense pattern on the ground, running forwards from the leader's aiming point. The breadth of the bomb pattern was the width of the formation at bomb release.

The few anti-aircraft gunners at Regensburg did their best to disrupt the attack, as did the few Messerschmitt fighters that had scrambled from the works airfield, but there were insufficient of either to blunt the force of the bombardment.

After bomb release, Latham's pilot disengaged the autopilot and set course for Algeria. Latham moved to a side window to observe the result of the attack he had led. He knew that he bore a heavy burden: the close formation of the B-17s behind him would guarantee that the bombs landed in a close pattern on the ground. The question was, would that tight bomb pattern fall

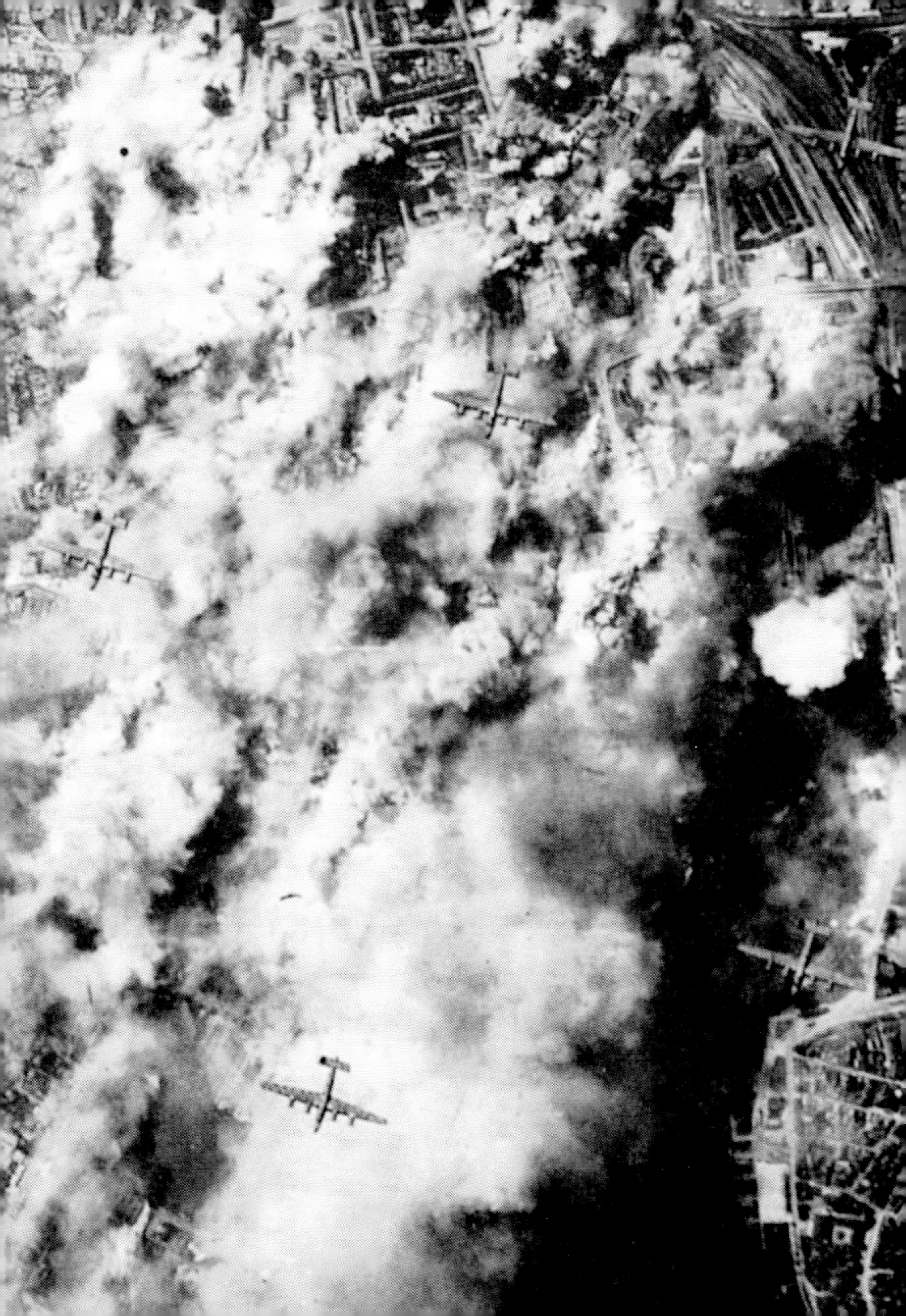

▶ Two Bf 110 Gs of ZG 26, fitted with a 37 mm heavy cannon in a blister under the fuselage. With this weapon the heavy fighter engaged a bomber formation from 1,000 yards, outside the range of the bombers' defensive crossfire. A single hit with its one pound high explosive shell was often sufficient to bring down a heavy bomber.

▼ Ground personnel work on fusing 21 cm mortars prior to loading onto a Fw 190. This formidable weapon weighed 152 kg excluding the launching tube.

squarely on the designated target?

With great satisfaction Latham saw his own bombs fall on the leading edge of the target, followed a split second later by those from the rest of the group. The bombs burst in a series of rapid, red-hearted explosions followed by a huge cloud of dust that grew ever larger as the bombs spread across the target.

The lead bombardiers of the next two bomb groups to pass over the target were also able to pick out their aiming points easily, and in each case their bomb patterns were tight and accurate. Then, as was often the case when a large number of bombers attacked the same target, smoke and dust thrown up by the numerous explosions drifted over the aiming points making them difficult or impossible to distinguish. This caused serious difficulties for two of the later Bomb Groups to attack, the 94th and the 385th. They found visibility so bad that they could not release their weapons during their initial bomb runs, forcing each to turn through a semi-circle, fly back along the route, then turn back towards the target and make second bombing runs.

Despite the problems with failing visibility, the B-17s laid accurate carpets of bombs over the factory complex. The plant area was hit hard; about 400 workers were killed and a similar number suffered injuries.

After leaving the target the B-17s continued south over the Alps, as they began their long flight to their recovery airfields in North Africa. On the way two badly damaged B-17s left the formation and headed for the safety of neutral Switzerland, the first of these aircraft to land there.

Of the 146 heavy bombers which set out from England, 139 penetrated occupied Europe, and of those, 115 went on to land in friendly territory. As was usually the case in a large-scale hard-fought air action of this

kind, the losses were not distributed evenly throughout the force. The 100th Bomb Group was in the most exposed position at the rear of the force and it took the heaviest beating. Of the 21 B-17s committed, nine were shot down. In sharp contrast the 96th Bomb Group, which led the raid, suffered no losses at all. Two other units, the 94th and the 388th Bomb Groups, lost only one aircraft each.

Just over three hours behind the first attack came the second, with four combat wing formations comprising 230 B-17s making for Schweinfurt. As before, the *Luftwaffe* fighters began their attack immediately after the US fighter escort departed. For the second time that day, a US bomber force reeled under a series of hammer blows. The fighters shot down 21 bombers on the way to Schweinfurt, and one more fell to Flak at the target. During the withdrawal flight to England, the raiding force lost a further 14 aircraft.

Thus, of a total of 363 B-17s which set out to bomb those two targets on 17 August, 60 were destroyed, yet that was not the end of the costly venture. When the Regensburg attack force returned to England a week later, attacking an airfield near Bordeaux on the way, it was missing 55 damaged aircraft which could not be repaired quickly enough at the poorly-equipped North African landing grounds. Three more bombers were shot

down during the return flight. In the short term the two attacks had, therefore, cost the Eighth Air Force 118 heavy bombers – nearly one-third of the force committed.

The *Luftwaffe* lost 25 fighters on 17 August, and although at each target the bombing was both accurate and concentrated, repairs were effected relatively quickly. Small scale production resumed within a week or so, and after a couple of months output had returned almost to normal.

The attacks on Schweinfurt and Regensburg, coming after the massive destruction inflicted on Hamburg and followed within a few hours by the raid on Peenemünde, shook the German leadership to the core. A couple of days later there was a further casualty, in the person of the Chief of the *Luftwaffe* General Staff, *Generaloberst* Hans Jeschonnek. He had suffered repeated tongue-lashings from Hitler and Göring, who placed on his shoulders personal blame for the deterioration of *Luftwaffe* fighting power and its failure to protect German targets from the increasingly destructive Allied air attacks. Given the much greater industrial resources of the Allies, and the continual expansion of their forces, Jeschonnek was unable to resolve these problems and, during a bout of severe depression on 19 August, he shot himself.

▲ A Bf 110G of III./ZG 26 stands ready for rearming for the next sortie. The Bf 110 was able to carry two 21 cm mortar launchers under each wing.

EYEWITNESS ACCOUNT OF THE REGENSBURG MISSION, 17 AUGUST 1943

Lieutenant Colonel Beirne Lay, a staff officer at Headquarters Eighth Air Force, flew as copilot in a B-17 of the 100th Bomb Group, a unit which suffered the heaviest losses during the Regensburg attack. Later he wrote a dramatic account of the action, excerpts of which are given below. The action began while the bombers were passing over Holland:

"At 10.17 hrs, near Woesdrecht, I saw the first Flak blossom out in our vicinity, light and inaccurate. A few minutes later, approximately 10.25 hrs, two Fw 190s appeared at 1 o'clock level and whizzed through the formation ahead of us in a frontal attack, nicking two B-17s of the 95th Group in the wings and breaking away beneath us in half-rolls. Smoke immediately trailed from both B-17s but they held their station. As the fighters passed us at a high rate of closure, the guns of our group went into action. The pungent smell of burnt powder filled our cockpit, and the B-17 trembled to the recoil of nose and ball-turret guns. I saw pieces fly off the wing of one of the fighters before they passed from view.

'Here was early action. The members of the crew sensed trouble. There was something desperate about the way those two fighters came fast right out of their climb without any preliminaries. For a few seconds the interphone was busy with admonitions: "Lead 'em more. "Short burst" ... "don't throw rounds away" ... "there'll be more along in a minute."

'Three minutes later, the gunners reported fighters climbing up from all around the clock, singly and in pairs, both Fw 190s and Me 109Gs. This was only my fourth raid, but from what I could see on my side, it looked like too many fighters for sound health. A co-ordinated attack followed, with the head-on fighters coming in from slightly above, the 9 and 3 o'clock attackers approaching from about level, and the rear attackers from slightly below. Every gun in every B-17 in our Group and the 95th was firing, criss-crossing our patch of the sky with tracers to match the cannon shell puffs that squired from the wings of the Jerry single-seaters. I would estimate that 75 per cent of our fire was inaccurate, falling astern of the target – particularly the fire from the hand-held guns. Nevertheless both sides got hurt in this clash, with two B-17s from our low squadron and one from the 95th Group falling out of formation and on fire and the crews bailing out, and several fighters heading for the deck in flames or with their pilots lingering under dirty yellow parachutes. Our group leader, Major John Kidd, pulled us nearer to the 95th Group for mutual support ...

'It was at 10.41 hrs, over Eupen, that I looked out of my co-pilot's window after a short lull and saw two whole squadrons, 12 Me 109s and 11 Fw 190s, climbing parallel to us. The first squadron had reached our level and was pulling ahead to turn into us and the second was not far behind. Several thousand feet below us were many more fighters, with their noses cocked at maximum climb. Over the interphone came reports of an equal number of enemy aircraft deploying on the other side. For the first time, I noticed an Me 110 sitting out of range on our right. He was to stay with us all the way to the target apparently reporting our position to fresh squadrons waiting for us down the road . . . No P-47s were visible. The life expectancy of the 100th Group suddenly seemed very short, since it had already appeared that the fighters were passing up the preceding groups, with the exception of the 95th, in order to take a cut at us.

'Swinging their yellow noses around in a wide U-turn, a twelve-ship squadron of Me 109s came in from 12 to two o'clock (head-on) in pairs and in fours, and the main event was on.

'A shining silver object sailed over our right wing. I recognised it as a main exit door. Seconds later, a dark object came hurtling through the formation, barely missing several props. It was a man, clasping his knees to his head, revolving like a diver in a triple somersault. I didn't see his chute open.

'A B-17 turned gradually out of the formation to the right, maintaining altitude. In a split second the B-17 completely disappeared in a brilliant explosion, from which the only remains were four small balls of fire, the fuel tanks, which were quickly consumed as they fell earthward.

'Our airplane was endangered by falling debris. Emergency hatches, exit doors, prematurely-opened parachutes, bodies, and assorted fragments of B-17s and Hun fighters breezed past us in the slipstream.

'I watched two fighters explode not far beneath, disappearing in sheets of orange flame, B-17s dropping out in every state of distress, from engines on fire to control surfaces shot away, friendly and enemy parachutes floating down and, on the green carpet far beneath us, numerous funeral pyres of smoke from fallen aircraft, marking our trail.

'On we flew through the strewn wake of a desperate air battle, where disintegrating aircraft were commonplace and 60 'chutes in the air at one time were hardly worth a second look.

'I watched a B-17 turn slowly out to the right with its cockpit a mass of flames. The co-pilot crawled out of his window, held on with one hand, reached back for his 'chute, buckled it on, let go and was whisked back into the horizontal stabiliser. I believe the impact killed him. His 'chute didn't open.

'Ten minutes, 20 minutes, 30 minutes, and still no let-up in the attacks. The fighters queued up like a breadline and let us have it. Each second of time had a cannon shell in it. The strain of being a clay duck in the wrong end of that aerial shooting gallery became almost intolerable as the minutes accumulated towards the first hour.

'Our B-17 shook steadily with the fire of its .50s and the air inside was heavy with smoke. It was cold in the cockpit, but when I looked across at Lt. Thomas Murphy, the pilot, and a good one, sweat was

pouring off his forehead and over his oxygen mask. He turned the controls over to me for a while. It was a blessed relief to concentrate on holding station in formation instead of watching those everlasting fighters boring in. It was possible to forget the fighters. Then the top-turret gunner's twin muzzles would pound away a foot above my head, giving a realistic imitation of cannon-shells exploding in the cockpit, while I gave an even better imitation of a man jumping six inches out of his seat ...

'Fighter tactics were running fairly true to form. Frontal attackers hit the low squadron and the lead squadron, while rear attackers went for the high [squadron]. The manner of their attacks showed that some pilots were old-timers, some amateurs, and that all knew pretty definitely where we were going and were inspired with a fanatical determination to stop us before we got there. The old-timers came in on frontal attacks with a noticeably slower rate of closure, apparently throttled back, obtaining greater accuracy than those that bolted in and in many cases seemed able to time their thrusts so as to catch the top and ball turret gunners engaged with rear and side attacks. Less experienced pilots were pressing attacks home to 250 yds and less to get hits, offering point-blank targets on the break-away, firing long bursts of 20 seconds and, in some cases, actually pulling up instead of going down and out. Several Fw pilots pulled off some first rate deflection shooting on side attacks against the high group, then raked the low group in the break-away out of a side-slip, keeping the nose cocked up in the turn to prolong the period the formation was in their sights ...

'Near the IP [the initial point for the bombing run] at 11.50 hrs, one hour and a half after the first of at least 200 individual fighter attacks, the pressure eased off, although hostiles were still in the

▲ This reconnaissance photograph shows an aerial view of Regensburg a few hours after the heavy attack with extensive damage to the workshops. Some undamaged Bf 109s had been moved to the flying field near the hangars.

vicinity. We turned at the IP at 11.54 hrs with 14 B-17s left in the group, two of which were badly crippled. They dropped out soon after bombing the target and headed for Switzerland, one of them, '042' carrying Col. William Kennedy as tail-gunner. No. 4 engine was on fire, but it was not out of control. Major William Veal, leader of the high squadron, received a cannon shell in his No. 3 engine just before the start of the bombing run and went into the target with the prop feathered.

'Weather over the target, as on the entire trip, was ideal. Flak was negligible. The Group got its bombs away promptly on the leader. As we turned and headed for the Alps, I got a grim satisfaction out of seeing a rectangular column of smoke rising straight up from the Me 109 shops, with only one burst over in the town of Regensburg.

'The rest of the trip was a marked anti-climax. A few more fighters pecked at us on the way to the Alps. A town in the Brenner pass tossed up a long burst of futile Flak. Col. LeMay, who had taken excellent care of us all the way, circled the air division over Lake Garda long enough to give the cripples a chance to join the family, and we were on our way toward the Mediterranean in a gradual descent. About 25 fighters on the ground at Verona stayed on the ground. The prospect of ditching as we approached Bone, short of fuel, and the sight of other B-17s falling into the drink, seemed trivial matters after the vicious nightmare of the long trip across southern Germany. We felt the reaction of men who had not expected to see another sunset."

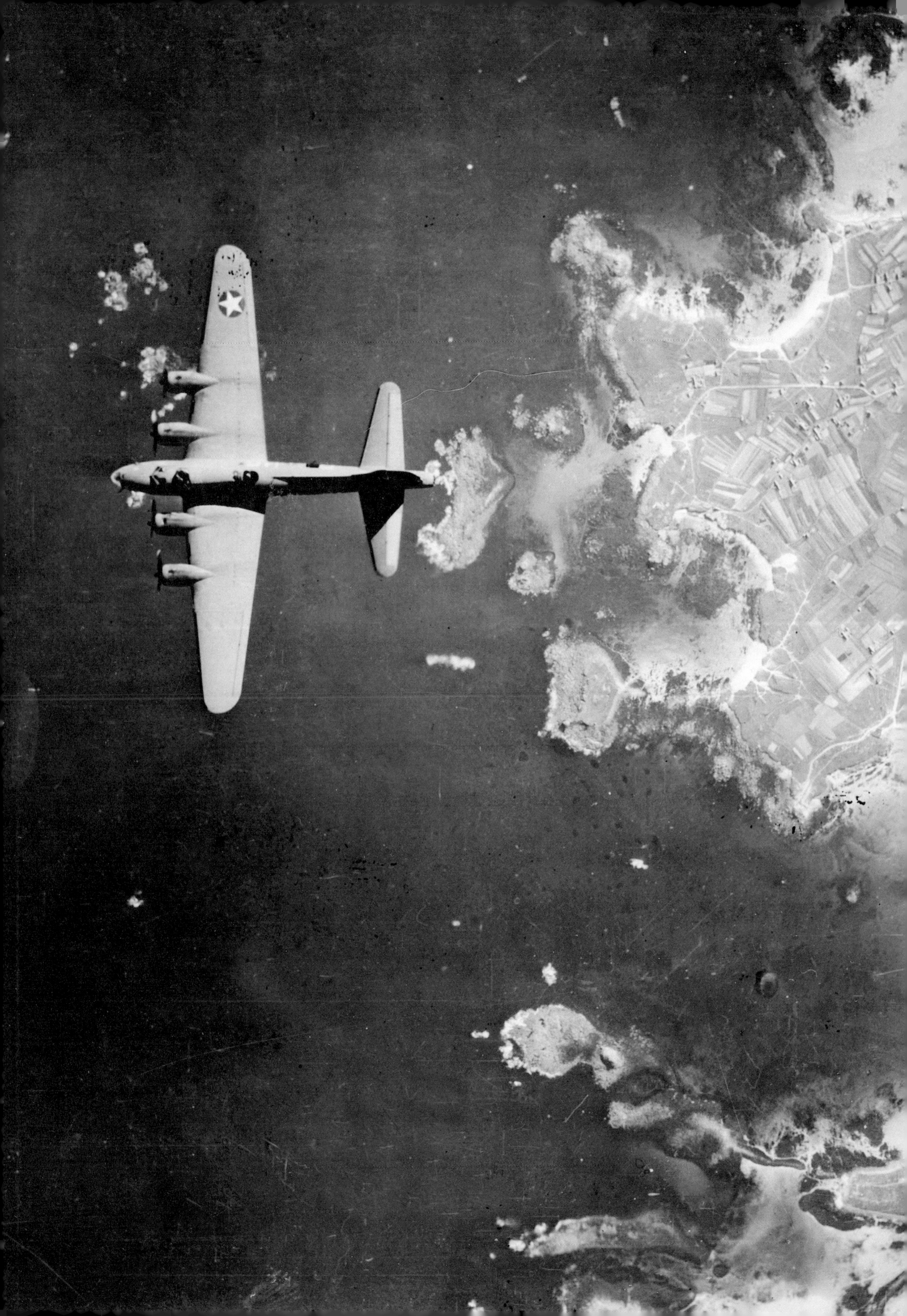

So far as the *Luftwaffe* was concerned, the needs of the future seemed clear enough. As *Generalfeldmarschall* Milch informed senior *Luftwaffe* officers a few days after the Schweinfurt/Regensburg actions:

"A large number of single-engined and twin-engined fighter Gruppen have now been pulled back to the homeland. In my view it was crazy that it should have been left so late but, at last, it has been done . . . The enemy cannot withstand losses of 25 or 30 per cent. This means that, if we can inflict such losses at regular intervals, he will be forced to desist from his attacks."

Milch pointed out that this would not be achieved so long as fighter production remained at its current levels, however. During July 1943 the German aircraft industry had delivered 1,050 single-engined fighters and some 200 twin-engined fighters. In Milch's view that was not nearly enough. At that stage of the war, fighter units on the Eastern and Southern Fronts were under heavy pressure, and their losses consumed most of the replacement aircraft. Also, the US attacks on aircraft production and repair facilities had their effect on fighter deliveries. As a result, in August he expected there to be 150 fighters less than had been delivered in July. As Milch saw it, the short-term answer was to give the greater number of the available fighters to the home defence units.

Despite its limited performance, Milch saw the Bf 110 as the most important type currently in large-scale production and which could be employed against the day bomber formations, commenting:

"Everything must be staked on the [Bf] 110. Only the 110 in sufficient numbers can give us the necessary relief at night. Moreover, the 110 can also be used by day. Compared with the other fighter types it has the great advantage of considerably longer range. After the raid on Regensburg, for example, the enemy bombers headed south for Africa. Our twin-engined [night] fighters pursued them to beyond Innsbruck and inflicted quite serious losses. That could not have been achieved with the [Bf] 109 or the [Fw] 190 because their limited endurance would have compelled them to land for refuelling and rearming long before that. Thus the 110 is particularly important for both purposes."

In the longer term, the only solution was to produce more fighters. Milch laid plans to increase production of all types of fighters to 2,000 per month, which he expected would be reached in February or March 1944. That, however, was all in the future. In the next Chapter we shall observe the effect of the short-term measures each side took in the weeks following the August actions.

◄ ◄ This B-17 named 'FDR's Potato Peeler Kids' from the 1st Bombardment Wing is seen leaving the French coast on its way home after bombing the U-boat pens at Brest on 27 February 1943.

▼ A Bf 109 G-6 fitted with drop-tank seen shortly after take-off.

TRADING BLOW FOR BLOW

September and October 1943

"You can squeeze a bee in your hand until it suffocates;

but it will not suffocate without having stung you."

Jean Paulhan

Between the beginning of September and the end of October 1943, RAF Bomber Command visited Germany in force on 15 occasions. On five occasions more than 500 bombers took part: three times on Hannover, and one each on Manheim and Kassel. Some 260 bombers were lost in the course of more than 6,500 sorties, a casualty rate of about four per cent. Bomber Command was receiving sufficient replacement aircraft and crews to absorb losses on that scale.

Although the raiders were not having such an easy time over Germany as many had expected after the successful introduction of Window, things were not as bad as the August confrontations over Berlin had suggested. The latter taught Bomber Command planners of the need to conceal targets from the defenders for as long as possible. In future the raiders would fly zigzag routes, with feint attacks to deceive the *Luftwaffe* fighter controllers.

During the autumn of 1943, RAF Bomber Command continued to introduce new equipment into service. The most important of these was the Mark III version of H2S, which operated on a much shorter wavelength (3 cm) and was thus able to produce a picture of terrain beneath the aircraft with greatly improved definition. With the new variant of H2S came the so-called 'Fishpond' modification, with an additional cathode ray tube in the wireless operator's position to allow him to scan a bowl-shaped volume of sky beneath the aircraft for enemy nightfighters attempting to sneak into a firing position.

In a bid to maintain the initiative, Bomber Command also stepped up its radio countermeasures campaign. The new *Luftwaffe* nightfighter tactics placed great reliance on ground radio broadcasts to inform crews of the progress of the bomber streams. Once this was realised in Britain, these broadcasts were subjected to a rising crescendo of jamming.

The 'Tinsel' system of jamming, which used the bombers' communications transmitter to radiate engine noises on the *Luftwaffe* high frequency fighter control channels, was updated into a new method designated 'Special Tinsel'. Under this system, radio-monitoring stations in Britain swept the ether to find the frequencies the *Luftwaffe* used for its broadcasts each night. That information was then broadcast in code to the bombers in the raiding force, whose wireless operators tuned their transmitters to the designated frequencies and jammed the enemy broadcasts en masse.

Special Tinsel was effective, but it did not cover the radio channels in the VHF band also used to pass orders to the nightfighters. To make good this deficiency, the Lancasters of No. 101 Squadron were modified to carry the high-powered R/T jammer code-named Airborne Cigar (and usually called ABC). The jammer radiated a raucous high-pitched note, similar to that of bagpipes, which proved effective in blotting out instructions. Each aircraft carried an extra crewman, who spoke German, to operate the ABC equipment. Using a search receiver he swept across the VHF band until he found a frequency the German controller was using, and tuned in one of his three jammers to blot out the signals. The operator then continued

◄◄ Bf 110Gs of 4./ZG 76 pictured on their way to engage a US raiding formation on 13 January 1944. The machine in front carries a 37 mm cannon.

▲ Lancaster of No. 101 Squadron fitted with the Airborne Cigar (ABC) equipment to jam the Luftwaffe nightfighters' radio control channels. Note the two large aerials extending above the fuselage, a distinctive feature of this device. (Manners, Garbett Goulding collection)

the process until all three of his jammers were blocking enemy radar channels. From early October, ABC Lancasters took part in most night attacks.

A further stratagem introduced at this time made use of the General Post Office's high-power radio transmitters at Rugby. Initially the intention had been to radiate noise jamming on the *Luftwaffe* high-frequency channels, but these transmitters could also radiate speech. If *Luftwaffe* nightfighter crews relied on instructions from the ground to find the bomber streams, might not false instructions from England lead them astray?

Under the code-name 'Corona', the idea of sending spoof orders was tried for the first time on 22 October, during an attack by 569 bombers on Kassel. The *Luftwaffe* controller realised what was afoot as soon as

"It isn't the Englishman who is swearing, it's me!"

the British 'ghost' controller started transmitting, and he warned his crews: *"Don't be led astray by the enemy"*. Becoming increasingly angry at the contrary instructions from the ghost, the German controller bellowed *"In the name of General Schmid, I order all aircraft to Kassel"*. Still the banter continued, until after an exasperating exchange the German controller swore into his microphone. That drew the immediate reply from the ghost, *"The Englishman is now swearing!"* The German controller shouted back: *"It isn't the Englishman who is swearing, it's me!"*

The bombers reached Kassel and delivered a destructive attack on the city, yet although the repartee on the *Luftwaffe* fighter control frequencies was an amusing diversion, it did not prevent fighters engaging

the bombers as they were leaving the target area. In the running battle that followed the nightfighters accounted for the majority of the 42 raiders which failed to return. The Bomber Command report on the attack noted: *"Many bombers were seen to go down in the target area without evidence of the cause"*. From *Luftwaffe* records, we know that many of these had fallen to nightfighters delivering attacks with the *Schräge Musik* upward-firing cannon.

For the next few weeks, Operation 'Corona' became part of the general irritation inflicted on German nightfighter crews, but by employing women and people with strong regional accents to broadcast orders to the nightfighters, it was usually possible to get these through to the crews. After a while the attempts to mislead *Luftwaffe* crews were abandoned. Instead, the 'ghost' took to reading long pieces of Goethe, turgid bits of German philosophy, and even playing records of Hitler's speeches, anything to raise the level of chatter and congestion on the control channels.

Taken together, the increased radio jamming cover, combined with feint attacks and evasive routing, held down losses to a bearable level. In the meantime, Germany's cities suffered further heavy blows.

———

In the autumn of 1943, five new electronic systems entered service in the *Luftwaffe*, aimed at improving the effectiveness of its nightfighters. *Naxos* and *Korfu* were special receivers set up at ground monitoring stations in Germany and the occupied territories, which gave bearings on aircraft radiating H2S signals. Both were passive systems that radiated no signals which would have betrayed their existence. The bearings from two or more ground stations were triangulated to give running fixes on the aircraft transmissions. At this time, in the RAF only Pathfinder aircraft carried H2S radar. Thus, by tracking the Pathfinders, the *Luftwaffe* signals organisation could confidently follow the movements of the entire raiding force. The Mosquitoes employed in feint attacks did not carry H2S; operating the new receivers would often distinguish between the real attacks and the feints.

SN-2 was a new nightfighter radar working in the 90 MHz band, a part of the frequency spectrum where the types of Window then in use were ineffective. Given the vulnerability of the earlier *Lichtenstein* radar to this countermeasure, this attribute was of crucial importance. Initially, SN-2 suffered from a serious disadvantage, however. Its minimum range – the minimum range at which it could detect targets – was

◄ During 1943, the RAF stepped up its measures to protect bombers from Luftwaffe nightfighters. This Lancaster of No. 9 Squadron, carries the transmitter aerial for its Monica tail-warning radar beneath the rear gunner's position. Note also the clear vision panel cut in the Perspex of the turret to lessen the chances of a surprise attack from behind. (Rogers, via Garbett Goulding collection)

▲ Nightfighter ace Major Rudolf Schönert, who commanded the test unit NJG 10, was one of the first pilots to employ the Schräge Musik upwards-firing gun installation in combat. He also pioneered the use of light-coloured camouflage schemes to make nightfighters less conspicuous. He ended the war credited with 64 night victories.

▲ ► Schräge Musik upwards-firing cannon installation with two Oerlikon MG/FF 20 mm cannon, fitted to a Bf 110 nightfighter. These weapons fired non-tracer ammunition, which enabled the Luftwaffe to keep the weapon installation secret for several months after its introduction.

▲ ▲ ► A close-up of the upward-firing cannon installation fitted in a Bf 110.

► A Dornier Do 217 fitted with Schräge Musik in the central fuselage position where the four barrels are just visible protruding above the surface.

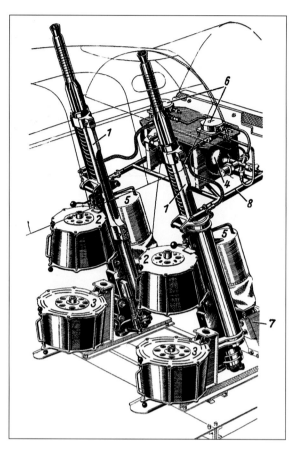

about 400 yards, which meant the radar could not show targets inside that distance. Yet 400 yards was somewhat further than a nightfighter crew could expect to see the prey visually, except on the clearest of nights. To bridge the gap between the radar's minimum range and the likely maximum visual range at night, some nightfighters carried both SN-2 and the earlier *Lichtenstein* device. This makeshift solution resulted in a forest of drag-producing aerials on the nose of the aircraft, but it was the best that could be done quickly until the radar's minimum range problem was solved.

Two new airborne radar homing devices were also developed to enable nightfighter crews to exploit the radiation from RAF bombers. *Naxos-Z* was a modification of the *Naxos* ground receiver and enabled nightfighters to home on the H2S radiations. A further airborne homing device, code-named *Flensburg*, enabled crews to home on signals from the bombers' Monica tail-warning radars. In combat, the two devices proved extremely useful, for they enabled *Luftwaffe* nightfighters to home on the bomber stream from distances far beyond the range of their airborne intercept radars.

◄ While the more concentrated bomber stream tactic used in 1943 reduced losses from enemy Flak and fighter defences, it led to some spectacular near misses. This Halifax was literally 'mounted' from behind by another bomber in the stream. Note the slashes in the fuselage, made by the other aircraft's propellers. (IWM)

Another important innovation in the summer of 1943 was the so-called *Schräge Musik* installation fitted in several *Luftwaffe* nightfighters. This comprised a pair of 20 mm cannon mounted in the fuselage or at the rear of the crew's cabin, arranged to fire upwards at an angle of between 10 and 20 degrees from the vertical. The pilot used an additional reflector sight, mounted above and in front of his head, to sight the weapons. The new installation enabled nightfighters to attack bombers from almost immediately below, a position where the bomber presented a large target but was itself almost blind and unable to defend itself. The ammunition drums of the *Schräge Musik* cannon were loaded with non-tracer rounds, so that bomber crews attacked with this weapon had no inkling of the danger until their aircraft shuddered under the impact of exploding cannon shells. As a result, *Schräge Musik* was kept secret for several months after its introduction.

At this time the majority of the German nightfighter units were equipped with the Bf 110 G. Earlier in the war this aircraft had an ample performance margin over the relatively slow Whitleys, Hampdens, Wellingtons and Stirlings, but by the autumn of 1943 these had been replaced in the raiding forces by the Lancaster and improved versions of the Halifax. The Messerschmitt was showing its age and was almost at the end of its development life. It now carried the new electronic devices and their drag-producing aerials, a heavier armament including upward-firing cannon, and the external fuel tanks to provide the range necessary for the *Zahme Sau* operations. As a result, the fighter had

◄ This Halifax of No. 158 Squadron was struck by a bomb which passed clean through the rear fuselage. The mid-upper gunner suffered a shaking and minor cuts, but otherwise was unhurt in his buckled turret. (IWM)

little performance margin over the heavy bombers it sought to engage.

The Junkers 88 C equipped a small, if growing, proportion of the force but its performance was little better than the Bf 110. The best nightfighter type available to the *Luftwaffe* at this time was the newly introduced Heinkel He 219, which had a maximum speed of 385 mph at 21,000 feet. However, with the German industry having to run at full tilt merely to replace losses in combat, *Generalfeldmarschall* Milch was loath to introduce this new type into large-scale production.

A significant element of the German air defence system, and one that grew in importance with the increased striking power of RAF Bomber Command's night raids, was the host of fire-decoys distributed throughout the Reich. The largest and most impressive of these was the V 500 decoy site situated some 15 miles north-west of Berlin, close to the routes often

▲ ► Eight victory markings painted on the tail of Fw. G. Wegman's Bf 110 W.Nr. 3412 belonging to ZG 26. The aircraft shows evidence of extensive repairs having been made to the vertical tail surfaces from damage inflicted during aerial combat.

used by raiders heading for the capital. The site comprised a cluster of twelve decoys spread over an area nine miles in diameter, and included a fake Templehof airfield.

To add realism to the decoys, the *Luftwaffe* developed special rockets to carry aloft coloured pyrotechnic candles; at a predetermined altitude a bursting charge expelled the candles, which ignited and cascaded to the ground. Although the distinctive colours of some British markers were difficult to replicate, on occasions the decoys seduced many bombs away from their intended targets.

With the introduction of the new freelance tactics, *Luftwaffe* nightfighters tended to delay their interceptions until the route and possible destination of the bomber stream became clear. As a result, the main actions took place beyond the reach of the short-range

► The The most heavily armed of the Luftwaffe fighters until late in the war was the destroyer version of the Bf 110. This example belonging to ZG 76 carried a nose-mounted armament of two 20 mm and two 30 mm cannon, supplemented by a further two 20 mm cannon in the under-fuselage weapon tray and four 210 mm mortar launching tubes under the outer wings.

◄ Recently promoted Oberleutnant Paul Gildner of 4./NJG 1, standing with jacket undone, in front of his Dornier Do 17 Z-10 showing 33 victory kills, at Leeuwarden in Holland on 9 June 1942. Having been awarded the Ritterkreuz in July 1941, by February 1943, Gildner was Kapitän of 1./NJG 1. He was killed in action on 24/25 February 1943, his score standing at 44 victories.

Beaufighters of No. 141 Squadron which carried the Serrate homer. There was a notable success on 29 September, however, when Wing Commander Bob Braham stalked and shot down a Bf 110 of *NJG 1*. Its pilot was *Hauptmann* August Geiger, a leading ace with 53 night victories to his credit. Geiger parachuted from his burning aircraft, but drowned when he came down in the Zuider Zee.

Following this victory there were a few more Serrate engagements, and in October the operations were discontinued. No. 141 Squadron began re-equipping with Mosquito nightfighters, which would enable the unit to return to the fray with increased effectiveness.

Following the suicide of Hans Jeschonnek, *Generaloberst* Günther Korten replaced him as *Luftwaffe* Chief of Staff. Korten had previously commanded *Luftflotte 1* in Russia, and he now regarded his first priority as the defeat of the US daylight bomber attacks. To bring this about he initiated a series of measures to improve the effectiveness of the home defence fighter force, grouped under four main headings: production, dispositions, tactics and armament.

Between November 1942 and July 1943 there had

been a steady increase in single-engined fighter production, from 480 to 800 aircraft per month. Including repaired aircraft, this meant about 1,000 single-engined fighters were available each month to serve as replacements and to expand the force. In that period the first-line strength of the fighter force

◄ A close-up of a fire decoy site. Such decoys were ineffective against daylight attacks but at night, if they produced realistic fires, they could look enticingly like the real thing and collected large numbers of bombs.

► During the summer of 1943 the Luftwaffe introduced the 30 mm Rheinmetall MK 108 cannon into large-scale service. The weapon is pictured with one of its high-explosive shells, which were very effective against light alloy structures.

▲ A Blenheim with its rear fuselage almost severed by a single hit during a ground test with a captured MK 108 in England.

▲ Big bombers were more resilient than the small ones, as can be seen from this photograph of a Stirling fuselage which suffered three hits during a firing trial. Although the holes in the outer skin were only about one foot across, there was considerable internal damage. On average three hits with 30 mm rounds were sufficient to bring down a heavy bomber.

increased from 1,250 aircraft to about 1,800.

Then, in the summer of 1943, came a period of heavy wastage of fighters in the Mediterranean theatre which placed limits on the expansion of the force. Production just kept pace with replacements and expansion, leaving few aircraft in reserve. After that date the US attacks on the fighter assembly plants began to take effect, imposing further limits on production.

As the seriousness of the situation became manifest, the *Luftwaffe* was forced to re-assign more fighter units to the defence of the homeland. That process proceeded apace during August, September and October 1943, and stripped *Gruppen* away from the Mediterranean, Balkan and Eastern fronts. The single-engined fighter units defending the homeland rose to about 800 aircraft in the middle of the year and 975 aircraft by 1 October.

Also during this time, Bf 110 *Zerstörer Gruppen* were withdrawn from the Mediterranean and Eastern fronts for re-assignment to the bomber destroyer role. These units were re-equipped with modified aircraft carrying an extraordinarily powerful armament comprising four 210 mm rocket mortar launchers, two 30 mm cannon and four 20 mm cannon. Furthermore, the first examples of the bomber-destroyer version of the

Messerschmitt Me 410, carrying the same forward firing armament but with a much-improved performance, began to appear. By the beginning of October the *Luftwaffe* had about 100 of the specialised twin-engined bomber-destroyers available for the defence of the homeland.

With the increase in fighter strength came some radical changes in fighter tactics. Previously, fighter units had gone into action as a *Gruppe* in formations of 15 to 20 aircraft, which was clearly insufficient to inflict major damage to bomber formations. By expanding the signals service and relocating radar units to provide better coverage of the interior of Germany, fighters could be assembled in concentrated forces with two or three times that number, and vectored to intercept the heavy bombers.

Also at this time there was a policy to up-gun single-engined fighters to give them the firepower necessary to engage the day bombers with greater effect. A larger proportion of the force now carried a 210 mm mortar launcher under each wing.

Following the August blood-letting, replacement aircraft and crews arrived to fill the gaps in the US bomber units, as the force prepared to launch further deep penetration attacks on targets in Germany. On 6

◄ This B-17 of the 100th Bomb Group was shot down during the abortive attack on Stuttgart on 6 September 1943 and is pictured after it crash-landed near Freiburg.

September, 338 B-17s took off to attack Stuttgart. Again the defenders reacted vigorously and effectively. Yet while the heavy losses suffered by the raiders on 17 August could to an extent be justified by the damage inflicted at the targets, there was no such consolation after the Stuttgart attack. The raiders arrived there to find it blanketed by cloud, and the aircraft unloaded their bombs on 'targets of opportunity' on the way home. That unsuccessful attack cost the Eighth Air Force 45 heavy bombers.

The failure of the Stuttgart raid highlighted a problem that had exercised Eighth Air Force planners since the beginning of operations over Europe. The continually changing weather pattern over north-western Europe imposed severe constraints on the daylight raiders, and forecasts of cloud over planned targets caused the frequent cancellation of missions. As the attacks on Regensburg and Schweinfurt had shown, US bomber crews would fight their way through the most powerful defences the *Luftwaffe* could muster, accepting heavy losses if they had to, to strike at important targets, yet no amount of fortitude or skill could enable them to place their bombs on targets they could not see.

The problem was distinctly similar to that faced by RAF night bombers a year earlier, and the solution was exactly the same: the day bombers also needed to carry radar bombing aids. In the summer of 1943 the first US Pathfinder unit, the 482nd Bomb Group, prepared for action. The Group comprised three squadrons, two with B-17s and one with B-24s. One B-17 squadron was equipped with the British H2S radar, and the others with the technically similar American H2X. During operations, the Pathfinder aircraft did not fly together in

formations of their own. Instead, the unit sent a couple of aircraft to occupy the lead positions in each of the wing formations.

US Pathfinders went into action for the first time during a shallow-penetration attack on the port of Emden on 27 September 1943. The 308 B-17s were divided into two divisions each comprising three wing formations. A pair of H2S aircraft flew at the head of the leading wing in each division. If the skies were clear, the bomb-aimers were to aim their loads visually, but if there was cloud cover at the target, the Pathfinder aircraft leading each combat wing was to carry out a radar bombing run, and the rest of the aircraft were to release their loads when the Pathfinder's bombs were seen to fall away.

▼ Daylight Pathfinders were necessary to lead attacks, because all too often cloud cover at targets made visual bombing ineffective. This photograph shows a B 17 fitted with a retractable radome mounted in place of the ball turret. (USAAF)

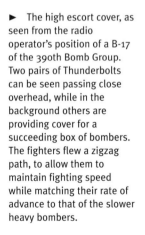

▲ A P-47 Thunderbolt of the 78th Fighter Group pictured during a practice mission over England in September 1943.

on targets even when they were blanketed by cloud.

The Emden attack was significant in another important respect: it was the first against an objective in Germany when the bombers enjoyed fighter cover all the way along their route to and from the target. More than 250 P-47 Thunderbolts, some fitted with the new 108 gallon drop tank, flew with the bombers. The presence of US escort fighters over home territory came as a nasty surprise to *Luftwaffe* pilots, and only seven bombers were lost. For their part the US escorts shot down about 20 German fighters, for the loss of one of their number.

Quite apart from forcing defending fighters to engage in dogfights instead of their primary task of attacking bombers, the presence of US escorts had two important secondary effects that also served to reduce bomber losses. Firstly, it meant that *Luftwaffe* fighter pilots no longer could afford to take their time in setting up an attack on bomber formations. When escorts were about, or thought to be about, each attack had to be pressed home at high speed and completed as rapidly as possible. This was particularly the case during head-on attacks. Previously, fighter pilots could throttle back when lining up for the attack, to align the weapons for an accurate burst. Now they had to deliver attacks flying at near full throttle, and the resultant high closing speeds allowed pilots little time to align

During the Emden attack, the raiders arrived to find that cloud almost completely obscured their target. The two H2S-led wings were able to bomb the target with reasonable accuracy, although those which followed did less well. This first attempt at daylight bombing through an overcast was, therefore, only partially successful. Yet it demonstrated that, given sufficient equipment to allow one or more radar-equipped Pathfinders to lead each combat box formation, the bombers could mount attacks

► The high escort cover, as seen from the radio operator's position of a B-17 of the 390th Bomb Group. Two pairs of Thunderbolts can be seen passing close overhead, while in the background others are providing cover for a succeeding box of bombers. The fighters flew a zigzag path, to allow them to maintain fighting speed while matching their rate of advance to that of the slower heavy bombers.

THE P-47 THUNDERBOLT AS AN ESCORT FIGHTER

Colonel 'Hub' Zemke commanded the 56th Fighter Group equipped with P-47s. He described the aircraft, and the best ways to employ it in action against the German fighters it met in combat, in these terms:

"[It was] a rugged beast with a sound radial engine to pull you along. It was heavy in firepower [eight .5 inch guns], enough to chew up the opponent at close range. It accelerated poorly and climbed not much better, but once high cruising speed was attained the P-47 could stand up to the opposition. Strangely, the rate of roll and manoeuvrability were good at high speeds. "At altitude, above 20,000 feet, the P-47 was superior to the German fighters. In my book you use your aircraft as advantageously as you can. In the dive, my God, the P-47 could overtake anything. Therefore I made it policy in my group that we used the tactic of `dive and zoom'. We stayed at high altitude, dived on the enemy, then zoomed back to high altitude before the next attack. To try to engage 109s and 190s in dogfights below 15,000 feet could be suicidal – that was not playing the game our way."

▲ During the late summer of 1943 the American long-range fighters became increasingly active in supporting bomber attacks on Germany. This P-47D Thunderbolt of the 361st Fighter Group was photographed when it moved in close to a B-24. The empty shackle for the drop tank is clearly visible. This aircraft had a maximum speed of 429 mph at 30,000 feet. Normal maximum take-off weight was 17,500 pounds. Offensive armament comprised eight Browning .5 inch machine guns.

REPUBLIC P-47D THUNDERBOLT
Serving with the 361st Fighter Group from Bottisham, Cambridgeshire during 1944. Overall standard finish of Olive Drab over Neutral Gray undersurfaces. Note the white bars on the tail and tailplane, introduced to avoid confusion with the Fw 190 during combats.

their weapons on the chosen target. If the fighters flew at 300 mph and the bombers at 175 mph, that gave a combined closing speed of 475 mph. The *Luftwaffe* pilots had time for only a short half-second burst, before they had to break away to avoid colliding with the bomber. To press home such an attack required considerable flying skill as well as a cool head. Range estimation proved beyond all but the best pilots, and those with less experience either broke away before they were within effective firing range, or left it too late before they had to break away without opening fire.

The second important effect of the presence of escorts was that no longer could *Luftwaffe* fighter pilots expend their entire complement of ammunition in a series of attacks on the bombers; instead, they now had to withhold a proportion of their rounds in case they had to engage the escorts after delivering their attack and fight their way past them.

Five days later, on 2 October, the Eighth Air Force launched another escorted attack on Emden, along similar lines to the earlier raid on the port. This time the defending fighters showed a marked reluctance to

THE P-38 LIGHTNING AS AN ESCORT FIGHTER

'Hub' Zemke also few the P-38 in action, but in his view this aircraft was the least effective of the US fighters in the escort role:

'The turbo-superchargers were controlled by an oil regulator and at altitude the oil had a tendency to congeal, which caused serious problems. On two occasions I recall entering combat with enemy single-seaters and it became a matter of life and death to get away and survive, though I had started with the advantage. On both occasions the engines either cut out completely or over-revved when the throttles were cut or advanced.

'A further problem with the P-38 was that its airframe was not strong and it had a relatively low maximum diving speed. If German fighters broke off combat by diving steeply the Lightning pilots could not follow.

'Yet the P-38 did have one outstanding feature. As a gun platform it was as steady as a shooting stand. With the two engines there was no torque. With a little trim to build up speed in a dive a pilot could ride directly on to a target. As to the armament installation, I have seen no better: four machine guns and a cannon mounted close together directly in front of the pilot. Because guns and sight were close together, there was no need for the weapons to converge their fire as with the more usual wing-mounted guns.'

◄ Four P-38 Lightnings of the 364th Fighter Group, seen flying the loose finger-four formation favoured by most air forces by the middle of the war. (USAF)

LOCKHEED P-38L LIGHTNING

Serving with the 364th Fighter Group from Honington, Suffolk, 1944.
Overall standard finish of Olive Drab over Neutral Grey
undersurfaces with codes and yellow noses to the engine booms.

engage the heavy bombers, and only two were lost.

On 4 October a force of 155 bombers made a deep-penetration attack on Frankfurt am Main. The escorts went with the raiders to a point just past the German frontier, and held losses to only eight bombers. Near Cologne Thunderbolts of the 56th Fighter Group, operating at the limit of their radius of action, caught a *Gruppe* of Bf 110s moving into position to launch their 210 mm mortars into the rear combat wing. The escorts shot down more than ten of the heavily laden bomber-destroyers, without themselves suffering losses.

A few days later the twin-engined Lockheed P-38 Lightning fighter began flying escort missions. Carrying two 165 gallon drop tanks it had a radius of action of 600 miles, and was able to penetrate deeper into enemy territory than the Thunderbolts.

After the one-sided action on 4 October the *Luftwaffe* restricted its twin-engined day fighters to operations east of the line Bremen-Kassel-Frankfurt, in a bid to keep them out of reach of the US escorts. That shift marked an important turning point in the air war: it was clear proof that the *Luftwaffe* had lost control over a large swathe of the airspace over its homeland.

In addition to the far-reaching changes made to the *Luftwaffe* day and nightfighter forces, during 1943 there was a major reorganisation of the Flak defences. During that year the number of heavy gun batteries increased from just over 600 to nearly 1,000. In order to bring greater firepower to bear against the close-flying American day bombers, and also to make greater use of the limited number of fire-control radars available, the size of the gun batteries was increased from four to six, and later to eight guns.

To add firepower to the defences, especially at the more important targets, so-called great-batteries – *Grossbatterien* – were formed, comprising two or three of the enlarged batteries all controlled from a single predictor. This meant that as many as 18 heavy guns engaged the single bomber selected as target. In the case of a daylight action, the unfortunate aircraft chosen was invariably the formation leader, for it determined the accuracy of the attack by the whole formation.

Now that the US bombers operating by day were attacking targets through cloud, the defending Flak units needed to use their *Würzburg* radars to provide fire control information. If those fire control radars could be jammed, then the accuracy of the Flak – and bomber

◄▲ Early in the war German engineers launched a vigorous programme to protect important potential targets. The Deutsche oil refinery near Bremen is shown with the larger oil storage tanks protected by their own blast walls.

▲ The same refinery, after it had been camouflaged. The storage tanks have been covered with netting to reduce their conspicuous outline.

▲ On 9 October 1943, 96 B-17s of the US Eighth Air Force delivered a concentrated attack on the Fw 190 assembly plant at Marienburg. Pre-strike reconnaissance photographs revealed that the target had only weak anti-aircraft gun defences. Bomber crews were ordered to deliver their attack between 11,000 and 13,000 feet, considerably lower than usual, to achieve accuracy. Photographs taken after the attack showed that most buildings had suffered heavy damage. Yet the all-important heavy machine tools and production jigs survived, unless they suffered direct hits. Production resumed within a few days of the attack, and by January 1944 production was running at pre-attack levels. Two B-17s were lost during this attack.

A SCHOOLBOY
IN THE FLAK ARM

Having begun the war as one of the elite branches of the *Luftwaffe*, the Flak arm had suffered a steady reduction in its status. There had been a steady draining of talent, as able-bodied men were transferred to the battlefronts. Only a rump of experienced personnel remained, to direct the ill assortment of personnel drafted in to fill the gaps in the ranks; schoolboys, youths of the Reichs Labour Service, men over-age for military service, factory workers and even turncoat Russian prisoners.

Luftwaffenhelfer (*Luftwaffe* Auxiliary) Hans Ring was one of a class of 15 and 16-year old schoolboys sent to help man a Flak battery in Berlin. The boys' schoolteachers accompanied them, and when there was no action the boys were expected to resume normal lessons.

"Our battery was a heavy one with four, later six, 105 mm guns, in an emplacement at Spandau-Johannisstift on the western suburbs of Berlin. The battery establishment consisted of two officers, 30 NCOs and other ranks, about 100 of us boys and some 30 Russian prisoners. The soldiers and the prisoners did the heavier manual jobs. The boys carried out nearly all the other tasks, from radio operator to gunner – even the K-3 [gun loader]. You can imagine that it was hard work for a 15 year old boy to load a gun with 105 mm ammunition during rapid fire [each shell weighed 90 pounds complete with cartridge case] often with the barrel pointing upwards at an angle of 40 degrees or more. The most skilful job was that of range finder, often a boy too. Sometimes the Commander would allow one of us to give the fire commands, the most exalted position of all: "Achtung!....Gruppe! ...Achtung! ... Gruppe!" [Attention!... Salvo!].

"If the battle was short the fire discipline was usually very good, but woe if the battery fired more than 80 or 100 rounds! Each gun crew had the ambition to be the best and to fire the most ammunition. Instead of a fine unison crash there would be guns firing off all over the place. We boys were most enthusiastic, and it was a bad day when there was no British activity. Our feelings were not completely selfless, since after a night raid we were allowed to sleep-in in the morning and did not have to go to school. I clearly remember that on one occasion towards the end of 1943 our battery fired about 40 salvoes at a very mysterious target; it had been detected by radar moving very slowly, and our commander thought it might be a glider with enemy agents on board. We afterwards learnt that the easy target which had refused to be shot down was in fact a large cloud of Window.

"We were in an odd position, sometimes treated as soldiers and sometimes as schoolboys. We were not allowed to see adults' films – and goodness knows, German adults' films at that time were harmless enough! We were expected to shoot down enemy planes with our 105 mm guns, but we were not considered old enough to carry rifles when we went to round up enemy aircrew who came down by parachute."

losses – would both be reduced.

Earlier in the year the USAAF had ordered into production the APT-2 'Carpet' equipment, designed to radiate noise jamming on the *Würzburg* radar frequencies. In the autumn of 1943 the first jammers arrived in England and were fitted to the B-17s of the 96th and 388th Bomb Groups based respectively at Snetterton Heath and Knettishall.

Each Carpet radiated only a narrow band of jamming, so the jammers in a combat-box formation with 20 bombers were pre-tuned with a 500 kHz spacing between each. In that way the formation as a whole radiated jamming evenly across most of the *Würzburg* band running from 553 to 566 MHz. The radioman in each aircraft switched his Carpet to transmit when the formation entered the Flak zone, and ceased transmitting when the formation left it.

On 8 October, a force of 170 B-17s of the 3rd Bomb Division attacked Bremen. Included in the force were 42 Carpet-fitted aircraft, only one of which was lost (2.4 per cent of the force). The 129 aircraft without the device lost 13 of their number (ten per cent of the force). This and subsequent attacks made it clear that Carpet provided useful protection against radar-laid guns engaging the raiders through cloud. As a result, Headquarters Eighth Air Force issued a requirement for sufficient Carpets to fit one into each heavy bomber. Several months would pass before this ambitious program could be realised, however. In the meantime, Carpet would have a relatively small effect on the total number of heavy bombers lost. Two-thirds of the losses were still to fighter attack, and Carpet could do nothing to hinder this. Its day would come, but later.

The success of the attacks on Germany during the first week in October encouraged the Eighth Air Force to extend its sphere of operations. On the 9th the bombers

▲ An Fw 190 caught by the camera gun of a US escort fighter.

LUFTWAFFE FIGHTER FORCE ACCOUNT OF THE ATTACK ON SCHWEINFURT ON 14 OCTOBER 1943

Author's Note: This is an abridged translation of the account in the War Diary of I. *Jagdkorps* (Fighter Corps).

Radio direction finding [on radio traffic] reported the assembly of a strong enemy bomber force in the area north-east of London at 10.30 hrs. Towards 12.30 hrs about 200 to 300 bombers in a large formation launched the attack heading in a south-easterly course from the Sheerness - Harwich area. They crossed the estuary of the [River] Scheldt and, taking a direct course, flew via Antwerp and Brussels to the Frankfurt - Würzburg area. The main attack hit the ball bearing plants at Schweinfurt, though some bombs fell on Frankfurt am Main. About 200 enemy fighters accompanied the bomber units during the period from 12.50 hrs to 14.10, as far as the area of Aachen.

The bombers return flight from the Schweinfurt area began at 14.45 hrs. The last bomber unit left the mainland at 17.15 hrs, between Berk sur Mere and Dieppe. An enemy force with 30 to 40 Liberators flew above the North Sea at 04.45 hrs, presumably with the intention of diverting German fighters away from the main attack force.

Between 15.10 hrs and 15.25 hrs, four Mosquito reconnaissance machines flew via Remagen to the area of Saarbrücken.

Effect of the Raid
In Schweinfurt the raid lasted from 14.35 hrs to 14.46 hrs.

Material damage:	100 buildings destroyed
	150 buildings heavily damaged
Personnel losses:	180 dead
	220 wounded
	10,000 homeless

The production of ball bearings was temporarily halted.
Heavy damage within the city limits and at the main railway station.

Commitment of I. Jagdkorps
All day fighter units and nightfighters suitable for daytime operations from the 1st, 2nd, 3rd, 4th and 5th Fighter Divisions. Clear skies facilitated the commitment of friendly forces. Since the enemy fighters turned back early, the bombers could come under uninterrupted attack from German fighters and destroyers in the area Frankfurt am Main - Schweinfurt - Metz. Reich air defence units gained a great defensive success on 14 October 1943.

Total aircraft committed:	567
Enemy losses:	74 Fortresses and 5 Thunderbolts definitely destroyed
	43 Fortresses probably destroyed

Notes
a. *Feldwebel* Monska of II./JG 27 shot down 5 aircraft.
b. An American bomber attempted to escape into Switzerland via Stuttgart - Memmingen. After an aerial combat it made an emergency landing near Mittenwald.

Own losses:	27 machines
Personnel:	6 dead, 9 missing, 11 wounded
Weather:	Holland:	fog, lifting towards the afternoon
	Germany: clear

Author's comments:
The total US losses during this action were 60 B-17s destroyed and 138 damaged, one P-47 destroyed and two damaged.

In addition to the *Luftwaffe* fighters' and destroyers' claim of 74 Fortresses and five Thunderbolts definitely destroyed, Flak claimed the destruction of 42 enemy aircraft that day. That supposed total claim of 121 enemy aircraft destroyed would rapidly be whittled down in the weeks to follow, however. The *Luftwaffe Abschusscommission* (Commission for the adjudication of victory claims) carefully examined the evidence for each claim. Since the great majority of US aircraft shot down on that day fell on German-occupied territory, a pilot or a Flak battery unable to point to a wreck or remains on the ground had considerable difficulty in getting a claim confirmed. The *Luftwaffe* gave individuals no credit for shared or probable victories. If more than one fighter engaged the aircraft shot down, the individual judged to have played the main part in its destruction received the credit.

After the action *Feldwebel* Otto Monska had his claim reduced to 3 bombers. He was killed in action in May 1944, when his victory score stood at eight enemy aircraft, of which three were heavy bombers.

FLAK ENGAGEMENT AT SCHWEINFURT, 14 OCTOBER 1943

Report from the 4th Battery of the 382nd Flak Battalion, an 88 mm gun unit situated near to the small village of Sennfeld and covering the southern approaches to Schweinfurt. The battery commander, *Leutnant* Kolhogen later wrote:

"One wave of bombers came in at 14.56 hrs, and we engaged it from 14.56 hrs to 14.58 hrs; target altitude 6,400 metres [20,800 feet] and speed 110 metres per second [240 mph]. The wave consisted of 36 aircraft and flew as though on exercise, with no recognisable evasive action. The sky was clear of cloud as the 8.8-cm Flak 37 guns opened fire, rapidly and by salvoes. The machine we had engaged dropped out of the formation over Schweinfurt itself; it dived in a steadily tightening curve towards Pusselsheim. After the crew had bailed out, it crashed at 15.06 hrs. Munition expenditure: 23 salvoes."

Author's Note: subsequent examination of the wreckage revealed a white square with a blue 'A' on the bomber's tail, the marking of the 94th Bomb Group.

▼ To provide greater firepower to knock down the tough, heavy bombers, the Luftwaffe increased the armament of its day fighters. This Bf 109 G of JG 11 carries underwing launchers for a pair of 210 mm mortars.

made their longest ranging penetrations so far, with near-simultaneous strikes on targets at Danzig, Gdynia, Marienburg and Anklam in eastern Germany by more than 300 bombers. On the 10th the bombers attacked Münster in similar force. In each case the losses averaged just under ten per cent of the force engaged.

If the *Luftwaffe* High Command was worried about its ability to counter the US attacks on the homeland, it showed little evidence of it. When US bombers next ventured over Germany, on 14 October, they were met by extremely determined fighter opposition. On that day a force of 291 B-17s was sent to finish off the target that had been damaged at such great cost in August: the ball bearing production centre at Schweinfurt. After the earlier raid on that target, its very name had come to strike fear in bomber crews. At the end of the mission briefing for the 385th Bomb Group based at Great Ashfield, Colonel Elliot Vandevanter concluded: *"This is a tough job, and I know you can do it. Good luck, good bombing, and good hunting."* At that, someone at the back of the room quipped, *"And good-bye"*. The comment drew nervous guffaws from the assembled crews.

As in the previous attack, there was little action until the leading bombers passed Aachen and the escorting Thunderbolts had to turn back. Then the *Luftwaffe* fighters struck in a manner that, in the words of the USAAF official historians, *"was unprecedented in its magnitude, in the cleverness with which it was planned, and in the severity with which it was executed"*. Among the successful German fighter pilots that day was

Unteroffizier Hans Seyringer, a 'greenhorn' no longer. With his *Staffel* he stormed through a B-17 formation from behind, and watched the bomber he had hit topple from the sky with its starboard wing and motors shot to pieces.

It was a badly mauled force that finally reached Schweinfurt: 28 bombers had been shot down while others had suffered battle damage and could maintain formation only with difficulty. As the Group box formations slid into line astern for the bombing run, it was the turn of Schweinfurt's ground defences to go into action.

The bomb-aimers in the leading waves found their aiming points easily, and placed their loads with great accuracy. Subsequent waves had the problem of smoke from the fires obscuring the aiming points, but throughout the attack the bombing remained good and the three bearing plants all suffered heavy damage.

After rapid refuelling and rearming, the *Luftwaffe* fighter units were ready to go into action against the bombers during their withdrawal. The return flight was almost a repeat of that to the target, with sustained attacks from the vengeance-bent fighter force. The attacks lasted until the raiders reached Aachen, where the protective screen of Thunderbolts arrived to

shepherd the battered survivors back to England.

As during the earlier attack on this target, the bomber formations suffered crippling losses: 60 B-17s were shot down, 17 suffered severe damage, and a further 121 returned with moderate damage. Thus, out of the original force of 291 bombers, 198 had been either destroyed or damaged. For their part the bombers' gunners, and the US fighters which covered the initial part of the penetration and the final part of the withdrawal, accounted for some 38 German fighters and caused damage to 20 more.

After the action, following examination of the wreck of the B-17 Hans Seyringer had claimed, three officers in the unit also laid claim to it. However, *Hauptmann* Schroer, the *Gruppenkommandeur*, had witnessed Seyringer's attack and on his insistence the latter received credit for the 'kill' (the *Luftwaffe* had no system for sharing victories).

Following the second attack on Schweinfurt, there was another break in the US deep penetration attacks on targets in Germany. After that bout of bloodletting, each side drew different lessons for its future conduct of the air war. These will be described in the next Chapter.

▼ As the evening approaches the activity on this unidentified Bf 110 nightfighter base increases to ensure the aircraft are ready for action at any moment.

7

TAKING STOCK

End of October 1943

"When men are equally inured and

disciplined in war 'tis, without a miracle,

number that gains the victory."

Admiral Sir Cloudesley Shovell

Following the October day and night slugging matches over Germany, each side drew significant, but different, lessons. To the *Luftwaffe*, the outcome of these actions seemed to confirm the effectiveness of its new tactics and weapons.

By day the recently introduced twin-engined Messerschmitt 110 bomber-destroyers, armed with batteries of heavy cannon and rockets, seemed to offer the best chance of countering enemy day bomber formations that ventured beyond the range of their escorting fighters. If bombers could be damaged sufficiently to make them leave the protection of their formation, these isolated machines were relatively easy to finish off. As a means of knocking bombers out of formation, the hefty 210 mm mortar had been a useful improvisation. Yet this low-velocity missile was relatively inaccurate and, since it was detonated by a time fuse, fighter pilots had to judge the range of the target to within fine limits before launching them. That proved extremely difficult, and the majority of rockets exploded either short or past their target.

For the future, the *Luftwaffe* planned to build a fleet of 'super-destroyers'. These would be twin-engined Messerschmitt 410 fighters fitted with 50 mm cannon, able to engage US heavy bombers from outside the range of their defensive fire.

For the longer term future the *Luftwaffe* planned to introduce the Messerschmitt 262 jet fighter into large-scale service in the spring of 1944. This revolutionary new aircraft, with a top speed of 540 mph, carried a battery of four 30 mm cannon that was powerful enough to knock down the heaviest bomber. Should the US 8th Air Force continue its deep penetration daylight attacks on targets in Germany,

which at that time was open to question, the bombers would suffer crippling losses.

For its part, the US 8th Air Force learned a quite different lesson from the October battles. It saw the solution to the problem of defending the bombers in a massive expansion of the escort fighter force, and more P-47 Thunderbolt units were arriving in England. The first units were forming with the North American P-51B Mustang fighter, fitted with the Rolls Royce Merlin engine and extra internal fuel tanks; it was hoped this fighter could provide full-route protection to targets almost anywhere in Germany.

Also at this time, the USAAF sought to exert further pressure on the already over-extended *Luftwaffe* fighter force. The Fifteenth Air Force was establishing itself at a clutch of airfields around Foggia in the south of Italy. From there its heavy bombers could reach a spread of targets in southern Germany and the Balkans, without the bombers needing to run the gauntlet of the air defences of north-western Germany.

In the case of the night actions, *Luftwaffe* commanders had good reason to believe they had weathered the storm following the Window debacle. During August, September and October 1943, RAF Bomber Command had launched a series of heavy raids on Berlin and other cities. It sought to repeat the pattern of destructive attacks that had laid waste to large areas of Hamburg. Yet although the German capital

◄◄ A formation of P-47 Thunderbolts of the 56th Fighter Group, without their long-range fuel tanks, on their way home after a mission.

USE OF CAPTURED ENEMY AIRCRAFT IN ACTION

During the war scores of Allied aircraft came down in German-occupied territory in a repairable condition, and the *Luftwaffe* flew evaluation trials with many of them. From Allied aircrew there were persistent reports that captured aircraft, sometimes in their original markings, had engaged them over Germany.

These stories have no basis in fact. *General* Adolf Galland, the Inspector General of the *Luftwaffe* fighter force and the man without whose approval such a stratagem could not have been used, has assured this author that captured aircraft were never used in the defence of the Reich. Quite apart from the ethical considerations, the use of enemy aircraft would have been unsound tactically: in a confused combat situation it is difficult to tell friend from foe. For a *Luftwaffe* crew to fly a Fortress or a Liberator singly in the vicinity of an American bomber formation would have meant a high risk of being shot at or shot down by 'friendly' fighters. Similarly, any fighter approaching a bomber formation in a manner that looked aggressive, no matter what its shape or its markings, almost invariably came under fire from the bombers' guns - as many a US escort pilot found to his discomfort.

In short, the *Luftwaffe* would have had much to lose and little to gain from employing captured aircraft against the raiding formations. Yet however shaky its basis, the notion of German-manned Fortresses and Liberators trying to infiltrate the bomber formations had wide credence in the USAAF. It is easy to see how such beliefs gained ground. The complex process of assembling the bombers into their huge formations seldom passed off smoothly, and often a few bombers failed to join up with their own groups. When that happened, the standing orders were to join up with another group and fly to the target with it.

Captain Tom Marchbanks of the 398th Bomb Group recalled an occasion when he was late taking off in his B-17, and he had to join up with another bomb group on its way to the target. Crews in the host formation thought his presence very suspicious, and all the way to the target the other aircraft in the formation flew with their guns trained on his aircraft. He told his gunners to be very careful not to point their weapons at other bombers, or do anything else that might be mistaken as a hostile action.

The impression that the Germans were infiltrating the bomber streams in captured aircraft was also prevalent amongst RAF crews operating at night. Yet, here again, German senior officers questioned by the author are adamant that this was never done. As in the case of the daylight bombers such a move would have been counterproductive. It was difficult enough to get a relatively fast radar-equipped fighter into the bomber stream, it would have been impossible to vector heavy bombers into the streams as a matter of course.

Nevertheless many crews returned with stories of having been fired at by Lancasters, Halifaxes, Wellingtons or Stirlings, almost certainly the result of poor recognition on one side or the other. The German ace Heinz-Wolfgang Schnaufer recalled one occasion when, as he manoeuvred into position to attack a Lancaster, another heavy bomber in the stream opened fire on it; 'Schnaufer's Lancaster' opened fire in reply. In obedience to Napoleon's famous dictum "Never interrupt an enemy in the middle of a mistake" the German pilot held clear while the two bombers fought a pitched battle that ended when both went down in flames.

▲ A Short Stirling which was captured in Holland in September 1942 stands behind a Bf 109 G, on show at the Luftwaffe Experimental Centre at Rechlin. It was extensively repainted in yellow and given the Rechlin identification number of '6+8' painted in white. This aircraft was repaired and test-flown before being scrapped.

▲ Initially the SN-2 radar equipment was unable to track targets at ranges less than 400 yards, a major disadvantage. To overcome this problem, some night fighters carried the older Lichtenstein equipment as well, (see the central aerial array), but this clumsy arrangement created further drag.

◄ Flame dampers fitted to a Bf 110 G nightfighter. These fittings, in addition to the carriage of radar and additional fuel tanks, added more drag and further reduced the aircraft's already inadequate performance.

THE BATTLE OF KÖPENICK

October 1943 ended for the *Luftwaffe* on a lighter note. On the 20th, a force of 119 B-17s attacked Düren in north-west Germany, and withdrew. For the *Luftwaffe* the action did not end there, however. Ground observer posts reported hearing the engines of aircraft flying above the layer of cloud, heading into Germany. In fact the sounds came from *Luftwaffe* fighters heading for home but *Reichsmarschall* Göring, who happened to be on an inspection visit at a fighter control bunker, decided to take personal command of his fighters.

He diagnosed the Düren attack as a feint and, noticing that the 'enemy' flight path was similar to the route taken to Schweinfurt a few days earlier, he pronounced that as the probable target. More fighter *Gruppen* were ordered into the air and sent after the 'bomber force', to add to the engine noises previously reported by the ground observers. Pushed for details, the radar stations confirmed that a force of aircraft was indeed heading towards Schweinfurt. Yet, mysteriously, the fighters airborne reported no contact with the 'raiders'. The 'enemy formation' flew past Schweinfurt, and in turn Göring judged the target to be Leipzig, then oil refineries in central Germany, then the Skoda armament works at Pilsen in Czechoslovakia. Finally, as fuel ran short, the fighters were forced to land and the 'enemy formation' petered out.

It soon became clear that there had been no hostile machines over southern Germany that day, merely German fighters. Once the truth was established, Göring saw the humorous side. He sent telegrams to all involved congratulating them on the 'great victory during the air attack on the fortress of Köpenick'. (In 1906 a shoemaker dressed in a Prussian army captain's uniform strutted into the barracks at Köpenick near Berlin and took control of a squad of troops who obeyed his orders without question. He marched the men to the local treasury, captured it, then walked off with the money they had seized. From then on, in Germany the term 'Captain of Köpenick' has been synonymous with 'confidence trickster').

NEW USE FOR 'WINDOW'

For the aircrews involved, the battle over Germany became ever more complex during 1943. This was a campaign fought mainly by wartime-only NCOs and junior officers. A year or two earlier these hastily trained men had not even heard of radar. Add to this the blanket of security that covered many aspects of the battle, and it is not surprising that some odd ideas gained currency.

To the crews that had seen the initial impact of Window on the Hamburg defences in July 1943, the value of the countermeasure was never in doubt. But the new crews who would later replace them in Bomber Command, the business of releasing bundles of strips the whole time they were over enemy territory seemed a futile chore. In many bomber squadrons nobody explained the reason for it.

One bomber navigator told this author that in his crew there was a debate on the value of dropping metal foil on the enemy: "That wasn't going to hurt them, was it?" So, the men arrived at a compromise. It was agreed to drop the Window bundles as briefed, but during the flight to the target the bomb-aimer would 'prepare' several bundles for use: he urinated on them, then placed them against the side of the fuselage to freeze solid. During the bombing run the 'doctored' Window bundles were released. The author was told: "They fell like little bricks and that way, we thought, they might do a bit of good!"

► The Heinkel He 219 was the most effective nightfighter type to enter service in the Luftwaffe, but due to the lack of spare industrial capacity it could not be produced in large numbers.

▲ Nordholz airfield had its runways, taxiways and the distinctive 'ladder' servicing ramps toned down to make them less conspicuous.

▲ Some six kilometres north of Nordholz airfield lay its attendant decoy site, with runways, servicing ramps and other features painted to look conspicuous.

suffered serious cumulative damage, it was scattered over a wide area and it was in no way comparable to the fate Hamburg had suffered.

In the relatively clear autumn nights, the night fighters' new *Wilde Sau* and *Zahme Sau* tactics had proved extremely successful against the bomber streams. Production of the new SN-2 nightfighter radar was proceeding apace, and it equipped a small but growing proportion of the force. For the future, the *Naxos-Z* and *Flensburg* airborne homing receivers promised to make it much easier for nightfighter crews to home on the bomber streams.

Meanwhile, RAF Bomber Command also continued to expand. It was in the process of forming a major new unit, No. 100 Group with about a hundred aircraft, to

serve in the night bomber support role. Part of the force would comprise heavy bombers loaded not with bombs but with radar and radio-jamming equipment, to hinder and divert defending nightfighters away from the raiding forces. The rest of the force would comprise squadrons of Mosquito long-range nightfighters, equipped to hunt down and engage their enemy counterparts over their home territory.

Thus, in the late autumn of 1943, both sides expected to see further hard-fought air battles over Germany during the year to follow. And each side had good grounds for believing that it would prevail over its opponent. In the second and final Volume, we shall observe how events progressed in this, the largest and hardest-fought air campaign in history.

Appendix A　　　Ranks

Royal Air Force	USAAF	Luftwaffe
Marshal of the RAF	Five Star General	Generalfeldmarschall
Air Chief Marshal	Four Star General	Generaloberst
Air Marshal	Lieutenant General	General der Flieger
Air Vice Marshal	Major General	Generalleutnant
Air Commodore	Brigadier General	Generalmajor
Group Captain	Colonel	Oberst
Wing Commander	Lieutenant Colonel	Oberstleutnant
Squadron Leader	Major	Major
Flight Lieutenant	Captain	Hauptmann
Flying Officer	First Lieutenant	Oberleutnant
Pilot Officer	Lieutenant	Leutnant
(leading cadet)	(leading cadet)	Oberfähnrich
(cadet)	(cadet)	Fähnrich
Warrant Officer	Warrant Officer	Stabsfeldwebel
Flight Sergeant	Master Sergeant	Oberfeldwebel
Sergeant	Technical Sergeant	Feldwebel
-	-	Unterfeldwebel
Corporal	Staff Sergeant	Unteroffizier
-	Sergeant	Hauptgefreiter
Leading Aircraftman	Corporal	Obergefreiter
Aircraftman	Private	Gefreiter
First Class	First Class	-
Aircraftman	Private	Flieger

In addition, the *Luftwaffe* used the term 'Hauptfeldwebel'. This was not a rank. A Hauptfeldwebel (colloquially called 'Spiess') was the NCO administrative head of a company or corresponding unit (Staffel, battery etc.). His rank could be anything from Unteroffizier to the various Feldwebel.

Appendix B　　　Combat Flying Units

Establishment of aircraft in the combat units of the Royal Air Force, the United States Army Air Force, and the *Luftwaffe*. Since the establishment varied considerably over the course of the Second World War, the figures given are only approximate.

RAF (Bombers)

Basic unit: the Squadron, comprising 16, later 30 aircraft.
Between 10 and 16 Squadrons comprised a Group.

USAAF (Fighters and Bombers)

Basic unit: the Squadron, comprising some 16 bombers or 25 fighters.
Four Squadrons of bombers, or three Squadrons of fighters, comprised a group.
Three Groups of bombers or five Groups of fighters comprised a Wing.

Luftwaffe (Fighters)

Basic unit: the Gruppe, comprising three or four Staffeln each with nine aircraft, plus a Stab (Staff) unit with three. Three or four Gruppen comprised a Geschwader.

Appendix C　　　Code-Names

ABC-Airborne Cigar. British airborne transmitter to jam the German fighter control frequencies.

Boozer. Radar warning receiver fitted to RAF bombers, to provide warning of illumination by signals from Würzburg or Lichtenstein radars.

Carpet. Airborne jamming transmitter fitted to US and later RAF bombers, to jam Würzburg fire-control radars.

Corona. RAF operation to transmit spoof messages on *Luftwaffe* nightfighter control frequencies, using transmitters located in England.

Epsilon ('Y'). Device fitted to German fighters to allow specially equipped ground stations to track their movements.

Flak. Abbreviation of Fliegerabwehrkanonen, 'anti-aircraft guns'.

Freya. German early warning surveillance radar.

GEE. British long-range navigational aid.

Giant. Würzburg German nightfighter control radar.

Helle Nachtjagd. German system of nightfighting, using searchlights to illuminate enemy bombers.

Himmelbett. German system of ground radar controlled nightfighting.

H2S and H2X. British and American systems of ground mapping radar to aid bombing at night or through cloud.

Lichtenstein. Airborne radar fitted to German nightfighters.

Mammut. German early warning radar.

Mandrel. British jammer to counter Freya and other German early warning radars.

Monica. British tail-warning radar.

Naxos. German airborne and ground direction finder, which gave bearings on H2S transmissions.

Oboe. British blind bombing aid using ground stations in England.

Schräge Musik. German upward-firing cannon installation for nightfighters.

Serrate. British airborne device to enable nightfighters to home on the radar signals from their German counterparts.

Tinsel. Scheme for jamming the German nightfighter control frequencies, using the bombers' communications transmitters.

Wassermann. German early warning radar.

Wilde Sau 'Wild Boar'. German scheme for using single-seat fighters to engage bombers over their targets.

INDEX

A selection of Classic aviation titles

The JADGWAFFE Series

VOLUME ONE

Section 1
Birth of Luftwaffe Fighter Force
0 952686 75 9, PB, 303mm x 226mm,
96pp, c250 photos £12.95

Section 2
The Spanish Civil War
0 952686 76 7, PB, 303mm x 226mm,
96pp, c250 photos £12.95

Section 3
Blitzkrieg & Sitzkrieg 1939-40
0 952686 77 5, PB, 303mm x 226mm,
96pp, c250 photos £12.95

Section 4
Attack in the West 1940
0 952686 78 3, PB, 303mm x 226mm,
96pp, c250 photos £12.95

VOLUME TWO

Section 1
Battle of Britain Phase 1:
June-July 1940
1 903223 05 9, PB, 303mm x 226mm,
96pp, c250 photos £14.95

Section 2
Battle of Britain Phase 2:
Aug-Sept 1940
1 903223 06 7, PB, 303mm x 226mm,
96pp, c250 photos £14.95

Section 3
Battle of Britain Phase 3:
Sept-Oct 1940
1 903223 07 5, PB, 303mm x 226mm,
96pp, c250 photos £14.95

Section 4
Battle of Britain Phase 4:
Oct-Dec 1940
1 903223 08 3, PB, 303mm x 226mm,
96pp, c250 photos £14.95

VOLUME THREE

Section 1
Strike in the Balkans:
April-May 1941
1 903223 20 2, PB, 303mm x 226mm,
96pp, c250 photos £14.95

Section 2
Barbarossa: April-May 1941
1 903223 21 0, PB, 303mm x 226mm,
96pp, c250 photos £14.95

Section 3
War Over the Desert - North Africa
June 1940 - June 1942
1 903223 22 9, PB, 303mm x 226mm,
96pp, c120 photos, col a/w £14.95

Section 4
The War in Russia
January - October 1942
1 903223 16 4, PB,
303mm x 226mm, 96pp,
c120 photos, col a/w
£14.95

VOLUME FOUR

Section 1
Holding the West 1941-1943
1 903223 34 2, 303mm x 226mm, PB,
96pp, inc 120 photos, colour artwork,
£14.95

Section 2
The Mediterranean 1942-1943
1 903223 35 0, 303mm x 226mm, PB,
96pp, inc 120 photos, colour artwork,
£14.95

Section 3
War in Russia 1942-1943
1 903223 36 9, 303mm x 226mm, PB,
96pp, inc 120 photos, colour artwork,
£14.95

Section 4
The Mediterranean 1943-1945
1 903223 46 6, 303mm x 226mm, PB,
96pp, inc 120 photos, colour artwork,
£14.95

VOLUME FIVE

Section 1
Defending the Reich 1943-1944
1 903223 44 X, 303mm x 226mm, PB,
96pp, inc 220 photos, colour artwork,
£16.99

Section 2
War in the East 1944-1945
1 903223 46 6, 303mm x 226mm, PB,
96pp, inc 200 photos, colour artwork,
£16.99

Section 3
Defending the Reich 1944-1945
1 903223 51 2, 303mm x 226mm, PB,
96pp, inc 200 photos, colour artwork,
£16.99

Section 4
Jet Fighters & Rocket Interceptors
1944-1945
1 903223 52 0, 303mm x 226mm, PB,
96pp, inc 120 photos, colour artwork,
£16.99

LUFTWAFFE CAMOUFLAGE & MARKINGS 1933-1945
Volume 1

Kenneth A. Merrick

The first volume in this unique work commences with a technical and historical background to the German paint manufacturing industry and colour interpretation, together with an overview of German factory standards. A major part of this volume deals with official camouflage patterns and unit codes of all major civilian and Luftwaffe aircraft types.

Also covered is a highly detailed study of the colours and markings of Luftwaffe day fighters including the legendary Messerschmitt Bf 109 and Focke-Wulf Fw 190 'workhorses', the Messerschmitt Bf 110, Me 210 and Me 410 'destroyers' and 'heavy fighters' and the Messerschmitt Me 163 and Me 262 rocket and jet-powered interceptors in all theatres of war.

There is an Appendix on the use of various laquers and the text is supported by hundreds of rare and previously unpublished photographs showing how paints were applied, masking methods, equipment and coding practices as used and adopted by all German units and aviation arms.

1 903223 38 5
303mm x 226mm Hardback
224pp, inc over 300 photographs,
colour chip cards and appendices
£50.00

DEFENDERS OF THE REICH
Eric Mombeek

The Luftwaffe's premier fighter defence unit, Jagdgeschwader 1, included some of the Luftwaffe's leading fighter aces. Eric Mombeek's classic history of JG1 is republished in three substantially revised volumes. Many of the 750 photos in this edition are new, and are accompanied by 90 new colour aircraft profiles.

Each PB, 303mm x 226mm, 96pp, c270 photos, 30 colour profiles

JG 1 Volume One: 1939-1942
1 903223 01 6 Available £16.95
JG 1 Volume Two: 1943
1 903223 02 4 Available £16.95
JG 1 Volume Three: 1944-45
1 903223 03 2 Available £16.95

1 903223 14 8, HB,
303mm x 226mm, 224pp,
250 photos, 30 col profiles, maps
£35.00

1 903223 26 1, HB,
303mm x 226mm,
176pp, 250 photos, colour artwork
£27.95

Classic tiltes can be obtained direct from:
Midland Counties Publications, 4 Watling Drive, Hinckley, Leics LE10 3EY   Tel: 01455 254450   Fax: 01455 233737   e-mail: midlandbooks@compuserve.com   www.ianallansuperstore.com
or in the United States of America from:
Specialty Press Publishers & Wholesalers, 39966 Grand Avenue, North Branch, MN 55056 USA   Tel: +1 651 277 1400   Toll free: +1 800 895 4585   Fax: +1 651 277 1203   www.specialtypress.com